TO FATHOM HELL OR SOAR ANGELIC

BY BEN SESSA

First published by
Psychedelic Press
Falmouth, Cornwall

ISBN: 978-0992808839

Cover illustration by Emma Watkinson
Printed in Cornwall, United Kingdom

For more information:
www.psychedelicpress.co.uk

This is a work of fiction.

Any resemblence to reality, or any person or object in reality, is entirely coincidental.

This book is dedicated to the three least psychedelically-experienced people I know: Sarah, Fred and Erica. Three people, nevertheless, who through their collective wisdom and unconditional love have taught me more about the human experience than every pill, potion, herb and fungus on the entire planet.

Acknowledgments:
Massive shout to Robert Dickins at Psychedelic Press UK for basically everything. Big Up Emma Watkinson for her Ethereal theta-genic warbling.

PART 1: MAKING THE SCORE

PART 2: THE COME UP

PART 3: THE PLATEAU

PART 4: THE COME DOWN

PART 4: THE AFTERGLOW

In 1957, whilst deciding upon a suitable name for a new class of psychotropic compounds emerging in the field of psychiatry, the mystic writer Aldous Huxley and the British doctor and early pioneer of LSD psychotherapy, Dr Humphrey Osmond, enjoyed an exchange of poetry. Huxley came up with 'Phanerothyme', but it was Osmond's suggestion that eventually lead to the birth to an entire new cultural genre.

AH: *To Make this Mundane World Sublime,*
Take Half a Gram of Phanerothyme.

HO: *To Fathom Hell or Soar Angelic,*
Just Take a Pinch of Psychedelic.

PART 1

MAKING THE SCORE

THE CLINIC MUST GO ON

This incessant screaming just has to stop, so Dr Austell tapes Ms Rattick's mouth shut and tightens butcher's twine around her wrists. He has had enough of her complaints - all that endless drivel about mental and physical health problems. No, this is it, Ms Rattick, it's time to make a clinical decision. Austell stands before his patient and rubs his chin pensively, eyeing her with curious regard. He then approaches his cabinet of surgical instruments, his eyes widening as he surveys the rack of glimmering scalpels. Taking his trusted double-bladed Stanley knife, he sinks the instrument into the flabby throat of his patient and severs both her jugular veins.

As her blood drains onto the clinic floor, the doctor glances nonchalantly out of the window and remembers his GMC membership is up for renewal next month. Then when the lifeless patient's shuddering ceases, he wipes his instruments clean, opens her medical notes and straightens his bowtie.

People think psychiatrists go around analysing people but they are paranoid to think that. For Dr Austell the discipline of psychiatry is more about apathy than analysis. He was always destined to spend the rest of his life in mental institutions, so he decided early on to prostitute himself to the medical industry. At least that way he would be on the right side of the couch, and get paid for it.

Ms Kathleen Rattick, obese and riddled with Catholic guilt, is a mild-mannered woman in her late forties. She suffers with social anxiety disorder and has been coming to see Dr Austell for over ten years. She thinks highly of her psychiatrist. He is such a professional, and *such* a lovely man.

'So do you think I am doing any better, doctor?'

Austell looks at her warmly from the other side of the desk where they sit. He sees a sad and desperate woman before him, smiling as she asks for release from a lifetime of mental illness that is not of her own doing. To him Rattick is nothing but a twisted writhing sack of petulant irritation. Still, no time to dwell on such things, the clinic must go on.

'Well, yes, indeed, Ms Rattick...'

'Oh, doctor, please do call me Kathleen.'

'Of course, Kathleen. It looks as if putting up the Prozac to 40mg has been a good move. I am pleased to hear you are sleeping better and that getting to the shops has been easier. You are certainly beginning to make some improvements. Might I suggest I see you again in, say, three months?'

She thanks him nervously as she stands to leave. Austell walks her politely to the door, wishes her well and then returns to the pile of notes before him. He has seen only twelve of the morning's clinic of twenty-two patients and is already experiencing his murderous, intrusive daydreams.

The fantasy of killing his patients was developed by Austell when he was a junior doctor in order to protect himself from their overwhelming projections of despair. In recent months, however, the technique has transmogrified into more sinister premeditated attacks. And it is not just towards Ms Rattick. It's the whole bloody lot of them; Rattick, Patterson, Claire Castle, you name them, he wants to murder them. Unable to control his thoughts, after half a lifetime of exposure to so many wretched people, all Austell can do is imagine the violent deaths of his patients.

As a young child his gloominess was less well pronounced. The

8

blackness emerged during his adolescence - those teenage years of conflicting emotions where on the one hand he was desperately bored by his social isolation, painfully aware of his inadequacies and wishing to be more part of the 'in' crowd, yet at the same time repelled by their puerile activities, which he did not understand and towards which he had no instinctual attraction whatsoever. So by the time he got to medical school he had learned to effectively isolate himself from the chuckles of the more immature students. He had acquiesced to the reality of settling into middle age and waiting to die: figuratively, spiritually and existentially. For this doctor, negativism is an art, not merely a developmental stage that will pass next year. Feelings are little more than knee-jerk, superfluous trinkets.

After all though, he lacks the guts to commit a real murder or develop anything as rousing as a real mental illness. He is a nobody, and there are countless others like him. They may not be doctors with tweed jackets. They may be standing in tracksuits outside pubs smoking cigarettes, or they may be housewives or businessmen, worn out parents dragging children around supermarkets or even the children themselves, glued to screens and piling on the adipose. But they are all the same; tumbling towards the same meaninglessness.

The intercom bleeps and Austell pulls another folder from the top of the pile - the next tax-payer sponsored victim to be fed by the NHS directly into his abattoir. Fodder for the good doctor. A pawn for the pharmaceutical industry. The almighty leader of the drugs industry, *Arable Pharm Ltd,* dictate that there must be constant copious prescription from their broad range of available products, all of which Austell knows are utterly useless. He could carry out his clinical consultations blindfolded. All he had to do was read

9

from a script.

'Come in Patient X, how are you?'

'Bit depressed, doctor.'

'Oh deary me! Here, let's start you on Mirtazepine. Special offer this month. Let's bump you right up to the 45mg dose, shall we? Anything else?'

'Bit anxious, doctor. Can't sleep.'

'Not to worry, how about a drop of Zopiclone? Splendid! 7.5mg each night.'

'And I find my moods go up and down a bit. Sometimes I feel happy, sometimes I feel sad. Perhaps I have bipolar disorder?'

'Yes, yes, sounds like it. Here, what about some Lamotrigine? Smooth out those troughs and peaks a little?'

'Thank you doctor. But what about my back pain?'

'Tramadol!'

'And something for my nerves?'

'Gabapentin!'

'And I keep getting thoughts that people are out to get me…'

'Sounds like a job for Quetiapine! Come on, Patient X, there must be something else I can help you with? I have plenty more sweeties in my clinical jar!'

Just an ordinary NHS foot solider working diligently in an ordinary English town. He follows orders, obeys the clinical guidelines rolled out by successive governments, directs his patients through evidence-based algorithms, as instructed and then pushes them back along new text-book dictated clinical pathways when the fashions change. His only job is to maintain a caseload and practice according to the policy-making powers. Aside from his patients, nobody knows he exists.

INDESCRIBABLE PACE
AND COLOUR

In Big Sur California, another British psychiatrist, Dr Joseph Langley, sits precariously on the edge of a cliff and faces out to sea. In the distance, rising out of the fog, the towers of the Golden Gate Bridge glisten in the sunshine. Behind him, from his tepee, there stirs the discordant twang of a sitar. His mind flows with indescribable pace and colour; an energy beam of cosmic particles cascades between his chakras, gushing from his pineal gland to his solar plexus.

Dr Langley draws in a prolonged inhalation of pine air, closes his eyes and settles into a deep state of meditation, in which he empties his mind of all superfluous thoughts. At the base of the cliff, way below the pony-tailed psychiatrist, the dark blue Pacific waves surge, crashing onto rocks, tapping into his brain's antennae, registering in his internal matrix as subtle changes in cosmic vibrational energy fields. The doctor opens his heart and gushes forth with boundless love, which he shares with the great prehistoric leviathans cruising through the bay below.

Deep in the mental throes of a simple but tremendously complex molecule called LSD, Langley has not allowed himself to be ground down by the plague of modern life. Not yet, not completely. He still has hope, and still has his life. But he has died, metaphorically and spiritually, and watched his ego dissolve and self fritter away into nothing but a river of effervescent specks of infinite light. But, Jesus Christ, he could really do with a drink right now.

Born in Somerset, England to parents of Pagan stock, he was whisked away as an infant to California and raised under the infinite totems of giant redwoods in the bohemian community of Palo Alto's Perry Lane. Langley senior was one of a breed of young longhaired men whose psychedelically-inspired programming and creative imaginings shaped the counterculture and societal changes of a generation.

A pioneer of early electronic engineering, Langley's father was the first to master molybdenum silicon chip etching that gave forth to modern computing. He met Langley's mother when she was a go-go dancer in a Venice Beach club. And with their marijuana and magnetic-storage semiconductors, Joseph Langley's Wicca-driven parents were part of the bright young things that gave birth to Silicon Valley.

Langley junior, the foetus, gulped acid and Benzedrine through his placenta at happenings filled with Beatniks and proto-hippies; parties that pushed back boundaries and broke rules that didn't even exist. His childhood was one of bearded digital geeks and performance artists whose language was sex and currency chemical. As an infant he could roll a joint before he could use cutlery.

It is, Langley believes, his solemn duty to fire love from his finger tips to the four corners of the world, turn on his patients to the beauty of the cosmos and make sure he has a darn good time while he's doing it. Every living breathing moment of his existence has been about the turbulent connectivity between stillness, reflection and having a ball. There is the perfect balance to his life, a great tattooed eagle on his back and doeskin moccasins on his feet. But, good God, could he do with a drop to drink.

He opens one eye and sighs heavily. Having just endured an

expensive divorce from his third love-mate, this weekend is an opportunity to get away from the shackles of San Franciscan life and spend a little time up country. With the warm sun on his arms and the breeze of the ocean tingling on his exposed testicles beneath his smock, he breathes in deeply and appreciates the emancipation he has earned.

Private practice psychiatry in contemporary California for the children of the children of the sixties is not all it's cracked up to be. Obsessed with their place in the capitalist sun, starved of the values their forefathers fought so hard to win, Langley is deeply cynical about the way the world is heading. He tries to be positive; it is in his nature to be so, but the kids these days just don't get off on the things that pumped his juice when he was their age. The drugs don't even work on him anymore, except alcohol of course, which he has embraced wholeheartedly, despite his hypocritical preaching against it. And the spectre of ethanol death prowls his liver and brain – he knows it, he can feel the bilious rot burrowing in the back of his throat, throwing up bloodied mucous and suicidal headaches that jerk him awake in the lonely night.

'Where is that bottle?' he grumbles to himself.

With a life's work of alternative healing and world-renowned research into psychedelic therapy under his belt, however, Langley is in hot demand. The movie stars and hip artists of Southern California flock to his door, demanding their moment of blurry-eyed cognitive impairment in his presence, praising him for his pioneering approach to tackling mental illness and shoving his books under his nose to sign along with their lines of finest Columbian cocaine. But it all just falls off the edge of the abyss and into the vacuum.

The open-mouthed flock of sheeple lapping up his words, which they tweet, blog and disseminate as memes into the cybersphere are clawing for a moment with his machine elves, hanging on his every word, waiting to see what mind-blistering annunciation he will spew forth next. It's all a load of baloney, of course, a shaky indefensible last-stand against the inevitable collapse of humanity into a seething pit of McDonald's flavoured Starbucks. He closes that damned eye again and tries to unite with the otherness, determined to make the acid work. Emptying the mind of all worldly distractions is harder than it looks. And after more uncomfortable minutes of shifting he admits defeat, calls bollocks to the chakras and crawls into his tent to look for that bottle.

CATCH 24

'Ah, Austell,' Dr Hunter sneers over half-moon spectacles. 'I see you are still yet to take any study leave. We have all taken our ten days this year. You really must.'

'I don't want any, Maurice. You have mine.'

'It doesn't work like that,' Hunter snorts.

Maurice Hunter, a semi-retired psychiatrist, has one eye on the golf course and the other on female students thirty-five years his junior. He should have gone years ago but his neglected, cheated-upon wife's penchant for expensive holidays forces him back for lucrative locums, which are abundant in this badly managed NHS service.

'Besides,' he adds, 'if you don't take your fill we are at risk of losing the lot. Those finance buggers are snapping at our heels, you know. Personally I couldn't give a toss if nurses only get a quarter of the training budget we get; that's their problem, they should have listened in school if they wanted to be doctors.'

'Quite.'

'So take it, Robert,' he says. 'Find yourself a conference or a course or something to justify the budget. Surely there is a topic you are interested in? What about the pharma industry? There's heaps of wonga in that game!'

'Wonga, maybe, Maurice, but not much in the way of efficacy.'

'Efficacy?' splutters Hunter, almost dropping his Daily Mail. 'Look, SSRIs have consistently been shown to improve rates of remission of core depressive symptoms by up to 65%!'

'But Maurice, the placebos they are tested against achieve 55%

15

remission on their own. Are all those side effects worth it just for that extra 10%?'

'Oh, come on now. You'll be telling me it's all a conspiracy by the pharma industry next!'

'Well, when one takes into account the massive publication bias – the fact that all the clinical studies are sponsored by the pharma companies and that they deliberately suppress any data with negative outcomes…'

'Bollocks to that!' shouts Hunter. 'Bloody left wing commie twaddle. Come on, give 'em the drugs, Robert, you stingy blaggard! That's what they want. Besides, if you have such a problem with our psychiatric medications why do you dish them out so copiously? I don't see you holding back.'

Austell pauses, focusing on the drug company freebie pen he holds in his hand. 'I don't know why, Maurice. I really don't. I suppose one must do something…'

'Ha! See! Anyway, enough of this,' sneers Hunter, folding his paper and rising to his feet; six foot five of public school tweed towers over Austell. 'Have you seen that new filly on the front desk? What about a bit of that for yourself, Robert, eh? Beginning to wonder about you, what!'

With that Hunter dashes off. He has patients to see, and besides, that new young secretary isn't going to drool over herself. Or maybe she would? Now that would be an exciting prospect, he thought.

The pile of notes in Austell's room looks up at him threateningly. First up is John Patterson, a fifty-seven year old with severe anxiety disorder and marked obsessive-compulsive traits. One of the few certainties in psychiatry, or in life for that matter, is that if one mistreats a child they grow up with problems. Patterson's father was a violent alcoholic who held his mother in dependent fear. Her capacity to protect her children from her husband was impaired by her use of heroin and prescribed tranquilisers. John and his siblings were subjected to systematic abuse at the hands of their tyrannical parents. Life was tough. Pleasures were scraps thrown from the table and the children's suffering was so commonplace it became monotonous - though no less traumatising. On one occasion John, aged six, and his younger sister, were left as collateral with his mother's heroin dealer for three hours while she went off to turn tricks to pay for her score. Suffice to say, at the hands of that dealer's house mates, the terrified children were treated to a range of activities that go beyond the typical spectrum of domestic hospitality. Memories of that sort are better off repressed, buried deep.

By the time Dr Austell met John six years ago his wife had left him and he was burnt out by years of failed treatments with inept medication, which caused side effects such as sedation, impotence and incontinence. Long since abandoned by his long-suffering children, John had spiralled into isolation and self-medication with booze. He has become everything he believes he ought to be; a useless piece of shit with no redeeming qualities. And he knows his doctor knows it.

As he walks in Austell grabs his arms and ties him to the specially constructed medieval rack in the corner of the consultation room. Then without looking up from his notes the psychiatrist smiles and musters a limp, 'How are you today, John?' then starts cranking the rack wheel.

'Don't think I've made much progress, to be honest, Dr Austell,' sighs Patterson; his shoulders letting out a dull pop as his arms are

17

wrenched from their sockets.

'Oh, I am sorry to hear that, John. Let's have a look at your drug chart, shall we? How are you doing on that new dose of Aripiprazole?' The ropes tied to Patterson's ankles dig deeper with each turn of the rack. Now the thighbones are beginning to give way. This is getting exciting.

'Things are not too good, doctor,' says Patterson. 'I still can't go out, except at night to the garage to get my tobacco. I don't like seeing people. Prefer not to. I'm not so sure the higher dose has made much difference.' By now Patterson has been fully dismembered. Austell turns to his knife cabinet to choose the best instrument for the next act: disembowelment.

'Hmmm, yes John, I can see that. Not to worry. We'll have to think again.' The psychiatrist sits back in his chair and places his hands behind his head, viewing his patient carefully. 'And how much are you drinking at the moment?' There was no hiding John's breath, which gives away the Dutch courage required to get him to the appointment. Looks like it will have to be the 18-inch scimitar. That always does the trick, no messing.

'Maybe I need more counselling, doctor? Do you think that will help if I try it again? The drink is the only thing that works. I know I must give it up, but I need the drink to stay alive. It's the insulin to my diabetes.'

'I like the analogy, John, but it is the drink that is killing you.'

'I know, I know. I need it! I'm in a real Catch 24 situation.'

'Ah,' smiles Austell. 'You mean Catch 22.'

'No, no, doc, it's way worse than that.'

Having cleanly dismembered the remaining twitching stumps of John Patterson and revealed yards and yards of glistening loops of bowel, spilled onto the clinic floor, Austell looks around for his petrol can. Ah, there it is! Standing over him with a lit match, enjoying the almost lifeless grimace on his patient's face, Austell says calmly, 'Well, unfortunately, John, the waiting list for psychotherapy is currently standing at eighteen months. It takes that long to get an initial assessment with the psychologist. Then, if accepted, the patient gets a measly six sessions of Cognitive Behavioural Therapy. Thereafter it is a one-strike-and-you're-out policy. Miss an appointment and it's straight to the back of the queue.'

Truth is, thinks Austell, it's not just the patients that deserve to die. It's the whole system, every last wretched bit of it.

'But hey ho! Maybe it's worth another go,' he chirps. 'I'll have a word with the psychologist and see if we can get you bumped up the list. She's supposed to be in later and there may have been a dropout. Perhaps she can see you this side of Christmas.'

Pushed into a corner and for want of a better idea, the conversation inevitably turns to psychopharmacology. One knows where one is with drug treatments. Maybe adding another mood stabiliser will help? Failing that there is always psychosurgery. It might be old-fashioned, but it is still a possible outcome for some patients with severe and unremitting neurosis. *Better a frontal lobotomy than a bottle in front of me,* as they used to joke in medical school. If only he had a rusty scalpel he'd attempt it here and now in the clinic.

'I'll have a word with the psychologist.'

Patterson thanks his doctor and lumbers from the room clutching a new prescription. He now has the journey home to contend with; two bus rides, hostile streets and up five flights of stairs to his pitiful flat, where he'll fall into his armchair and chain-smoke in front of the television, perhaps to emerge again at nightfall. Mr Patterson is not insane. Lacking the cushion of madness that protects the psychotic patient from reality he knows his fears only too well and this insight makes him worse.

The phone rings. 'Dr Austell…I'm going to make myself a cuppa. Do you want a coffee or shall I send in the next patient? It's Claire Castle.'

'Claire Castle,' Austell sighs to himself.

'Send her in please, Sylvia. Let's have her.'

Sod it. Send them all in. What could possibly go wrong now?

Claire Castle is just over twenty, with a sallow visage that betrays exposure to an unspeakable history. To call her early years a childhood would be misrepresentative. There was no attempt to protect her innocence, she was never nurtured or encouraged to learn. She was methodically shattered by her father and her mother's duplicitous failure to act in her daughter's defence. Her only hope of survival was to build a dissociative fortress. She locked her mind away and her identity became a fragmented distortion of 'Clairness'.

Austell regards her as she walks towards him. Tremulously clutching a plastic cup, Claire takes a seat as Austell attempts a smile and asks her how she has been. 'Not good,' she mumbles, her young teeth ravaged by amphetamine abuse. She has carried on with the tablets he prescribed at the last appointment but is feeling no better. Terrified to go out sober, she trudges the streets in a state of hyper-vigilance, seeing a potential abuser at every corner.

'I can't sleep.'

'No? Not even with the Temazepam? I suppose we could always increase…'

'Don't bother. No amount of sleepers is going to block it out.'

'Well, Claire, there is this new one just out; *Snoozazepam*. A recent study showed it…'

'I said don't fucking bother! I try and sleep after a drink, and then spend two fucking hours with my head on the pillow staring into space with the lights on full.'

'And then you drop off?' Austell is clutching at straws now.

'When I do eventually get to sleep all I get is endless, repetitive nightmares. Going over those fucking memories again and again… the fucking site of…him…the smell of whisky on his breath…the scratch of his stubble on my neck.'

As she speaks, Claire scratches at her forearm, picking at the patchwork of self-harm scars, new upon old that cover both her arms.

'And all the time he is whispering how much he loves me...'

Her voice trails away as she digs at the wounds. The skin breaks and a trail of fresh blood trickles off the ventral surface of her forearm and runs down her wrist, weaving in channels to pool in her hand. Looking straight ahead, not at the doctor but staring right through him, her lips move but she makes no sound as she describes her dead father's visit. Her leg jiggling manically with her speeding breath and the colour in her face draining away.

Presently the scratching slows and she draws up her knees, wrapping her arms into a foetal position on the chair. Slowly her breathing resumes a normal pace as she returns from intrusive memories and back to the room with her psychiatrist, sobbing loudly into her sleeve. Dr Austell holds a tissue towards the curled up figure of his patient, now rocking rhythmically on the chair.

'Claire…'

It is some time and many Claires later before she suddenly comes round with an abrupt jerk, flashing an angry look at the doctor.

21

'Don't fucking Claire me, like you give a fucking shit! It's just your fucking job!'

She then bursts into tears with defensive emotional instability to show the world she can survive. Attack others before they get the chance to attack first - or rape.

'True, this *is* my job...but...but you deserve my attention.'

'Are you calling me an attention seeker?'

Austell exhales impotently, 'Claire, you are an emotional black hole. You swallow up love and affection but you will never have enough to fill the vacuum left by your parents' failure to protect you. You are a hopeless, useless piece of shit. They fucked you up good and proper, they really did. And all you can do is make life a misery for those around you. I applaud you for this. You are true evil personified.'

How much of this the doctor actually says and how much of it he merely thinks is uncertain. Austell's spirits are jaded, clouded by his professional judgment. In some appointments he rejects her and throws out barked authoritarian commands. Or he lectures her about the need to take responsibility and grow up. He always medicates her with one drug or another. Sometimes he sections her. Always hiding behind the medical model, he blinds her with his knowledge, raping her with his professional opinion.

'We must discuss your medication, Claire. That is all. I will leave the psychotherapy to the psychologist. She is much better placed to help you with these dynamics than me. After all,' and he now laughs, 'what the hell do I know? I mean, look at me.'

This is perhaps the first honest exchange he has had all day, all week perhaps, which is why Austell actually likes Claire, if such a thing is possible for him, or indeed her. She smiles and agrees that as far as doctors go (and they are all cunts) he is alright. Austell feels an omnipotent sense of triumphant achievement; a dangerous counter-transference seducing him into a polarised position of 'all good' as opposed to 'all bad'. Now Austell is the father, seeking love and retribution for his assault. There is an uncomfortable frisson and the doctor is forced to retreat back into the security of the medical model.

'Let's talk about your medication.'

Psychiatry can be a complicated landscape. Claire huffs and curls up again, rocking. Austell, sitting back in his chair, intentionally disengages to a professional distance and sorts through his paperwork, giving her space to re-engage. He flicks through the pages of notes detailing the years of psychiatric drugs she has been on. It makes for depressing reading.

'Thing is, Claire, you are pretty much at the end of the line regarding psychopharmacotherapy. You have had five courses of antidepressants to lift your mood – all the SSRIs and most of the old tricyclics.'

'They were all shit,' Claire responds.

'I've tried you on three different anti-convulsants to try and stabilise your mood swings.'

'They were rubbish.'

'We have used benzodiazepines to blunt the edges…'

'I liked the Valium,' says Claire. 'But you never gave me enough of them.'

'Too moorish, Claire. I suggest we steer clear of them. I could see you getting a taste for the benzos…' He thumbs deeper into the notes. 'So then we moved on to the antipsychotics, which we used to partially manage the dissociative episodes…and finally we have tried at least three different hypnotics to help you sleep.'

'But none of them are enough,' she replies. 'These fucking nightmares and flashbacks rule my life. At best all of the drugs you give me just mask my symptoms, none of them actually treat or cure me.'

Impressed by her insight, miserable though it is, she is one of the few patients with whom Austell can be frank.

'Psychiatric drugs are a sledgehammer for the brain when what you really need, Claire, is a fine-tooth comb, a guided psychopharmacological bullet that gets to the heart of the problem. But truth is – there is no such thing.'

'I'm drinking too much,' she says. 'And there are a lot of people coming through the flat now that Darren is dealing again. There's a lot of crack and gear moving through. He's a fucking nutter. Bastard, that's what he is. But he's alright.' Austell knows Darren is violent towards Claire.

'Still with Darren then? I thought he got sentenced to...'

'I love him. He loves me. End of. Got a fucking problem with that?' And so it goes on.

After Claire leaves, clutching her prescription, Dr Austell stares out of the window for a full ten minutes. His cynicism for the system is an insidious cancer. These are the most victimised members of society. People on the bottom rung of the ladder whose lives have been ripped apart since before they were born. They lack the most basic emotional security that normal people take for granted. What *is* love to someone like Claire Castle other than a meaningless abstract term other people use to describe their attachments? Love is something to be stamped out before it gets you first. Austell has had twenty-five working years of this and he is not sure whether he

24

can take it anymore.

Day after day Sylvia comes into his office with more armfuls of files. She doesn't say anything as she gathers up the towers of discarded notes and leaves a fresh pile of post on his desk. Austell is becoming a statistic, soon to be taken by one of the four recognised grisly Russian roulettes, the four Ds that plague all psychiatrists: Death (from suicide), Divorce, Drugs and Drink.

Glancing disinterestedly at his letters he sees the usual demands for work and trashy invites to expensive presentations given by doctors on the pay role of the pharma industry. They are all the same. But one of the letters stands out from the others. It is an austere pamphlet, which is not like the typical drug company advert, a small postcard that says simply:

DOCTOR, ARE YOU FULFILLED?

Austell blinks at the card, about to immediately reject it as nothing but a clever advertising ploy, but then turns it over and reads:

If you are disillusioned with your psychiatric practice then you must attend:
The Opening Minds Annual Meeting in San Francisco, California, USA.
www.josephlangley.org

Ok, so it *is* a blatant piece of advertising. But intrigued, he has to hand it to the organisers of Opening Minds, they sure know how to target a disenchanted doctor. He wonders how many other psychiatrists as desperate as him are reading this card. Can't be many. Advertising slogans aside, the meeting looks interesting. He picks up his phone.

'Sylvia, how much annual leave do I have?'

'*Erm*...this year Dr Austell, you still have 19 days to take... that is until next month when the year's rota starts again. You can probably carry some days over into next year, but then you did that last year. I think it would be good if you actually take leave at some point...'

'OK, fine. And study leave?'

'Pretty much whatever you need. Dr Hunter has been asking about your study leave. He is encouraging you to spend...'

'Yes, yes, I know, I have found a conference I would like to attend.'

'Really?' her astonishment palpable.

'Yes,' says Austell, just as surprised as her to hear himself saying it. 'I think I'm going to have some leave and go to a conference... in America.'

AS COMMON AS THE COMMON COLD

Sitting on the edge of his immaculately made bed in Atlantic Heights' best suite, California's foremost psychedelic researcher Dr Joseph Langley looks at the flimsy papers of his keynote speech. He *must* get this finished. He reads aloud from the tremulous script.

'We toil on, with far from perfect treatments for our sick patients. But with the benefit of our rich pharmacopeia and after a hundred years of focused psychotherapy - is any of it any good?'

Langley wants his message to be concise and hard-hitting. Just like the psychedelic drugs he so wholeheartedly believes in. He wants to get to the heart of the delegates. But it is all so tiring.

'And what are the traditional psychiatric drugs that we currently have to offer? All of them – from the benzodiazepines, through the antipsychotics, mood stabilizers and hypnotics to the antidepressants – all of them are nothing but useless brain depressors. All they do is nullify, muddle and at best *numb* the brain!'

He takes another swig of whisky from a mini-bar plastic bottle. Maybe whisky is not such a bad thing, he wonders. What's so wrong with a bit of numbness? People need numbness. He didn't get a wink of sleep last night after some hot-shot juvenile chemist insisted he sample some newly synthesised chemical that had been reverently named after him, '*Langlethalmine*', which he naturally felt obliged to take. Langley had no idea what effect it was supposed to have on these people but for him it produced a sustained sense of edginess followed by several hours of nausea and sleepless anxiety. So today he knows about feeling numb. And now he has to talk in front of

27

this writing mass of tie-dye. He won't leave the room till it is done.

'The drugs don't work, my friends. At best they soften the edges and mask the symptoms. Sure, some of them have some active qualities but the results are not spectacular. Indeed, they are a very long way from spectacular. And they are certainly not a cure. In fact we are so disheartened in psychiatry today that we have become conditioned not to expect too much. We dare not even use the word 'cure' in reference to mental illness. It is a taboo. Why? Why *shouldn't* we talk about a cure? Where has the hope gone in contemporary psychiatry that we dare not even utter the possibility of such a thing?'

He glances out of the window. An elevated view over the streets out towards the ocean greets him. In the distance the Golden Gate Bridge thrusts its towers out of the fog. He truly wants this conference to work. It has been a long time in the planning. He and his colleagues in the new renaissance of psychedelic research have waited years for this moment. The medical establishment is in need of the challenge. Psychiatry is failing its patients. Langley feels an urgent need to win over hearts and minds. But perhaps he is trying too hard? Maybe that is the problem? The truth is *he* needs this conference to save himself. Another swig of whisky and he carries on.

'Mental disorders are not rare. It is not as though we are looking for cures for some weird and wonderful tropical diseases that happen so infrequently as to be insignificant to the public at large. The mental disorders that are ravaging society today are not the sort of stuff that only makes the front page in the popular papers and the amusing 'Eponymous Syndromes' column on the back page in the medical journals. No, *mental illness is as common as*

28

the common cold! If the same patient had a fracture, an everyday acquired infection or any other familiar ailment there would be an *expectation* for the medical profession to be doing a better job than this. What a sorry state of affairs we are in!'

He likes the way it is going. He wants to pitch it just right; enough knowledge to feed their imaginations, enough controversy to keep them engaged. It is impossible to preach on this subject without bringing politics into the debate. They want politics, this lot, and some radical energy. He stands up and paces around his room, gesticulating wildly to his imaginary audience, wondering, for a second, whether the Langlethalmine might be beginning to take hold.

'But of course it's not just psychiatric medicine that is in pieces. Oh no! Everywhere we look society is sliding into oblivion. It's all happening. We've got religious wars, corruption, plagues, floods, starvation and obesity. We have uncontrollable migration of whole populations, genocide, rising seas, sinking glaciers. We've got seven billion over-weight TV addicts gorging on consumer driven culture and we have barely even started! Nor have we even noticed what is going on. We may *think* we have noticed. We may all *talk* about it constantly. But are any of us actually getting out of the rat race? How many of us self-righteous, educated, enlightened know-it-alls can really see the wood for the trees and are truly making steps to *drop out*?"

No one answers his question. There is only silence and the hum of the air-conditioning, which he welcomes. He takes another swig. Damn teeny-weeny portions! Throwing open the mini-bar door and fumbling for another bottle – brandy this time – he unscrews the lid with his teeth and spits it across the room.

Anyone For Entities?

Austell's journey to the Californian conference was taken without preparation or any background reading for the event. 'It may as well be about hallucinogenic toad-licking for all I care,' he mused to himself as the aeroplane left the coast and climbed through the ivory sky over Bristol. Accompanied by his violent fantasies, three-quarters of the aeroplane's odious passengers had been brutally murdered by the time they touched down in San Francisco. He was spending the night in a large wooden-fronted hotel called The Red Victorian in a district beside Golden Gate Park, crowded with dogs and sleepy hobos clutching bottles. Everyone looked tired and bloodshot. Nervy tourists paced along the sidewalk beside shop fronts displaying peculiarly ornate chemistry glassware.

After several hours distracted by jet lag, studying the morphing abstractions of a lava lamp, it became clear he would be unable to sleep and so strolled the night-time streets, eventually ending up back in a bar near his hotel. A barmaid from Oregon set up bourbons for him in return for stories about child abuse and cricket. She called him 'old man' and told him she liked to shoot meth, which Austell assumed must be an easier version of snooker for the American market. Eventually sleep caught up with him and he wandered off to bed with a sleepy drunken head.

The next morning, Haight Street is up early except for two elderly folk asleep in the hotel doorway. On a hired bike Austell passes more homeless people congregating around the entrance to Golden Gate Park. It is an extraordinary sight; this endless pouring of young and old – mostly obese – laden with shopping trolleys, shuffling through a labyrinth of small paths in the park. He has never seen so many dispossessed gathered with such solidarity. He is used to seeing people living on the streets but in England they always seem so isolated. Yet here in San Francisco there are dozens, perhaps hundreds of people mingling together with a cohesive identity - a force to be reckoned with.

For someone from rural Somerset the sight is mildly daunting, and wishing to avoid interaction Austell fixes his attention on the twisting path ahead and cycles on. But it is too late, one of the raggedy men spots him and calls out, 'Hey dude, got a lid?' Or it could have been 'Wanna lid?' Neither makes any sense to him, and he pretends he hasn't heard and peddles on briskly. But up ahead a gathering of a dozen or so people block the path, with more positioned in the bushes. There is no escape. 'Nugget?' someone calls out. He wants to pick up pace and blast his way through the line of ragged zombies but is forced to slow down and roll to a stop in front of the crowd.

In the dappled morning the men (and on closer inspection a few women too) have the genuine appearance of those who sleep in bags under stars. They are free; living outside traditional life. He doesn't see their cynical expressions and dirty fingernails but only their lack of restrictions. To Austell these people represent a form of social emancipation that he has never known. This is the San Francisco, the hippies, he had read about.

The Free crowd around his bike, oozing liberty, and enthusiastically invite him to sit with them. Terrified, but seduced by the idea that this is as romantic as it is risky, the doctor drops his bike and takes a seat on the grass. A dog licks his face and a young fat guy with a goatee and baggy pants introduces himself

32

as 'The Ace'. Fuelled with the naïve invincibility of a tourist, Austell's gestalt connections transform these vagrants into colourful characters. Early morning light streams wraithlike through the trees behind the figure of The Ace. These are not tramps in the park. They are Beat poets.

'So, dude, you wanna buy a lid? Jo Jo left his home in Tucson Arizona for this shit!' says The Ace, drawing in a rich lung-full from his hand-rolled cigarette and passing it on to Austell, who being a non-smoker turns it down. They are all very friendly people and most welcoming. So not wishing to appear rude or ungrateful the doctor feels duty bound to eat half a peanut butter sandwich that gets passed his way. It has a strong herbal taste, most unlike English peanut butter.

Time passes surprisingly slowly for Austell, then quickly, then slowly again. Before long – or maybe not - the tramps peel away and part company with him amiably. There are hugs all round then Austell mounts his hired steed and continues on. His heart is racing and blood courses through his veins in rhythm within the great vessels of his chest. He is aware, in a manner that is alien to him, that the bike's pedals are fused to his feet, extensions of his thoughts. By imagining this, he is able to glide with ease through the lush cloudscape of San Francisco's Golden Gate Park.

The air is fresh with misty zephyr driving in off the ocean as the road winds its way beside lakes and sports fields. Art galleries in the park are opening their doors and there are dogs everywhere taking their joggers for walks. Perhaps it is the environment, he rationalises, maybe I am preconceiving a zeitgeist because I'm here in San Francisco? I don't know, but The Ace and his 'dudes' were so friendly. They said if only the whole world would smoke weed everyone would live together in peace and harmony. Austell likes the sound of this, but without comparing The Ace's cohort with a demographically identical control group he cannot make a fair assessment as to the validity of the statement. Nevertheless, it sounds impressive.

Trees circle the spiralling psychiatrist and tropical birds call out. Lost in a maelstrom of cognitive distraction Austell almost *sees* a field of connectivity reaching out from his bicycle into the space around him. It is happening at a level of consciousness that is not simply *un*conscious but more sort of *super*-conscious – whatever that means. He giggles to himself, then giggles more at the thought of giggling to himself, as he glides on past a Japanese garden, a polo field, countless baseball pitches and themed arboretums; ploughing the bike through the thick San Francisco air, the machine clicking along obediently at his command.

There is a network within his brain that seems to know nature intrinsically, everything shooting past with silver-streaked flashes. These American's have really got their bikes well trained. Peddling energetically along the road under endless pyramids of green he rattles down another steep hill and bumps his way through a cathedral of giant trees stretching into the clear sky, and then emerges from the park onto a broad city boulevard. Succulents sprout up from coarse sand lining the road. A cool breeze blows up him as his bicycle bumps over tramlines and hurtles downwards towards the ocean, standing out starkly as a dark band of distant sea, intermittently visible between the criss-crossing streets.

Traversing the Great Highway, Austell wheels his bike down onto Ocean Beach. Fog hangs over the water, rolling down to obscure the horizon in both directions. He stands for a moment listening to the waves with sublime tranquillity. This is a degree of peace that the psychiatrist has never known. Down at the ghostly waters' edge, hanging fog moistens his face and when he turns his head the screech of the biting wind obscures the city's distant traffic. He has the briefest of thoughts that the inevitable fragility of his life is something to be celebrated, not mocked, as he has done so often.

Immediately forgetting his thought – though wishing he could remember it - he takes stock, checking his map and orientates himself in the direction of the Atlantic Heights Hotel. He is suddenly eager to get there in order to let the world know what the universe is all about. He is not sure what he means by this, but it drives him on and he peddles harder than ever. He must tell someone about this feeling, but by the time Austell reaches the venue he has forgotten about his world-changing mission.

There is a small crowd of smokers gathered in the street below the glass building, which is adorned with banners proclaiming 'Opening Minds: Where Magic Meets Medicine'. Suddenly overwhelmed by anxiety, feeling uncomfortably self-conscious, as if every eye in the place is watching him, the psychiatrist is ushered in through the rotating doors by a nervy-looking security guard. As Austell stands in the great vestibule gone is the relaxation and emancipation of earlier. In its place is an emerging paranoia. It dawns on him that he is very far from home.

Globular shapes of purple glass dangling from the ceiling distract Austell's gaze. A giant structure is turning slowly above him, lit by strobe lights and ethereal music. He is drawn to a colourful poster on the wall explaining that this sculpture is a model of the LSD molecule. *LSD*? Austell has heard of it of course. He learned about all the dangerous drugs of abuse as part of his psychiatric training.

And as far as he can remember LSD is a particularly nasty one. It causes menacing hallucinations and makes people jump out of windows believing they can fly. It can turn people crazy. Lost in the rotating sculpture and angelic music, his attention is grabbed by a voice in his ear.

'Ain't she beautiful?' He turns to see an elderly lady following his gaze up to the hanging sculpture. She appears as out of place as Austell feels. Leaning on a walking stick the old lady chuckles as she views the revolving glass installation. He feels like he ought to say something.

'This sculpture? Well, yes. It says it is LSD! But I have no idea what it is all about.'

'It's all about *everything*!' laughs the old lady. 'It is because of *Her* that we are here.'

'It *is*?'

'Yes of course! The magic molecule; glittering in hyperspace, spinning, drawing us in and welcoming all these beautiful people to this momentous event. We do, after all, owe it all to Her, do we not?'

'We do?'

'Oh yes, indeed.'

She moves off, pulled into the hallway by mingling crowds streaming in from the street. Austell makes his way to the registration desk. Perhaps he has got the wrong venue? He needs answers. This is certainly not a typical medical conference, or at least not how he imagined one would be. But his name is on the list. This is definitely Open Minds. He signs in and receives a glossy welcome pack. But scanning the literature merely confuses him further. Although many of the lectures appear to be discussing psychiatry, loosely, the programme is also filled with descriptions such as *energising*, *realising* and *illuminating*. These are not the sorts of treatment goals with which he is familiar.

There are no lectures about antipsychotic drugs. Nor is there anything on mood stabilisers or benzodiazepines and not even a sausage on antidepressants. Instead, it appears, this is a medical conference dedicated entirely to the use of *hallucinogenic drugs*. Psychedelic Therapy they call it. These people are seriously talking about prescribing powerful mind-altering drugs to mentally ill patients in order to enhance their experience of psychotherapy! *Really*? But psychedelic drugs are lethal, dangerous things.

Feeling profoundly out of his depth, Austell wonders how many of the other delegates are experiencing the same emotion. To Austell, the idea of psychedelic drugs as medical treatments is so ludicrous as to be laughable. He confesses to himself that he is completely oblivious that this subject even existed.

Who are these people? Looking around, the crowd is so varied it is impossible to say what genre they represent. There are academics in corduroy patched jackets and polar-necks, wearing wire-rimmed spectacles chatting to suited doctors and sober-looking research scientists, nothing unusual about that for an academic meeting. But unlike your average conference there are also an unusual number of scraggly-looking hippies filling the place with their explosions of fluorescent-dyed, dreaded hair. And alongside the cyberpunks is an extraordinary collection of silver-haired elderly people, like the lady he met earlier, dressed in the fashions of their day; propped on walking sticks in flea-eaten suits or dated floral attire from the 1960s, who stand alongside their bloodshot teenage grandchildren with serene wisdom, surveying the mass of fledgling acidheads at their feet. This is a generation connected to Mother Earth by fibre

37

optic umbilical cords.

These people are a seething network of interneurons dendritically absorbing the throbbing evolution of psychedelic culture from the streets and transmitting the cosmic message back through multimedia tendrils to the pulsating universe. All of this is about as far from Taunton as one can possibly get.

Taking stock, Austell retreats from the crowd, stepping over a cluster of face-painted kids in group-embrace. He slips past a post-apocalyptic couple wearing gas masks and goggles and ducks surreptitiously into a small seminar room beside the main hall. Leaning against the back wall in darkness his eyes accustom to the gloom, he realises there is a lecture being delivered to a small gathering of semi-recumbent delegates. The speaker is an exceptionally tall gentleman with long grey hair in a neat ponytail and a hypnotic West Coast accent.

'... we are talking here, folks, about Mushroom Medicine, Fungal Chemistry and The Vibration Principle in the Practice of Holistic Self-Transformation. Within this realm all human DNA is connected. *Inter*connected. The double helix gliss-openings percolating into our grid cubes transmit to us from mutated cadence entities. Using a synesthetic code derived from two-dimensional forms we exist simultaneously in identical universes. We jump in real time using fractal wave structures between this, our everyday world and the Other - where nothingness is connected with ourselves, the spirits and our environment.'

Christ, thinks Austell. If he were hearing this in his clinic in Taunton he would be reaching for a pink form by now to recommend immediate hospital detention. He looks around at the other listeners expecting to see equally unconvinced looks on their faces but to his surprise they are all transfixed.

'...after all,' drones the speaker, 'matter itself is trans-linguistic, isn't it? Substance is merely the visual experience of *deep blue imagery* making connections through the *i Ching*. It allows us to do this. I mean, who here has seen alien entities in their travels? Entities anyone?'

There is a murmur of recognition from the seated crowd, many of whom are clearly familiar with entities. Austell has never come across them. He makes a mental note to himself to address this shortcoming in his education. It frustrates him to think there are mental phenomena out there about which he has no knowledge.

'We *must* learn to extrapolate from the ternary to the binary in order to emerge into tomorrow's eschaton. To do so we must concentrate on being the spiral children of our time...'

There are more affirming nods from the crowd. The pony-tailed man goes on.

'In my own practice I employ the following utensils: LSD, DMT and the iPad - as well as the Wii controller and 2-CB. These tools help me balance the interactions between software, psychedelics and language. Interspecies communication with animals and extra-terrestrials all happen in our ineffable landscapes...but who are these entities? And what do they want from us?'

The audience stares in silence; a sea of bloodshot eyes waiting on the speaker's next words.

'They are almost certainly alchemical connections from another planet speaking to us, though our fractals, about the year 2023. Why? Because, my friends, that's where it's all going, man! No, not 2012, even Terence is allowed to make mistakes. No, the D-Day we are now for waiting is Summer Solstice 2023. That is when the world will awaken to a new consciousness. It's make or break time, folks and by then we'll know! Thank you for listening. My name is Mountain Spirit. Check out the website and remember to keep watching the skies. Thanks.'

There is an affectionate round of applause and Mountain Spirit bows gently to the crowd making the prayer gesture, smiling warmly.

'Does anyone have any questions?'

A lady to Austell's left tentatively stands up, nerved by the mass of faces.

'Thank you for your talk doctor…'

Doctor? Bet he's not a real doctor.

'I am interested in what you were saying about real-time hallucinations. I…er…I have a friend who's been using tryptamine entheogens on a regular basis for many years and she takes a measured DMT trip every three days as a means of communicating with the entities…'

'Great, great,' purrs Mountain Spirit. 'Beautiful start-out material, DMT.'

'Right. Well her heavy use has resulted in decoupled retinal-waves interrupting her normal linear rendering. Can you tell me anymore about this? Is it likely that she is accessing a space usually reserved for synergy dreaming?'

Mountain Spirit is relatively unperturbed by the question.

'Thank you for your thoughtful enquiry. Please tell me, is your friend familiar with the multistate landscapes accessible through Ethoxy Salvidivinorum?'

The enquirer looks for validation from the crowd. She isn't going to find any from Austell, but one or two others nod knowingly.

'Then in that case,' smiles the Spirit with a knowing grin, 'I would say your *friend,* ' and the audience sniggers with shared knowledge, 'has most likely gone and de-coupled her non-linear projections. Tell her not to worry. Sure, she may be putting some of her primitive spiritual pathways at risk, but hell who hasn't done that before!' The audience laughs. 'No, it's nothing to fear. The spiralling effect of DMT *wobblers*, as we call them, is easily undone by simply administering an intramuscular dose of acetylcholine before taking the psychedelic agent; thereby reducing her pressure phosphenes from working overtime. It's a basic trick we used to use to prevent perceptual splitting back in the day at the Easylay Institute in Big Sur. Works every time. OK? Great. Any more questions? No? Cool. *Om Shanti.* Goodbye for now. And remember friends: don't miss Joseph Langley this afternoon!'

The crowd shuffle out leaving Austell at a loss. How does one judge this? Is it a medical conference or not? Usually his nihilism would crush a new experience such as this. But there is something so completely mad about it all that it leaves him curious to learn more.

Emerging from the symposium Austell mills through the crowded lobby and finds a psychedelic bookstore full of topics such as therapy with LSD, Ketamine, magic mushrooms, DMT, and cannabis. There are books on South American Indians drinking ayahuasca, Mexicans eating psychedelic fungi, Shamans from Russia doing something with reindeers' urine and hippies everywhere chewing bark and even licking toads.

The psychedelic revolution, it seems, exploded big time with the discovery of LSD in the mid-forties. A remarkable molecule by all accounts, stumbled upon serendipitously by a Swiss chemist and initially proposed as a tool for psychiatry. Austell had no idea the

41

drug was used in psychotherapy in the fifties and sixties. How come he was never told about this stuff in medical school?

Being such a thorough and autistic learner the more he reads the more cheated he feels. This is an entire area of medical history that was absent from his education. And seeing it all now he wants to know more; if for no other reason than he can't bear that everyone else in this place seems to know more about it than him. Here he is, a qualified psychiatrist, surrounded by a bunch of stoned hippies with greater knowledge than him. There is also something about the anti-establishment stance of the subject that appeals to Austell. On the surface the concept of deliberately giving a patient a psychedelic drug is so alien. It goes against everything he's been taught. Usually when Austell gives a patient an antidepressant or antipsychotic drug he isn't expecting them to actually feel anything; at least not right there and then. But these powerful psychedelic drugs, it seems, cause immediate and profound alterations in consciousness, huge distortions in thinking, which are about as far removed from normality as it is possible to get.

In his zest for knowledge he purchases four books and plans to escape this madness and return to his enclave on Haight Street to learn more about psychedelic drugs. He has decades of psychiatric training to make up for; an education, it seems, he was cruelly denied at university.

As he makes his purchases a lady dressed in flowing green silk looks over his shoulder with the typical over-familiarity Austell has come to expect at this conference and comments on his hoard of purchases. She introduces herself as Betsy, originally of Eastern Bloc origins and a nurse by training but now living in San Jose and practising as a psychotherapist. She is maybe in her late thirties although it's hard to tell with these hippie women. She could just as easily be sixty, or an adolescent. Betsy's parents were veterans of the field, she says. She grew up amidst an atmosphere of 1960s LSD therapy and has since taken on the mantle. She talks about the 'new renaissance' of psychedelic research that is happening.

'It's great to be back doing the work of my mom and dad after all these years. The authorities are finally takin' notice!'

He admires her positivity and is embarrassed at his ignorance, confessing the subject is entirely new to him. He wonders for a second what his Taunton colleagues might think about all this. Imagine Hunter's face if he could see him now.

'Thing is,' he says. 'I'm a bit...well, you know, stuck in my ways. I don't see much opportunity for psychedelic therapy in my everyday work. Difficult to see where it would fit in.'

She smiles back warmly. 'Do you love your job so much that you wouldn't want to change it at all?'

'Oh good God no, I'm not saying that. It's just that...well...I really can't see this sort of thing happening ...in *Taunton*...can you imagine it?' And as soon as he says this he realises he has never actually told anyone face-to-face that he is dissatisfied with his job. In fact he has never even acknowledged it to himself. But there is something about the way this Betsy looks at him that draws out his thoughts.

'If you really want to know what this is all about,' she smiles, 'then you must make sure you see Joseph Langley's keynote talk. That's the one that will really sway it for you. He's on at four o'clock.'

'Ah yes, Joseph Langley. I saw his name on the programme. You recommend him do you?'

'He's *the man*,' says Betsy, wandering off to a group of people she spots on the other side of the bookstore. She waves goodbye to Austell, calling over her shoulder as she floats away, 'If anyone is going to make it happen this time around it's Langley.'

Presently, Austell becomes aware of a humming noise coming from the main hall. Intrigued, he tiptoes closer to the doorway. A poster on the door says it is an 'Experiential Session' by a local band called *The Third Eye of Perception*. From the hall there is the sound of a throbbing electronic wave rising and falling through the blackness. He opens the door and peers in. The dark space is severed by sharp beams of green laser light, casting an undulating plane in time with the music. There are some three-dozen people sitting cross-legged under the rolling canopy of light. A voice reverberates through the hum.

'...Friends, you are hearing the sound of the sacrament...my computer is linked by an electric probe to this vial of liquid acid on the table...it is transmitting the sound of the vibrational frequency of LSD...the molecule itself is producing these tones from within its core...listen to the voice of our ancestors, each life and memory of generations of countless millennia...all of us tied-up within the molecules of our bodies...and within the molecular structure of LSD...'

Hovering in the doorway Austell notices he is spoiling the ambience somewhat by casting a shaft of white light across the otherwise darkened hippies on the floor. A few heads turn to see who is interrupting their cosmic voyage. Nodding an apology, Austell slips off his shoes, crawls inside and sits down on the floor. Again, if only Hunter could see him now...

'...and this is how we start our day,' drones the voice over

the fluxing sounds distorted by special effects, '...*we will be here each day to start the conference with some cosmic transmissions from Planet Love...tap into it...melt...become part of it...open your mind to new dimensions of consciousness...this is where we lay the foundations for a new beginning. Connect with the plants and animals of the planet...here is where the collective human psyche re-enters...a chance to survive the destruction of the planet by transcending physical matter...listen to the molecule...ride her peaks....yes...she speaks to each of us...listen to her voice...what is she telling you?'*

Austell feels terribly self-conscious but it would be rude to leave. Everyone else seems to be taking it incredibly seriously. A number of them are twisting through a series of yoga moves. Others are face down. There is no turning back so the Taunton psychiatrist lies back and closes his eyes. The pulsing vibrations of the molecular structure of LSD-25 flow through him. He promptly falls into a deep and dreamless sleep.

A CAPTIVATING NUT CASE

Austell's sleep is broken by the sound of scraping chairs. Bright-eyed mind-benders, fellow delegates like he, are excitedly filling the hall for the keynote speech and now he has a front row seat. Rubbing his eyes he remembers his name as it is called into his ear.

'Hey, Dr British! You made it back here for Langley's talk then? Great spot! Mind if I join you?'

Betsy pulls up a seat just as the lights dim. Someone approaches the podium and taps on the microphone. 'Ahem...testing, testing... OK, great...Hello everyone! Welcome to the Opening Minds International Conference! And how are you all? Did you have a good night? Anyone still yet to go to bed?'

There are giggles from some dark-spectacled young revellers sitting at the back, prompting Austell to wonder what kinds of exciting lives the other half live. He is just waking up to the fact that he is half way across the world surrounded by hippies at some bizarre gathering about psychedelic drugs - by accident. Betsy pulls excitedly at his sleeve, 'This is it! Oh, man, you're going to love Joseph Langley. Everybody always loves him...my Joseph!'

'You know him?'

She laughs, 'Yes, I know him!'

The MC continues, 'So without further ado let's get started. Joseph Langley, who is he? A psychiatrist, a psychedelic visionary, a man both before his time and beyond his time. Psychonaut and psycho-taught, this is *the* man to bring you kicking and screaming into the modern renaissance of psychedelic research. Langley has a story to tell. He believes, as I do, that psychedelic drugs, and not pharmaceutical company products, hold the key to our survival.'

A few shouts fly out from the audience. Austell tingles with anticipation. He has been brought to this conference by the need to escape from a nervous breakdown and the need for some random study leave. And although he is not a superstitious man, far from it (he is the antithesis of such things), since touching down in San Francisco he wonders whether there are forces beyond his current understanding. The MC, blissfully unaware of Austell's conflict with such mysterious energies, carries on.

'Joseph Langley is the brains behind Opening Minds, the future of psychedelic research, and this entire program. He is the founder of an educational project many of you may be familiar with: Devout Mind Training (DMT), from which he and I developed the Opening Minds, or 'OM' project. These developments are churches. No, they are *chances* for us to see what is right there in front of our very own, very shut, eyes. What there is to know about psychedelic drugs, Joseph Langley already knows. What is not yet known, Langley is looking for.

'But who is Dr Langley the man? Well, he is a doctor, a chemist, a mycologist, an ethnobotanist, an accomplished visual artist, a self-taught Zen master, a member of the coveted Magic Circle of Wizardry and, believe it or not, a registered deep sea diver. A qualification he sought in the seventies in order to gain access to an alleged hallucinogenic sea anemone living deep off the coast of Borneo. He found it of course, brought it up, categorized it, isolated and synthesized the active component of the mysterious beast. And now it goes by the name of *Anenomeous langlyolous*. Jesus! The guy's even got a sea anemone named after him.

'And so here we are. Taking in the vibe on the first day of

the international Opening Minds conference. The next few days represent the pinnacle of all our years of preparation. It really is happening. Each and every one of you is contributing to the dream that one day we can see these fascinating chemicals become prescribed medical treatments!'

A cheer goes up.

'So anyway, you didn't come here this afternoon to listen to me. You are here to see Joseph Langley. Ladies, gentlemen, doctors, psychologists, stoners, wizards, fairies, gnomes, elves and the occasional Elvis, I give you: Dr Joseph Langley!'

Applause ripples through the auditorium as the MC strides over, pulls Joseph Langley from the wings and they embrace warmly. Dr Langley takes to the podium and waits for the noise to settle then looks out at the throng of eager faces.

'Ahem...hello...thank you, thank you. It is amazing to see so many of you here today. And thank you for that wonderful introduction.'

Applause again. Austell wonders why everyone always has to do so much evangelistic whooping? All through the introduction there were people in the audience who felt the need to show their approval by letting out seal-like yelps. Such lack of decorum. So American, he thought.

'I am grateful to be part of this momentous event. Thank you all for attending and coming here to hear me give the keynote speech. I am just like you. We are here because we, all of us, share the same dream: We all want to see psychedelic drugs harnessed by the medical profession as viable treatments for mental illness. Is that such an unusual thing to ask? All we want is a decent, worthy, effective treatment for our patients. We want to see clinicians

49

prescribing these medicines so they can be used safely, effectively, cleanly, cheaply and widely on our patients. I believe LSD, Psilocybin, Ketamine, Cannabis, DMT, MDMA, 2C-B, Ibogaine and the magic sage Salvia divinorum *can* and *must* be used by the medical profession. I feel we owe that much to our patients.'

Austell listens intently. What a strange looking man he is in his loose fitting linen suit and a flowing ponytail of greying blond hair hanging down his back. Of an indeterminate age, he looks young, or at least no older than himself, but there is a timeless exuberance about him. And rather incongruously Langley appears to be wearing a pair of old tennis shoes. Nice touch. It is exactly the sort of thing Austell himself might do if he were to ever stand on a stage like this and give such a talk, which, of course, he will not.

'At heart I am a simple doctor. I have seen patients with mental illness all my working life. And let me tell you, no two people are the same. There is only one form of schizophrenia: it's the one in the patient before you. But Houston, we have a problem.'

He gives a pregnant pause and all eyes fix on him, including those of the spellbound Austell.

'I, and my medical colleagues, have become lost. The entire profession is lost. Politicians and the general public are the same. The public is *worse* than lost. They are…empty…gone. They, we, are the losers. Look at the Western world: apathetic, brainless, ignorant, mindless zombies. No one cares any more. We can't even be bothered to fight. Where have the street protests of the sixties gone? What could be more vacuous than a protest via Twitter? The sad truth, ladies and gentlemen, is that we are sitting in a tepid bath and it is not getting any warmer. And for those of you who work with psychiatric patients, (and I know there are plenty of you out there today), you *know* that the traditional tools we have at our disposal are woefully inadequate for the job. Am I right?'

The audience is silent. There are murmurs of validation and a few heads nod; Austell's being one of them.

'Mental illness is an infection. You are born with a genetic susceptibility, you pick up the pathogens from your environment and then you pass them on to others. None of our psychiatric drugs are antibiotics. None of them get inside the brain and neutralise these micro mind-organisms infecting the cells. At best our treatments mildly treat the symptoms of the disorder; like an aspirin numbs pain without treating the cause of a headache, or a handkerchief mops up your running nose without actually attacking the virus. In psychiatry we have nothing that actually kills the cold. So our doctors struggle along in their clinics. We follow our follow-ups. We soldier on. Our sugar pills soften the blow and return our patients to some level of functioning but the infection grumbles on. Tell me, you psychiatrists out there, does any of this sound familiar?'

From the crowd comes a greater sea of nods and few more of those inevitable whoops. Austell is nodding, transfixed. It is as if Langley can read his mind. The speaker recognises the hopeless rot festering in Austell's brain, projecting out for all to see, and he delivers back exactly the same message in his speech.

'Come on doctors, wake up! Shake up the brain. We need to focus on consciousness in a way that is both subtle and yet staggeringly beautiful. We must reveal the consciousness of illness. We need to pick apart the psyche. Things are really messy and tangled up down there. The human race is in a pickle and don't we know it. We have to get right down inside those untidy thoughts and give the house a proper spring clean. And I don't mean just straighten the rug; we

51

need to lift up the cushions and go down the back of the sofa.'

He pauses and takes a gulp of water. Langley is on fire.

'What I do want to do is put things in perspective. It is not possible to approach the subject of psychedelics without understanding the context in which these drugs are floating. You will hear many people talking to you in lectures this weekend about the role of drugs in human history. You will hear about ancient civilization using sacramental plants and fungi and you will learn about remote non-western cultures still employing such practices. The world outside this conference will tell you that psychedelics started in the 1960s; they are synonymous with hippies and dropouts. LSD has brought us Deadheads, acid casualties and, as far as the media are concerned, probably schizophrenia itself. The media will tell you that nobody wants to experience any other state of consciousness except this typical waking state.

'But don't be fooled! In fact, this notion that the drug-free state is the purest or most spiritual is a relatively new concept. Spiritual psychedelic practices have persisted for hundreds of thousands of years in virtually unchanged rituals all over the world. Mushrooms are much older than beer as an intoxicant for humans. The drugs and plants that produce these visionary states are part of life. Not just human life but all life; they grow all around us, anywhere you care to look. In fact, you know what? I passed a lovely patch of *Psilocybe cyanofibrillosa* as I walked here this morning. So beautiful! Yes, they are living amongst us.'

Laughter jumps over the crowd.

'And for ancient people, these special plants and fungi formed an important part of their society. It is only very recently that the Christeo-centric idea has emerged to tell us that only through sobriety can we reach God. Those indigenous populations, who the media tell us are crazy, who still use these plants to commune with their spirits think *we* are crazy for sitting week after week in our cold empty churches, or in front of our computers, wondering why we are not experiencing the life of the spirits. But of course we use this argument to validate our *own* cause. We say they are heathens, less civilized and less advanced than ourselves. We think *they* are backward. But look at where *we* have advanced. Pop Idol? The shopping mall? Spiritually, mentally and culturally, have we advanced at all? Or have we have actually receded? And are we very soon about to die?

'And all this because in the centuries since the pioneering words of Jesus, Buddha, Mohammed and all those other bare-footed shaman, their less-inspiring followers have twisted their messages, mixed their sermons with the politics of power and somehow come up with the idea that we would be better off if we were sober when we commune with God. Sober from the effects of a truly transformational potion. But the Bwiti in Africa, the Shamans in Siberia, the Native Americans in New Mexico and the Amazonians and druids everywhere wonder how we could possibly imagine reaching God *without* the sacrament. And yes, we look at them and they look at us and we say to each other: *how very ignorant you are*!

'Let's face it, the western world is struggling. It's hard to say when the regression started: maybe the beginning of the industrial revolution, maybe more recently? Who knows? But it's certainly on the way down, and at a terrifying pace. For all our technology and liberal understanding it is greed that blinds us. The ego, the human brain, that elusive spark of sentience that held such promise as a unique resource, is now letting us down. We sit by and gorge ourselves to death on our own self-importance whilst the true communalistic understanding of archaic civilizations is being lost.'

He pauses and frowns at the captive spectators. Are they getting this? Are these the chosen people to carry his message forward? Stepping away from the podium Langley strolls to the front of the stage.

'Maybe I'm being too harsh. I suppose it's not all bad in the modern world. Technology has brought us some advantages. We generally have less disease, improved infant mortality (if one is lucky enough to live in the west) and I would even grant that some aspects of modern society have advanced a little too. But after several thousand years of increasingly complex political and religious systems and repeated attempts at organizing populations into manageable structures, we still seem so far from a Unified Theory of Everything, a universal dogma of understanding that all humans can access in order to find our common roots. The Islamists, Jews, Buddhists, Christians and the rest; all of us are at odds with one another and all of us are in decline. Neither capitalism nor communism has worked. In fact, without wanting to sound like a scaremongering evangelist, it really does sound like the human race is doomed.'

The audience love it. But in Austell's mind there is cognitive dissonance. What is this paranoid Conspiracy Theory pseudo-scientific new-age crystal-gazing tree-hugging mumbo jumbo hippie crap? Joseph Langley is clearly a nut case. But he has to admit; the man is a captivating nut case.

'But look, I am no new-age crystal-gazing tree-hugging mumbo jumbo hippie,' says Langley. 'We will leave the evangelism to the Scientologists. I respect that many of you here, like me, are *scientists*. And psychedelic drugs have a place in the world of science and medicine.'

Wow, thinks Austell, more than a little spooked at the morphic transmission of thought going on between him and the speaker. He wants to hear more about psychedelic drugs though, not Langley's naval-gazing prophecies for the planet's future. The Taunton psychiatrist looks at his watch and wonders about the impending coffee break.

'So before you look at your watches and wonder when it's time for coffee, I want to bring us back to the topic of this conference: psychedelic drugs. The 1960s drug revolution was an important time in history. Sure, people back then had some fun for a few brief years. These fascinating chemicals stripped away their egos, exposed their true selves and flung open the eyes of those brave enough to take them. A few select voyagers opened the door to a past dream and pointed the spotlight on the modern world. But then that door shut again so quickly and the fantasy faded. The cancer of oblivion set in and nothing, certainly not kids on LSD at rock concerts, was going to halt that tide.

'The politicians who repressed the sixties protests had an easy time of it. The hollers of stoned kids fell on deaf ears and the hippie movement dug its own grave. The authorities, blinded by their greed and an erroneous belief that money would save them, didn't need much to get back on top. And relying on the drugs themselves to open the eyes of the disbelievers was naivety in the extreme. Nope, the dream was over and the drugs had failed. These drugs, which could have been part of society's survival, were not enough to halt the decay once the ball was rolling and the dollar had set in. Critics of LSD, of course, used its lack of success at changing the world as validation that the drugs don't work. They were right. LSD did not enlighten the world, at least not enough of it and not for long enough.

'But…' and Langley thrusts a single finger into the air, 'that was not the fault of the drugs and nor was it a measure of LSD's lack of efficacy. The simple reason we failed to turn on the world fifty years ago was because there were not enough of us. Sure, there were handfuls of zonked kids on acid trudging the sidewalks and there were a few writing poetry and pop songs about it. But how many were truly altered by the drug's effects? How many had enough of an enlightenment to not be seduced back into the machine?

'LSD was great but it was too little too late. The truth is, my esteemed delegates, that psychedelic drugs were then and still are today the appropriate moral choice for the survival of humanity. And this time around we need to be a lot cleverer about how we go about getting the message across. Last time LSD and her cousins merely whetted the appetite. They were nothing but a craze, a stylish trend. Society did not get the chance to allow the drug to sink in and change its consciousness at the very core. It got pretty close, for sure, and if Grace Slick had gotten past security that night in '69 and into that White House party with her secret pocketful of powdered LSD destined for the president's cocktail glass, it could have got a lot closer but alas…no, this time we need to use the field of medicine to get these spiritual sacraments into society. Sadly the dollar has won the first battle but we must not let it win the war.

'Spirituality will never compete with capitalism; whatever those religious fools out there tell you. It has never been able to and it certainly can't do it now. Money always wins. But what we can do is appeal to people's need for better, more efficient and effective health care and then…and only then, can we sneak transpersonal change in through the backdoor.'

A great cheer goes up and along with the rest of the crowd Austell joins in. There is real hope in the speaker's words.

'Psychiatry needs psychedelics and psychedelics need psychiatry. But we won't get there by harping back to the philosophies of the East. That was tried in the sixties and it didn't work; today the East's consumerism is worse than the West's. No, we need to embrace the cancers of the West with the modern developments of the West; with science and medicine. On the face of it psychiatry made the only choice it could when it developed alongside a gradual divergence from humanity's antiquated past. After all, it was probably better to live within societal norms than outside them. People don't want witch doctors, they want medical doctors.'

Langley returns to the podium and takes another gulp of water. His speech is coming to an end. Is this repetitive re-hash of old dogma ever likely to bring about real constitutional change? This is preaching to the converted, but they are the only ones that ever turn up. It would be nice for once to meet some real cynics at these kinds of events, someone with a willingness to learn and a healthy scepticism for the whole subject of psychedelic therapy. Drug geeks and students are all very well but when is the movement going to seriously challenge the authorities?

'I don't know about you, but personally I was always left frustrated by the likes of Leary. A genius, of course, but he failed to bolster my need for escape. His attempts to knock the West off course irritated me, left me wanting something more solid, more targeted. Indeed, the fact that Leary and many others attempted to turn-on the world and then failed rather adds to the gloomy state of affairs. After all, it was the children of the sixties who spawned the 1980s and right through to the present day where now any hope of rebellion is lost in the mists of time. I am a child of the 1960s, I grew up in the seventies and came of age in the 1980s. Is this present situation my fault?

'Today's generation of young people is dead; but they are not the Deadheads of the sixties. So let us not confuse the noble sixties sentiment of being 'laid back' with the modern curse of apathy. In the sixties people were laid back because they protested against having to do what was expected of them. They fought for the right to be laid back. Today's youth are content to just push the buttons and toe the line, so long as there is a steady supply of nullifying food, television and consumerist gadgets to distract their flabby brains from engaging with the wider world.

'We have ended up with Huxley's nullified utopia rather than Orwell's dystopia. For God's sake we could do with a little dystopia, it might liven us up a bit. Our kids today have the world on a plate but in front of the God damn TV. Brainless, hopeless, spunkless, empty lost-causes eating their TV dinners. And their children will be even more lost; measuring the passage of time between their next fix of junk food and purchases of no lasting value.'

The crowd is being pulled in all directions by this keynote speech. Not knowing between sentences whether they will cheer or just listen. Joseph Langley perseveres, speaking with clarity about desperate and gloomy things disconnected from psychedelics. He surveys his delegates. Are these the useless lost kids he is talking about? He hopes they are not. After all, they are here. There has to be some hope out there.

'But listen: *all is not lost*! I have a plan. We must bite the forbidden apple and allow its beauty, its visionary magic to show us the world as it truly appears. We, the most visionary scientists on the planet, have the power and resources to transform the medical landscape. For those of you who look at your psychiatric patients with a degree of despair then this conference is for you. So I'm going to shut up now, but remember, *you* are the future for psychedelic psychotherapy. We've been given the tools; now let's find a way forward to Open Minds. Thank you very much.'

There is the inevitable big applause and the MC returns to the stage and shakes Langley's hands warmly. The delegates shuffle away to their vaporizers and smart drinks, feeling they are pioneers on the crest of a wave that will be remembered by history. The doubting psychiatrist from Taunton stays in his seat and watches the crowd leave.

No Orgones Please, I'm British

The Atlantic Heights Hotel has never been so alive; peaking with High Priests and three generations of stoners, professors, multimedia artists, exhibitionists and Nobel winners. Pushing his way through the crowd, the new boy Austell comes to rest by one of the stalls.

'Morning, sir,' says a thin man with one of those obligatory long grey ponytails. Why do they all look like this? Austell surveys the stall's merchandise of sculptures, crystals, incense, oils and pendants. Behind the stall is a poster of an airbrushed dolphin diving through a rainbow rising from a fractally-distorted molecule hanging in space.

'Can I interest you in a Sonic Brainwave Karmic Equalizer©, sir? Each unit has been carved out of South American Shaman Wood; sculptured by indigenous craftsmen from Peru and fitted with a state of the art Orgone Accumulator of my own design. This baby here, The Thymatron 2000©, collects cosmic rays from the outer rim and transmits them directly into your frontal lobes. Would you like a demonstration?'

Austell soon finds himself strapped into a tie-dye booth staring at a pulsating dot. The tall cyber-man fixes an elaborate headpiece to his crown and plugs in a rank of twinkling gadgetry. The machine bursts into life and ethereal music is piped through headphones. Austell wobbles as the Orgone accumulates and the Alien Gray sways enthusiastically to his own internal beat.

'Feelin' good?' the man asks.

It is quite clear to Austell that all that is going on here is a pair of headphones and a dot on a screen. However, not wanting to appear ungrateful or overly British, and longing to break free from his cynicism, he perseveres.

'What exactly am I expecting to feel?'

'The vibes, man, the vibes! You gettin' it? Let go, man. Let it melt over you. Only when you allow your neuronal tangles to become unknotted will you clear the way for the entities.'

What is it about these people and entities? There is definitely nothing happening. At best he is feeling slightly nauseous.

'Can you see 'em yet? Close your eyes, man.'

'Well yes, one is trying…'

'Let go, man…Hey, are you British?'

'Yes, I am.'

Without saying anymore the man sighs and begins unplugging the machine.

'OK. No problem. Thank you, sir. Here you go, let me help you out.'

Austell is relieved but somewhat confused.

'What's going on?'

'It doesn't work on the British. Please step out of the booth, sir.'

'Doesn't work on the British? Why ever not?' The psychiatrist is disappointed. He was looking forward to an experience of altered consciousness, he really was.

'I don't know,' says grey-tail, shutting down the controls and ushering Austell out. 'Never has.'

Austell wanders off and makes his way over to the registration desk, manned by an efficient-looking student-type smelling strongly of the same noxious substance enjoyed by the vagrants in the park; the staple diet of purveyors of dreamery. He tries to make some enquiries about where to find Langley but the receptionist is unable to help him, or even remember much from one sentence to another. Apparently Langley was whisked away for media interviews. Everyone wants a slice of the keynote speaker.

'Yeah, dude,' says the dread-haired, tattooed, multi-pierced student. 'Yeah, Langley ain't 'round right now. He's got the BBC at twelve, followed by the New York Times. And then Fox News, who are doing a real nice piece on the conference together with the Scientologists. I'm looking forward to that one.'

'OK, so how can I catch up with Dr Langley?'

'Well, you can't. That's what I'm saying, I guess.'

'You guess?'

'Yeah. You a Brit, dude? You know that cat Schubert died from eating poisonous mushrooms? He was British. Should have stuck to the freakin' *cubensis*, man!'

Determined not be sidetracked by this man's toxic redundancy of brain cells, Austell continues, 'Is there no way of contacting Dr Langley? Can I leave a message for him? Only I am a doctor from the UK and I think we may have some interesting things to talk about.'

'Oh, man. Too bad, man. Hey, you want some acid, dude?'

'No. Thanks anyway.'

*

Robert Austell files surreptitiously out of the final symposium. The last speaker was an interesting man. It was a lovely touch to bring a toad along and invite people up to lick it. Austell veers left towards the lobby while the rest of the attendees file off in a chattering group to the elevators, heading back to someone's room to look for entities. As he cuts through the lounge to leave, Austell's heart palpitates when he spots Joseph Langley, the man of the moment, perched on a stool at the bar.

As he approaches the dizzying height of Langley's pedestal he is struck by how fragile the little man at the bar appears. And if there is one thing Austell can identify with it is fragility.

'Erm, excuse me...Dr Langley?'

'Oh...erm, yes, hello,' replies Langley, tired and drunk. 'Heading home? I hope you have enjoyed the day?'

'Yes indeed, thank you. It has been...noteworthy,' says Austell. He must be able to think of something vaguely interesting to say to the man. 'And have you enjoyed your day, Dr Langley?'

'Yes, yes, of course. You know how these things are. To be honest it is a pleasure to get away from it all and relax with a drink. It sounds like you're British?'

'Yes, I'm afraid I am,' replies Austell. He stands gawkily, partly walking on, partly loitering and racking his brains for something profound and erudite to say. Langley is too half-cut to notice.

'Me too,' drawls Langley. 'I was born in the UK. But been in this God damn place all my life since.'

'Really?' replies Austell. Then after a long pause adds, 'I am surprised to find you in the bar tonight. I had assumed you psychedelic lot would find alcohol a bit boring.'

At the mention of alcohol Langley perks up and calls the barman over. He notices Austell, perhaps for the first time, and gestures for him to sit down.

'Yes, yes, you're right, of course. Alcohol isn't cutting edge enough for these drug geeks today. Many of them would rather be cooking up some new experimental compound; ethylating this, methlyating that...it all gets very technical. But forget your 2C-9s and Bromo-bluebottles and whatever else; nothing quite beats a tot of whisky. Here, will you have one? What is it that brings you out here to the conference? And what's your name?' he slurs, sticking out a hand.

Austell can barely imagine he is here in the bar with the great man. But Langley is making it so easy for him he cannot refuse a drink, even though as a rule he loathes alcohol.

'Robert Austell,' he says formally, shaking Langley's tremulous hand. 'And the truth is I am completely new to this psychedelic thing. It's all a great revelation for me. You see I come from Taunton in Somerset...'

'You're from Somerset,' exclaims Langley. 'How tremendous! I was born in the West Country. Never been back there, mind, but I hear they have the best cider in the world. And honestly, don't worry about not knowing anything about psychedelics. Truth is, the subject is so small I could tell you everything you need to know in under twenty minutes. How have you found the conference so far?'

'Well, I'm fascinated. As a doctor I am open to anything that might work, as long as it's safe. Let's face it, the present solutions for mental disorders aren't much good, are they?'

'Very true, Austin.'

'Austell, Robert Austell.'

'Austell. Bob, can I call you Bob? That's exactly how I feel. It may sound loopy, but we have to do something for our patients, don't we? I don't know what your experience is like clinically...'

Austell takes a timid sip from his whisky. It is unpleasant and there is no way in hell he can drink it all. 'I see a lot of people stuck in the same old cycle,' he chokes. 'Disengaged from their treatments. They want to get better but can't. They take the medications I prescribe and they suffer horrendous side effects. So I encourage more psychotherapy but they can never really get into it. That's pretty much how it is. Basically it is palliative care, not curative.'

'Well, that's exactly what psychedelic therapy is all about,' says Langley, taking a considerably larger pull on his own drink. 'I've seen all kinds of stuck people make advances with hallucinogenic drugs. I think these drugs should be used first line, not just reserved for the most severe patients, but employed across the board for all kinds of mental health problems. Honestly, when you've seen the power of LSD in action you'll be amazed.'

'Really?'

'Yes, indeed! We may look back in 10 years time, when psychedelic therapy is mainstream, and wonder why we ever attempted psychotherapy without psychedelics. Can you imagine it?'

'No, I can't,' replies Austell, who finds the idea absurd. 'Do you really think it could eclipse traditional therapy altogether?'

'Sure, Bob, why not? Of course psychotherapists are bound to protest. The whole concept of combining drugs with talking therapy gets their backs up. Psychedelics turn everything we know upside down. So there is not much support from traditional psychotherapists, which is crazy because at the heart of psychedelic therapy is simply a beautiful relationship between patient and doctor. It's all about psychotherapy. So what about you, do you think there is a place for LSD in medicine?'

'Well, I couldn't possibly comment,' says Austell with embarrassment. 'I'm too new to have an opinion. But I know something is needed. Anything that offers promise is worth exploring. On the other hand, there are some good points about modern treatments. Not all of the prescribed drugs we employ in psychiatry are poor. They aren't all bad.'

Dr Langley smiles at Austell. 'Ah, well I think they are all bad, Bob. The problem is that us psychiatrists have become too used to poor clinical outcomes. We are so accustomed to failure that we believe psychiatry is primarily a palliative care medicine, like you say. We don't believe we have the power to cure anymore.'

'But I don't think we can actually cure people,' interjects Austell, 'not when their mental health problems relate to severe trauma from their childhood. How can anyone ever be cured of something like that?'

'Sure we can cure them.' protests Langley, thrilled that Austell is not just another meaningless yes man. And he certainly doesn't look like any of the hippies around here. 'Don't be so negative. We can't give in that easily. Why does a horrific childhood experience have to haunt you for the rest of your life? The problem is we have not yet developed an effective form of psychotherapy that gets to the heart of painful memories. We need not be permanently blighted by our childhood traumas. It doesn't have to be that way.'

Austell detects an evangelical pang in Langley's approach that he finds irritating – augmented by the development of his increasingly slurred speech. It reminds him of the whooping of the servile audience. The Taunton psychiatrist anticipates Langley's next claim will be about a conspiracy involving the pharmaceutical industry. He can feel it coming any minute now.

'And no, we're not talking about some elaborate conspiracy from the Pharma industry,' says Langley, tottering somewhat, his cerebellum clearly impaired but his pre-frontal cortex still on – or at least fairly near – the ball. 'They merely provide the market. Supply and demand. No, the real rot, the insult, is because of psychiatrists themselves. We have become blinkered, distracted from a very simple truth that is right before our eyes: the patient needs to revisit the trauma of their past and fight their demons head on. Not skirt the edges with traditional therapy whilst nullifying the senses with yet another depressant drug.'

'Like alcohol?'

'Ha ha! Yes, indeed! Forgive me. My only pleasure in life!' laughs the Californian, steadying himself on his stool and tremulously placing his glass back on the bar. 'But the truth remains that the fault lies with psychiatrists, and psychologists and psychotherapists, all of us who fail to dig deep enough. It's the closed-minded doctors who don't have the balls to put the real power into the hands of the patient. And of course the pharma industry is quite happy with the status quo; they benefit from the rut into which psychiatry has allowed itself to slide. Why should they complain? It is to their advantage that patients keep taking antidepressant drugs day in, day out, for the rest of their lives. Society is addicted to the medical model that supports the need for the drugs, and this plays beautifully into the profit-driven hands of the pharma companies.'

'Well yes, I agree with that…' murmurs Austell.

'The industry has invented its own dogma to ensure compliance with traditional methods,' continues Langley, tugging the arm of a passing waiter and pointing at his empty glass. 'And Pharma maintains its stranglehold on the business of medical research; drug companies are so economically powerful they get to dictate which projects get studied and, crucially, which ones *don't.*'

'Psychedelics?'

'Yes Bob, exactly.'

Austell sighs. 'It's true. No government or university research centre has anything like the funds available to the big drug companies,' he admits. 'There is no such thing as unbiased pharmaceutical research when it is sponsored by the pharma industry.'

'Of course,' Langley adds, 'and none of the drug companies have any interest in psychedelic therapy. Why would they? Why would they want to research a drug treatment that actually works?'

Austell can see that Langley is not talking about a well-organised conspiracy on the part of the pharma industry, but rather a product of convenient evolution that the drugs industry is able to reap the rewards of psychiatry's failure. He is genuinely in agreement with Langley and impressed to hear the point made so clearly.

'It's sad. Psychiatry really is that bad,' says Langley, draining his glass and ordering another two. Austell has still barely touched his and gestures no but Langley is insistent. 'Come on, old chap,' he calls in a mock British accent. 'Keep up!'

Austell takes another sip whilst Langley goes off into a pontificating monologue on aspects of high-level pharmacology intermingled with statements about energy waves. There is so much information it is hard for the Taunton man to keep up. But unlike those crazy hippies from the hotel lobby Langley's words are enthralling. He is becoming more captivated by psychedelics with every minute, which to him represent a fundamental new approach to the management of mental illness.

'There is so much I've missed,' says Austell eventually in a quiet voice. The statement is almost missed in the garbled diatribe of his partner. Langley drains his latest drink, gets to his feet and steadies himself on the bar.

'I've got to pee,' he slurs. For a second Austell is worried the keynote speaker might collapse. But Langley is still going strong. 'Hey, doc, who doesn't feel like that? My only regret is that I'm mortal. I feel cruelly cheated by the fact that I have to die. Look, I have crammed a lot into this short life. And if there is one thing I've learnt it's that it's OK to branch out and try something new. No one minds if you push the boundaries.

'There is so much I want to do in my life. So many things I want to be and see. Which is where psychedelics come in again. The experience itself, by definition, is beyond description. No words do it justice. That is why when people take acid they so often sit there in silence. There are a million things they are feeling but there is no way to verbalise their thoughts. This ineffable experience is so... timeless...you know what I mean?'

Austell sighs again. 'No. I don't know what you mean. That is the problem. I mean, I can understand the words…I can picture the scenario but I can't imagine the psychedelic experience itself. I do want to understand it but it means nothing to me.'

'Look, Bob, hold that thought. I'll be back,' and he trots off from the bar leaving Austell staring into his acrid drink and wondering, not for the first time, how he possibly came to be in this position.

The conference, Langley, the whole thing, they are all a million miles away from Austell's scene; if he even has one. The situation would almost be comical if it wasn't so tragic. What on earth am I doing here? he thinks. Joseph Langley must believe I am a complete idiot, a fraud. He decides he must finish up and get out of here, but before he can do so Langley comes bounding back.

'Right, another?'

'No thanks,' sighs Austell, feeling his familiar sense of uncomfortable anxiety; the old cynicism and despair have now truly taken hold again, 'I've really got to be going. I'd love to stay but…well the thing is, Dr Langley, I don't know about any of this…stuff. All I have is my patients. Unlike you I am just a boring everyday jobbing psychiatrist. I have nothing to contribute to your movement.' The energy drains out of him as he slumps in his seat. There, he's said it, but rather than being sucked into the misery of Austell's dirge Langley is animated.

'I envy that you have dedicated your life so wholly to your patients. That is the greatest accolade of all. It is psychiatrists at the coalface like you, Bob, that are actually dealing with these patients. It is people like you who should be driving this new renaissance in psychedelic therapy. Not the God damn hippies. I mean, Bob, do you think I'm impressed by all this madness?' Langley sweeps his arm across the glittering hotel vista. 'I am a scientist like you. Truth is I have no time for tree spirits and all that crap, I've hardly any time left myself,' he pauses, sad for a moment, before continuing. 'I want to know about real doctors working with real patients. And you, the jobbing psychiatrist, know better than anyone what works and what doesn't.'

Langley can sense his companion's despair. 'Look,' he says. 'We psychiatrists are the ones who are ill. We have become so depressed by our own ineffectiveness that we keep trying to justify our useless treatments. And the industry flatters us about how great we are, when the truth is we are not. But please, there is no need to be negative. Because there is an alternative.'

'LSD...' sighs Austell.

'Yes. But not just LSD. Also psilocybin, MDMA, Ketamine, Ibogaine...hundreds in fact. All of them represent a new class of medicine for psychiatrists. Medicines that can have our patients move on and give them a whole new way of looking at their lives.'

'But don't you see?' says Austell. 'Don't you realise how mad it sounds? To me these are drugs of abuse, dangerous substances that ruin people's lives.'

Langley looks at him incredulously. 'Come on,' he smiles, 'you don't really believe that do you?'

'I don't know,' insists Austell. 'I can't tell what the truth is anymore. I have been fed so much propaganda, on both sides, so persuasively, that everything is turned upside down.'

'OK, well you are right to feel confused and angry. And I'm glad your conservatism is rooted in ignorance and not arrogance. Because I'm telling you now, and forgive me for this, but the negative stuff they've told you about psychedelics, and most other recreational drugs for that matter, is all wrong. Psychedelic drugs are extremely safe. They are totally physiologically non-toxic and, if handled with care, can also be perfectly psychologically safe. Sure, you have to be cautious about their use. You can't just rush out and take a huge hit of acid without spending a bit of time in preparation. You need to know what you're taking, make sure the time and place is right. You've got to be with the right people and you have to know what you want to get out of the experience. But if you do pay attention to all those things then the experience can, indeed will, be the most profound and beautiful experience of your life.

'It is in fact the most fundamental, primitive human experience possible. The experience of God, birth, life and death all rolled into one. How can that not be beautiful and significant? How can it not be transcendent and profound? Psychedelics force one to ask all sorts of vitally important questions about yourself, your life, love, who you are, what is your ego, what does consciousness mean, what is it to be alive and what it will be like to eventually die. Tell me these are not important questions? Tell me this is not an experience that everyone should have at some point in their life?'

'But it's not natural...taking a drug. How can you talk about spirituality when it comes out of a bottle? Trust me, Dr Langley, I'm not a religious man, but surely you can't compare the drug-induced LSD experience with a pure religious experience?'

'What do you mean not natural? What could be more natural than eating a freshly picked mushroom that grows all over the world?'

'You know what I mean.'

'Look, psychedelic drugs are not drugs like alcohol. Now that really is unnatural. Psychedelic drugs are hard work. You can't take LSD as lightly as if you were in some bar and fancied getting blasted on whisky,' he says taking a sip from his own. 'It takes a great effort and great care to take LSD. It's like running a marathon or climbing a mountain. You wouldn't do those things without careful training and advice, would you? And like running a marathon or climbing a mountain, it can hurt at times. You may feel like giving up, it may even be the most difficult and challenging experience of your life. But once it's over, once you cross that finish line or reach that peak, oh boy! It's all worth it and your life is richer for the experience. Do you see?'

Austell nods his head.

'No one would say "Don't climb mountains" or "don't run marathons" just because they're hard, or even because they may be risky, would they? Humans like to do hard things. Taking LSD is the same. It's a challenge. Psychedelic drugs are certainly not a walk in the park.'

CAREER SUICIDE

'Dr Austell, I cannot possibly bring myself to approve of such a thing. None of us can. Can we?' says Hunter, turning to the circle of other doctors in their monthly meeting. There is no protest from the rest of the meeting but everyone avoids Austell's gaze. 'I mean, why you can't choose a proper subject like SSRIs, or sexual disorders or something like that? Why do you have to be interested in such a crackpot idea as this? Really Robert, it's just not cricket, is it?'

'Maurice, I don't think I have explained things as well as I could,' appeals Austell, scanning the incredulous faces of the medical colleagues before him. 'The point I am making is that, yes, these ideas, psychedelic psychotherapy, *are* at an experimental stage; this research is in its infancy...'

'I thought you just said it was started in the 1950s?' questions Dr Isabelle Plum, the doctor who covers the local patch consisting mainly of Londoners' second homes, as well as enjoying a comfortable private practice of the worried well. 'You said just now that this 'research', if one can call it that, is nothing new? And now you are saying it is experimental. Which is it to be Robert?'

'The work with LSD was banned, stopped, some forty years ago and now it is being revisited,' replies Austell, watching the sound of those three little letters cast a horrific scowl over their faces.

'Yes, banned, exactly. Nasty stuff. No, I don't like it at all,' she retorts, straightening her back with po-faced disapproval. 'Besides, what about the reputational risk of aligning oneself with such folly? It's just *not right*. Career suicide I'd call it.'

'Isabelle, this could be the next big thing in psychiatry! If you care to look at the data coming out of the studies going on in California you will see that…'

'Why are these ridiculous crazes always taking root in dreadful places like California?' cuts in another doctor, sending snorts of laughter around the group. 'No, I'm sorry, there is no convincing me either I'm afraid. Giving fragile psychiatric patients killer drugs like LSD and magic mushrooms? Have you lost your mind, Robert? I think you may have been sampling the wares when you were out there!'

Austell continues to attempt making his point, but as the laughter rises and further jokes and quips rally between the establishment doctors he gradually retreats. He sits through the rest of the meeting with boiling resentment and coloured cheeks then retreats to his office. His colleagues' condemnation merely strengthens his resolve.

Despite the many reasons to reject psychedelic therapy, Austell is reminded that he was convinced by a good deal of what he saw at Opening Minds. Not the glitz, but the science, and particularly his evening meeting with Langley, so he quietly begins to read around the subject some more. He looks up some of the papers from the researcher that Langley mentioned in his keynote talk in San Francisco, the UK's Roland Cox, an expert on neuroimaging with psychedelics. This latest research suggests the psychedelic substances have unique psychotropic qualities that set them apart from other medications. Notwithstanding the palpable objections from traditional medicine, Austell is fuelled by his memories of Langley, whose infectious enthusiasm for a bite at the psychedelic apple was inspiring.

Some weeks later a particularly desperate man, Austell's patient Andy, walks into his office wearing the standard uniform of the streets; baseball cap pulled down over a shaved head, grubby tracksuit, battered Reebok Classics, cheap bling and tattoos. His gait, which was once a self-assured swagger, is now a sedated shuffle. He drops heavily into the chair and his head drops into his hands. Austell says nothing and nor does Andy. For several minutes the two men sit in silence; the doctor reclining in his chair, holding his chin in thoughtful attention and the patient staring at the floor.

'Long time no see, Andy. Last time we met you had just started rehab. How did it go?'

The patient doesn't speak. He sniffs violently; noxious mucous slides down his throat. The slime of thirty Bensons and a half-gram of cheap speed, hefted off a key in the waiting room toilets. Austell remembers how last time he saw Andy he had attached electrodes to his testicles and given him thirty thousand volts before the consultation was over. It seemed like the only option for such a lost hope case as his. But now, somewhat surprisingly to himself, Austell looks at Andy in a slightly new light. Perhaps, just maybe, there might be a way through?

The product of a violent father and emotionally dependant mother, Andy grew up in a part of South London where unemployment, crime, alcohol, drugs and child abuse have been the staple existence for generations. All the men in the family are hardened criminals and all the women broken slaves. Drugs are the saving grace and crime the only opportunity for survival. Andy is an advert for violence, for sexual abuse, emotional neglect, subservient women dominated by aggressive men who are little older than boys; everyone bathed in alcohol and twisted by drug misuse. But Andy found a way out. He joined the army. He packed his childhood away into a rucksack, picked up a gun and carried his trauma overseas to

Iraq and Afghanistan. At first the camaraderie and support he found in the forces was a saving grace; he developed attachments and friendships that were able to mask the agony of his early years. But then his friends started dying around him. He suffered a catastrophic breakdown and was given discharge on medical grounds, which left him in limbo between civilian and military life. Disgraced and embarrassed (real men don't have breakdowns), he returned to England where he slipped into social decline, homelessness and drugs. Now all those frozen years of childhood are seeping back into his everyday life. But perhaps, wonders Austell to himself, when one has sunk to such horrific depths, maybe the only way is up, into the light? Langley talked endlessly of journeys out of the darkness and into the light. Perhaps this is what he meant?

'Yeah, it's been a while,' says Andy looking up at his doctor briefly then back down at the floor. How far away he must seem, this doctor, this man in a tie sitting at a desk with his university degrees on the wall and his shelves of books showing off his armoury of mental resilience.

'Where have you been? Did you finish the rehab?' Dr Austell flicks through Andy's notes without looking up. Andy looks back at him, then away again when Austell looks up. Eye-contact tennis.

'I've been inside.'

'Right. Since I last saw you?'

'Pretty much. Got out three weeks ago.'

'What were you in for?'

'Burglary and handling stolen goods.'

'I see.'

'And resisting arrest.'

'Right.' Dr Austell puts down the notes and sits back in his chair.

78

Despite Andy's long forensic history his crimes have been relatively non-violent; apart from a few scraps as a teenager and the inevitable, occasional, drunken ABH. Instead Andy tends to turn the violence on himself. Most of his crimes are connected with the need to find over £100 a day to fund his drug habits. There is plenty of money out there if you know where to look. Thanks to the government's War on Drugs the industry is thriving. 'Did you hurt anyone?'

'No.'

Austell shuts the notes and regards Andy carefully. He looks awful, worse than Austell has seen him for years. 'What are using at the moment?'

'Gear mostly,' says the patient in an obsequious tone, well practiced through years of institutional servility. 'And Vallies. And occasional crack when I can afford it.' Andy respects Austell. He even just about likes him, inasmuch as it was possible for Andy to like anyone, given the severity of damage to his early-life blueprint for measuring the quality of his relationships. This doctor is, at least, not someone who beats him up regularly, so in that respect there is room to afford some kind of emotional attachment. More crucially, the doctor seems to be there for him. Consistent. Containing. That has to count for something.

'Smoking?'

'Injecting.'

'Get any help with the drugs in prison?'

'Yeah, plenty.'

'No, I mean did you get...'

'I know what you meant.'

Austell makes them tea then sits and listens while Andy weeps. He knows Andy has only come in order to blag a prescription for diazepam, which he doesn't mind writing – the patient is going to take them one way or another, funded through crime, if he doesn't get the prescription. He offers to contact Andy's probation officer to see if he can help take the heat off, but Andy doesn't want this. He doesn't want to implicate Austell in his involvement with stolen property.

'I wanna change, doc. I can't take it anymore. I really feel like this time I'm going to do something...something really crazy...I fucking swear it.'

Andy pulls back his sleeves and shows Austell his scarred arms. Deep lacerations criss-cross his wrists and there are tell-tale circular welts of cigarette burns that dot the skin between the cuts and military tattoos. Austell gets up and leads Andy over to the couch.

'Come on, let's get this cleaned up, shall we?'

'Thanks, doc.'

Austell swabs and dresses the wounds. Andy doesn't flinch as the doctor picks the grime from the welts. 'None of these cuts are deep enough to require any sutures at this point, Andy, but here, let me give you a couple of suture packs and some new razor blades. If you are going to cut yourself again I'd rather you did it with clean instruments.'

'Cheers, doc. I appreciate that. I don't do it to kill myself, you know that?'

'I know, Andy. It's not about that. It's different. May I ask, when you cut do you find it helps? Does it work to relieve the pain and tension?'

'Yeah, for a while. But then it all comes back – twice as bad, cos I feel so shit for doing it. Guilty, you know what I mean?'

'I do, Andy, I do. Here, take this bag of swabs and bandages as well. Make sure you always keep the cuts clean. And also, remember to always cut transversely across your wrist, not longitudinally – not down the length of the arm. That way, if you are not intending to kill yourself you are less likely to hit an artery. Or if you do so it wouldn't be so catastrophic. The arteries lie deep, buried beneath the muscles and tendons. You'd have to really dig down deep with carefully dissected longitudinal cuts to do some real damage.'

'I appreciate your advice, doc. You're all right you are.'

'No worries, Andy. Harm minimisation, not prohibition is the name of the game, especially when it comes to self-harm. And the same goes for your drug use. Try and limit the harm caused by your heroin and crack use.'

'It's not that easy, doc,' says Andy, getting up off the couch and pulling his sleeves down over his now cleanly bandaged arms. 'Everything I do centres around getting that score. It's all I do.'

'I realise that, Andy. But once you've dealt with your score and you feel you are in a state in which you can reasonably function try and make use of that time. See if you can pay the rent and get to the shops to get some bread and milk in. Or try and do these things on the day you get your benefits *before* heading out for that first score. And when you are down to your last score always savour that final rock. But above all, cut down pinning the brown. Can't you chase instead?'

Austell makes up a 'one hit kit' goodie bag of clean needles and barrels, citric acid, filters and disposable spoons. Everything Andy will need if he continues to inject, as well as some heat-proof foils and straws to encourage smoking. All good stuff to reduce the harm of drug-using behaviour. But when it comes to a cure, there is no simple paraphernalia with which to send his patient home.

'I don't know what more I can offer, Andy. You've been on every medication I know, you've been through courses of psychotherapy, residential detox, care, rehabilitation and all forms of social inclusion exercises I can think of. You've had psychodynamic therapy, Cognitive Behavioural Therapy and Cognitive Analytical Therapy. The only thing we haven't tried yet is Family Therapy. Do you think we could encourage your mother or father to come up to the clinic and...'

'No, doctor, That ain't goin' to fuckin' happen.'

'I just don't know where to go with you, Andy. I really don't. Are you still getting nightmares?'

'Doc, when I do eventually get to sleep I just experience endless fucking gore and guilt. I can't tell you how it feels. Fucking bombarded with blood from exploded children scattered at my feet. All of it mixed up with images of my dad and the beatings. There is no escape, doc. It's just me,' says Andy. 'It's who I am. I'm made like this. I've been made like this. There is no bloody gettin' away from it, is there?'

He is right. It is everything. It's in his genes, his childhood, his environment, the lack of support and the continued influence of those around him.

Andy continues, now crying, 'I'm cracking up! I've tried everything. You've tried everything. Nothing works. Nothing gets to the heart of the problem. Everything I take just skims off the surface. What I really want doctor, what I really need, is a new brain. I want to cut the whole fucking thing out and start again.'

'Brain transplant is not an option. Sorry, Andy.'

The look of desperation and hopelessness on Andy's face slowly melts into a fixed stare, a blank, dissociated daze. He disappears from the consulting room and drifts off to another place, alone on a battlefield. Austell's thoughts follow him and in their shared fantasy realms they lament together the sheer utter despair of their retched lives.

'*The Glorious Dead!* That's what it says on the Cenotaph, Dr Austell. What a load of fucking bollocks that is. There is no glory in war. There is no space for wearing remembrance poppies and talking about wars and parading the broken fragments of victims to those crowds of admiring, pitiful well-wishers. War does not liberate or save. War does not herald regime change or push through revolution or foster democratic movements.'

'But it's not your fault, Andy. Some might say war is a means to an end.'

'Balls! War is not a 'necessary evil', nor an end-point of failed diplomacy or a political inevitability, or even an unfortunate by-product of man's inherent animalistic tendencies. War can't be explained by the frontal lobes or the heart, or in the aching balls of a man. War's not about pride or power or money or greed or countries or boundaries or land. War doesn't transcend religion and race. War is not something we try and avoid or something worth fighting for or something we cannot escape. War is nothing to do with drug abuse or prisons or pain or industry. It's not about men in pubs with Union Jacks or Stars and Stripes and families to feed, nor sovereignty nor queens.

'Have you ever smelt brains, doc? Have you ever had to wipe splattered brains off your face, tasting the inside of the head of your best mate when it explodes over you? Have you felt blood coming from your own ears and been catapulted forty feet across a market square crowded with bodies when an IUD explodes at your feet?

Have you seen limbs lying in gutters? War is not about any of these things.

'War is about children, Dr Austell. That's what it's about. Your daughter, his son, my daughter, your son, your wife, my mother, their father, his father. *Who fucking cares*! These fucking Arab bastards. The blood of my mates…the men I have lived alongside…we've slept together, eaten together, sat together, shit together, we've wished each other to die…we are one…we need to be there for each other…the best fucking mates in the whole fucking world…cut down like grass…no fucking Arab cunt is going to get me! Fucking, fuck you all…I'll fucking fuck the whole fucking lot of you…'

Snapping out of his fugue Andy weeps for some time 'There must be something you can think of,' he says through tears. 'Some new therapy? Please, honestly, I'll try anything. I'm desperate, I really am.'

'I know, Andy. And so am I. But all the available interventions just paper over the cracks until eventually the splits grow too big and the guts come pouring out.'

As he says these words Austell cannot help but imagine this very scenario happening to Andy. But try as he might the doctor cannot bring himself any degree of emancipation from the distress of the situation by imagining Andy's violent demise. In the past such fantasies were always a comfort to him. But something appears to have changed for Austell. Even his fantasy life has become frustrated.

AN EVERYDAY JOBBING PSYCHIATRIST

Further weeks of senseless grind begin to finally extinguish any remaining sense of optimism ignited in San Francisco as surely as if Austell had never been there at all. Then one afternoon Dr Maurice Hunter interrupts Austell from his brooding in the staff room.

'I see in The Mail that your hippie friends are at it again,' says Hunter, tossing his paper at Austell. 'They're really stirring things up in Whitehall. Bloody wasters. Dreadful things these drugs, what? I really cannot understand the argument that by being softer on drug users we will in anyway reduce the burden of these terrible people on society. Lock 'em up, that's what I say. Lock up the buggers and throw away the key. That'll stop them using their filthy drugs.'

'Oh, come on Maurice, you know it's not as simple as that. There are more drugs in jail than there are on the streets. What we need to do is take more time to understand the root causes of drug dependence. Drug addicts are not going to just go away by employing increasingly draconian methods of oppression.'

'I say drug test the whole bloody nation,' spurts Hunter, his face reddening. 'Anyone with a positive test for any illegal drug immediately loses their benefits.'

'And then what?' asks Austell, by now riled enough to be in this conversation just for the sake of playing devil's advocate. This is, he recognises, a new trait of his. There is something refreshingly enlivening about it. 'All you end up with then is a bunch of penniless, homeless addicts – disconnected even further from society; HIV and Hepatitis positive. Even *more* likely to break into your Range Rover for your stereo.'

'Not if we lock them up and never let them out. Bring back the bloody lash! The gallows!'

'Are you seriously suggesting we hang every person who tests positive for any illegal drug? Including cannabis?'

Hunter growls to himself, casting a derisive eye at Austell. The old man's gripe about Austell's hippie friends refers to a newspaper article describing the growing tide of support for what the left are calling, 'innovative approaches to medical research'. Naturally Hunter abhors such things. Austell, on the other hand, eagerly scans the article:

> *The UK government has unexpectedly declared its support for widening the scope of psychiatric medical research. Ministers are considering the possibility of UK-based research on the killer drugs Ecstasy and LSD, which scientists say could be developed as possible treatments for mental health problems. This paper believes any softening on the issue of drugs is sending the wrong message to young people, whatever the evidence of their relatively safe use.*

Austell stares at the article in disbelief. Cutting through the obvious blind rhetoric his thoughts turn immediately to Joseph Langley. He throws down the paper, pushes past Hunter and heads back to his office. Perhaps it is all coming to pass just as Langley had said? Austell logs on and searches for more breaking news. It doesn't take long to track down the story. People everywhere are in support of the scientists proposing this radical new approach to treating mental illness and Joseph Langley's name is already linked to the news, using this media attention to call for a new British research project.

With uncharacteristic haste Austell seizes the opportunity. Suddenly fired with an optimism he hasn't enjoyed since returning from San Francisco he rummages haphazardly through his desk and finds Langley's contact details, which he had written on the back of a flyer for a parapsychology conference in Palo Alto. Jesus, I must be crazy, he thinks, as he hurriedly types an email. He hits send and the message is away. Surely a stab in the dark. But when one lives in such gloomy halls as Austell any pinprick of light is enough to cause an illumination.

Sylvia keeps the onslaught of patients going all afternoon, a revolving door of victims of a failed service. All Austell can do is deliver the same dismal sermon but they love him for it; the placebo effect of his presence in their lives makes them think his treatments are active, so he carries on pushing the buttons that keep each desperate soul on the conveyor. Then as the last victim of the day shuffles out of his office there it is in his inbox, amongst the inevitable consumerist spam, a lonely message with the subject title, *'Psychedelic Doctor seeks Ordinary Jobbing Psychiatrist'*. Austell opens the message, scans the words and hastily reaches for the phone.

'Bob! Fantastic, it's you!' says Langley, breathless on the other end. 'Look, I've just landed at Heathrow. It would be great to meet up. I have some exciting news...you've heard, I presume? Right...

the UK is where it's at, not California after all. This is an opportunity like never before…can we meet? There are things we must discuss.'

'Yes, yes. I am interested, but as you know, I'm just…'

'…an everyday jobbing psychiatrist, yes, I know,' says Langley excitedly. 'That's precisely what we need.'

'Don't move, I'm coming to the West Country. I'm coming home.'

PART 2

THE COME UP

PRECISELY BECAUSE
IT WORKS

Two psychiatrists, one experienced and one naive, who can say which
is which, meet one evening in a cider farm outside Taunton. It's not
only San Francisco that has capacity for beauty in springtime. The
county of Somerset, which lies at the gateway to the South Western
peninsula of the British Isles, has no towns above a few thousand
people and far more sheep and cows than humans.

'I lived for a while in Greenwich Village before returning to
San Francisco to watch the tide of American culture rising up in
celebration of the millennium. But as the party faded and the fate of
humanity set in all I could do was sit in my tepee and chew the cud
on sacred mushrooms.'

'Really?' asks Austell. 'I think I stayed in for the millennium
celebrations and watched it on TV.'

'Of course by then LSD was already old news. Indeed, it had
little place in the world by the time I finally got practising medicine,'
says Langley. 'Then the ecstasy craze exploded in the late eighties,
which gave way to crystal-meth and left us with the crack-fuelled
consumerist post-rave generation we enjoy today. All I could do
was watch as all those hard-fought battles of the sixties slowly sank
away into apathy.

'Yes, America used to be a damn fine country,' Langley
continued, gazing out across Somerset. Rows of cider trees budding
with growth ache in fecund anticipation of the coming summer.
'There was so much promise. At one point the States was decades

ahead of England for all things psychedelic. She had new horizons. And new chemicals gave Americans a glimpse of the future. It was the land of promise. Man, we were doing things back then that didn't even have names.'

Austell tries to imagine what it must be like to have Langley's life. Surely everything has a name. It has been Austell's business to autistically categorise everything according to their designation, presentation and overall place in the taxonomic system. Many of Langley's words make no sense but he finds them intoxicating all the same. There is romance in his absence of logic. A part of Austell would love to live in a tepee and do something without a name.

'So, Bob, I am here now because I finally have a chance to put into practice all those years of studying psychedelics. After sixty years of pseudo-scientific frivolity we can now get back to where we started, looking at these drugs as medical compounds, not simply as chemicals to get loaded. This is an exciting time.'

'Yes, I felt that in San Francisco. You really think something is going to happen now?'

'It certainly is,' says Langley. 'And I'm back here in the UK to complete the next leg of the journey. You know, it all started here in England, not the USA. It was British doctors who first gave LSD to patients on a large scale. Can you imagine how that felt as a psychiatrist back in the 1950s? Patients who had been racked by untreatable conditions were suddenly amenable to this new treatment. It reduced their inhibitions and allowed them to access repressed emotional memories. For the psychotherapists of the day it was a miracle drug.'

'Yes, I could imagine that being really something,' says Austell, thinking of his own stuck patients. Hideous images of John Patterson and Kathleen Rattick being systematically tortured in his macabre chamber of murderous fantasy pervade his mind. But he doesn't dwell on these eidetic images. Langley's words bring him quickly back to the here-and-now.

'And now we have a chance to start again, to pay homage to the earliest pioneers of the psychedelic movement and bring the subject of conducting psychotherapy with psychedelic drug adjuncts back to the UK where it all began.'

'So why didn't it take off? Why did no one ever tell me about this stuff when I was a trainee psychiatrist? I can't believe all this was kept from me.'

'The reason you never heard anything about it,' smiles Langley, 'is because all this research ground to a halt. Governments didn't like the idea of doctors prescribing LSD to their patients.'

'Why not, if it works?'

'Precisely because LSD works, Bob. That's why.'

'No, I can't believe that,' scoffs Austell. 'That's just more of your conspiracy thinking. If something is shown to work then doctors are keen to promote it. Genuine treatments don't get abandoned just because of government conspiracies. There's no way doctors would let a socio-political agenda get in the way of evidence-based treatments.'

'I'm not talking about a conspiracy,' says Langley. 'I'm talking about a very real piece of history concerning the genuine effectiveness of LSD that led to its removal from the medical pharmacopeia. Because the drug works so well its life-changing effects escaped into the world and carried an entire generation towards revolution. This challenged governments and resulted in an authoritarian backlash that still exists today. That's what I mean when I say you were not told about the clinical benefits of LSD because it works.

'Once they had leaked from the medical community and become popularised by the likes of Aldous Huxley, Tim Leary, Ken Kesey and others, the genie was out of the bottle. Scenes of such indescribable beauty cannot be kept to oneself. The LSD trip produces an impetus to tell the world about what one has seen. It is like a religious experience; it *is* a religious experience! And once the news is out, once people know they too can have a taste of heaven who wouldn't want to go there? It was the perfect backdrop with which to challenge the tide of 1950s materialism.

'Back then there were two opposing cultures that hit each other head on: Vacuous consumerism on the one side and rock 'n roll on the other. And the result? Well, the result was the sixties; a beautiful expansion of minds and mass opposition. A generation of kids standing up to their parents and demanding better schools with new teaching methods, new ways of conducting medicine, new arts, and, of course, new politics. There was a call to return to an archaic way of life. Live off the land, escape the cities and build new communities based on trust and enlightened social values. People turned to the East, to Buddhism, Hinduism, the Kabala and Paganism – to anything that took them away from the establishment.

'The psychedelic experience isn't something you can simply be told about in a sermon by a priest. You have to have the experience yourself. And in the sixties it came down to those who had and those who hadn't. Society was split down the middle; torn at the seams. And all because of that tiny but immensely potent molecule, LSD. My God, a kilo of the drug could turn on an entire city!'

Austell goes to the farmhouse where an old lady is serving cider from oak barrels; just as generations of Somerset farmers have done before her. As she taps the cider into pint glasses for him she explains that cider is the most elemental of alcohols. More simple than beer and a world away from the complexities of wine; everything that is needed is right there in and on the apple. The skin carries the necessary yeasts and the juice of the freshly pressed apples contain all the sugar required for the process of fermentation. Simply press the apples, bottle up the juice and leave it to rot.

As he carries their drinks back to the table Austell considers the high, the intoxication, induced by alcohol, which he has never particularly enjoyed. He doesn't like the feeling of being out of control, but acknowledges it is something that has been favoured by many generations of people. There is something in the simplicity of pressed apples that feels more natural than LSD. This LSD is an altogether different entity. No doubt about it.

'Joseph, you were born in the wrong decade,' he says, returning with their drinks. 'Do you ever wish you had been there in the sixties to witness all this as an adult?'

Langley laughs. 'Well, yes and no. I'm just fine with right now. What I've got planned is going to be bigger than the sixties,' he takes a sip of his drink. 'Great cider by the way.'

The sun drops below the hills and the air carries a chill. Dr Langley pulls on his coat. He possesses a humanness that Austell admires. There are so many shades of grey. Langley's approach and enthusiasm challenges Austell's tendency to polarise people into their character extremes. With Langley there are myriad possibilities and being with him makes Austell feel more human; it cures him of his own autistic traits.

Looking up from his pint Langley says, 'So I'm back here now because I'm on a mission.'

'So I understand,' says Austell, happy to get to the point of their meeting. 'Tell me what it is you have in mind.'

'OK. You've heard about this opportunity with the UK government, right? There is now the chance for a limited period of research into the possible therapeutic potential for psychedelic drugs.'

'What kind of research?'

Langley is clearly excited, necking back his cider before continuing.

'Well, ever since LSD was banned back in '66 and MDMA in '85 we have been waiting for this break. The UK Home Office has agreed for me to set up a small, but potentially wide ranging, study in the UK. There is just twelve months to complete the preliminary project, using psychedelics on a named-patient basis and then report back. If the results are good they'll consider further research.'

'It's almost too good to believe,' says Austell. 'I never imagined the UK would sanction something like this. Is it funded?'

'Yes, by the UK government. It's a bit sad really. It's not about what's scientifically or clinically right but rather what is politically advantageous. Power motivates politicians. The British and American governments are hungry for war, for all the usual reasons, the need to grab some other poor bastard's loot, in this case oil, but the result is tens of thousands of shell-shocked causalities pouring back into society from the Middle East. Rates of post-traumatic stress disorder are skyrocketing.'

'Yes I know', nods Austell. His patient Andy McGovern is an example of the blood-for-oil cannon fodder of which Langley speaks.

96

'And the government are getting tired of pouring millions into disability payments for the post-combat vets. So they need a new treatment for PTSD. It's baloney, I know. They should really be doing this research because they can see the moral and ethical need for these new treatments, not just because they hope to save money and face from it. But look, I'm not complaining. I'm really excited. And the thing is Bob, I'd like you to be in on it too.'

Austell had felt this was coming. Although he respects and admires Langley, having fallen under his spell from their first meeting, there is a gulf of difference between being a distant admirer and getting involved in a research project. He barely knows Langley from Adam, or MDMA for that matter.

'Doing what, exactly?'

'Doing what you do best.' exclaims Langley. 'Being an everyday psychiatrist. I want you to do it because I think, I know, that you have exactly the qualities I'm looking for.'

'Me? Come on, Joseph, there must be a thousand people better qualified than me. I mean, I saw plenty of them at that conference with more knowledge and understanding about psychedelic drugs than I have.'

'Look, Bob, don't you see? I want you because you are inexperienced. My God, I don't want any of those characters at the conference with their baggage and navel-gazing. Crystal healing is the last thing I need. I need a medic, a traditional, unblemished doctor.'

'Unblemished?'

'Unblemished by the psychedelic community. When you walked in I just knew you were the man for the job. You have the most important quality of all...'

'Really?' Austell replied skeptically. 'What's that?'

'Hopelessness.'

'*Hopelessness*?'

For a brief moment Austell had entertained the fantasy that Langley thought there was something special about him, some positive quality that sets him apart, a latent talent or gift that could transform the future of psychiatry. He sighs.

'Hopelessness? Is that it? I suppose you're right...'

'Well, no. Not entirely. Not just hopelessness. Obviously there is more to you than that.'

'I'm very relieved to...'

'You also possess cynicism; a total lack of trust in the current system. You have no optimism for the future. All these qualities are very attractive. In short Bob, you represent the absolute epitome of everything that has gone wrong with modern psychiatry.'

'Hang on a second...'

'No, no, I don't mean it like that. You've not done anything wrong, far from it. You are a talented doctor in the front line of the NHS. But it's what you have become as a result of the system that makes you so special. Don't you see that? You've had enough. You have no hope in the available treatments for you patients. Psychiatry has failed them. It's failed you. It's not that you don't care – on the contrary, you do care, deeply – but your care has been eroded by years of repeated systemic let-downs.'

'Well, I suppose there is some truth in…'

'And I need someone who can come into this project with new eyes, with nothing to lose. Someone critical but open-minded, willing to try something new to improve the lives of their patients.'

'I can see where you are coming from,' says Austell, 'and it's true that I am pretty hopeless about my clinical work. But I don't want to be duped into this scheme merely as some half-wit lab assistant whose only quality is their total lack of effect on their patients. Just because the system is lousy doesn't mean that I'm completely incompetent.'

'Bob, I know you're not incompetent. I wouldn't be asking you if I thought that. You bring genuine NHS psychiatric authenticity to the project. And this is something I could never do. You see? I need you.'

They sip their ciders. Neither of them wants to fill every second with dialogue. Better to sit within the swelling background of silence and see what materialises. It is Austell that pipes up first.

'So what will the project look like? What is it exactly you intend to do?'

Langley downs another pint, looks up with glassy eyes and smiles at Austell.

'Bob, I thought you'd never ask.'

ACTING WITHOUT DUE CARE AND ATTENTION

'Come in!'

Austell gingerly enters the room and takes a seat. In front of him sits Douglas Gascoigne, his service manager, and the service medical director, Dr Maurice Hunter.

'Do sit down, Robert.'

The overworked manager's grey face betrays his chronic sleeplessness. Hunter's smiling visage is characteristically ruddy by contrast; his thoughts are with the young medical student who has been assigned to shadow the medical director for the week. She sits beside the senior figures with a look of suitable anxiety. Austell feels in the back of his throat an intense building of violence toward the smug Hunter. Meanwhile, in the depths of darkness beneath the manager's desk, a pair of slit-like eyes flicker and a forked tongue sniffs the air.

Gascoigne scans the letter before him. 'So I see you are requesting to take a year's sabbatical, to carry out a research study of sorts. What is this all about, Robert?'

Emerging from the shadows behind the desk, the horrendous monster, a thick, slime-covered snake, is stealthily slithering towards the two inquisitors. It coils its way up the chair legs and begins to wrap itself around Hunter's throat. The pompous toff is now turning purple as the killer begins to squeeze.

'Well,' says Austell, clearing his throat to swallow away the savage attack of the killer beast, 'it is essentially a psychopharmacology study. We will be examining the potential role for drug-assisted psychotherapy in the treatment of...'

'If I have understood this correctly you are talking about *psychedelic* drug-assisted psychotherapy,' cuts in the manager. 'LSD and the like, is that right?' Abandoning the half-eaten carcass of Hunter, the yellow-eyed serpent has now moved across the desktop, scattering papers in its wake, and is now coiling itself around the manager's midriff, preparing to tighten its grip and crush the life out of the heart and lungs of Gascoigne.

'Er, yes. Exactly. We are planning to look at a range of different substances across a variety of mental disorders. The purpose of the research is to gather data about the appropriate dosage ranges and assess the relative safety and efficacy of...'

'Oh, come on Austell!' pipes up Hunter. 'Surely you are not serious about running off to pursue this madness with magic mushrooms are you?' Hunter is having none of it. All the doctors in their practice know that it is Austell who has carried the bulk of the work for all these years. Having read his proposition Hunter is peeved by the extra on-call duties that would arise because of Austell's absence. He is not looking forward to being forced to pull his, quite considerable, weight. 'I cannot think for a minute why you want to bother with this ridiculous sabbatical. Why go anywhere? I joined the Trust here in Somerset thirty-eight years ago and never saw any reason to leave. Why can't you just be content to stay in the same job for life? Never did me any harm.'

But the manager is now looking more closely at Austell's proposal and comparing it alongside his spreadsheets outlining this year's spend on staffing costs.

'Hmmm, well, just a moment, Maurice. Let's not be too hasty

to dismiss the idea before we have given it proper consideration. It certainly *does* sound interesting. And you say you will be away from the Trust for a full 12 months, Robert?'

'Yes. That's the plan.'

'And that would mean coming off the payroll, of course.' The manager's insomnia is driven by nail-biting anxiety associated with the impossibilities of balancing the books. When he does eventually drop off, his sleep is tortured by strobe images of financial outcomes festooned in red figures. The cost of external medical locums is threatening to bring the whole system down. They must find ways to claw back some of the Trust finances. 'So,' he says, 'when, exactly, would you propose leaving us to pursue this research?'

'Well, right away if possible, Douglas. Obviously I would have to complete my three month leaving period. So basically I'd like to be gone by Christmas.'

The thought of another three months in this place is painful to bear. The snake, which concurs entirely, flashes a look of agreement and slithers from the desktop to start systematically pulling down the filing cabinets and fixtures in the room.

Hunter sits before Austell, pretending to scrutinise the papers but clearly trying to peer down the student's blouse.

'Be gone by Christmas! I really don't see how that is going to be possible, Robert. I mean, if one looks at the out-of-hours Christmas on-call rota…'

But Mr Gascoigne's shallow world extends no further than the Trust's shallow pockets. He ignores Hunter's harrumphing and interrupts.

'Well, thing is, Robert, the chief executive is due to deliver his annual statement next week and as you know there is a strong desire to complete this year's round of cuts. In brief, I am happy to support this idea of yours completely. That is on one condition.'

The snake, having eaten the plastic yucca and the sickly sweet photographs of Douglas Gascoigne shaking hands with the chief executive on the opening last year of the new, pharmaceutical industry sponsored, psychiatric intensive case unit, stops in its serpentine tracks and looks up, gazing between Austell and the manager. Hunter's lifeless body is no longer of any concern to either of them.

'And what would that be, Douglas?'

'That you leave right away,' smiles the manager. 'That we cut your pay from the end of this week.'

'What about the obligatory three-month notice the Trust usually requires?' asks Austell.

The snake is laughing now, pulling strings of sinewy flesh from its teeth, the last remnants of the manager and Hunter's corpses.

'Oh, don't worry about that,' smiles Gascoigne, having already made the savings calculations in his head. 'We would be prepared to support your important project by not wishing to impede it any further. Consider yourself free to push ahead with your plans.'

Aware he has turned a corner, for the first time in his life, Dr Robert Austell experiences the thrill of knowing he has just acted without due care and attention. He had imagined his dissatisfaction with life was sufficiently hidden by a glossy exterior of superficial care for others, but alas it is not the case. He is morose, a cynic, and in this state he knows he is no good to his patients. Joseph Langley, that maverick daredevil, was insightful to spot Austell's hopelessness and his associated potential for behaving drastically. Maybe Langley's peculiar hallucinogens *could* be the next big thing for psychiatry. He gets up from his seat and shakes hands with his interviewers, thinking only of getting back to his office to remove the dead weight of dated psychiatry textbooks from his shelves. Their musty pages have failed him. For now the medical model is over.

And as he walks out of the office, leaving behind the odious Hunter and all his other doubting colleagues behind him, there creeps across his face the faintest flutter of a smile, because the serpent has now transmogrified into a glorious dragon, adorned with great golden scales. It swallows the last remains of Austell's dogmatic colleagues and then rises up to engulf the whole office. The walls of the hospital are crumbling down, the pillars of the medical model with its algorithms and protocols are being obliterated by this wonderful beast. The dragon beats its great wings and lets out a flaming torch of expiration, setting alight traditional medicine and taking off into the sky above the smoldering remains of Austell's old job.

The pretty medical student, meanwhile, in the nick of time, just about makes it out unscathed. She has decided after today, however, not to pursue a career in psychiatry.

THE MAN ON
THE OUTSIDE

Every clinic needs a physical space in which to operate. Even those whose purpose is primarily psychological. Drs Langley and Austell found what they were looking for when they stumbled across a dilapidated farm site outside of Wiveliscombe in south-west Somerset. The owner, Morris, had fallen on hard times and even harder liqueur. Faced with the prospect of either injecting himself with 350mg of veterinary grade Ketamine and turning his shotgun on himself, or letting his property out to those with non-farming interests, he has made the honorable decision to do the latter.

The farm itself is the picture of bucolic delight, set in a lush sheep-chewed valley at the gateway to Exmoor. Last year Morris had briefly let one of his buildings to a Vietnamese couple who had been employed in some kind of cultivation business. They had patched up the barn and installed an elaborate indoor grow system consisting of powerful lights, ventilation arrangements and a sophisticated irrigation set-up. Such things were beyond the imagination of the traditional Somerset farmer but Morris did not ask any questions. The mysterious growers paid in cash and left as quickly and as silently as they had arrived and worked. So by the time Austell and Langley approached Morris to explain the nature of their project they found a nicely refurbished building, decent wiring and a landlord who was used to keeping his nose out of his tenants' business.

While the two are inside painting walls on a rainy Somerset

afternoon, transforming their space into a room fit for mind expansion, Langley says, 'Bob, nothing will help you understand. You *have* to take the sacrament yourself. It's the only way.'

Austell is well aware of the Day-Glo elephant in the room but he is cautious. He does not want to take a psychedelic drug himself because he wants to remain a blank slate, unsullied by any personal experience. Although Langley understands and respects this, his wealth of experience in these matters tells him that any doctor conducting sessions with psychedelic drugs must have personal experience. It is *de rigour*.

'Thing is, Bob, you can't expect a patient to dive into the swirling pool unless his guide knows the signposts. Your job is to make them feel relaxed. They need to know they are in the safe hands of an experienced pilot, someone who has been into the same dark cave and who knows where the dragons lie. How can you do that if you have not experienced this state for yourself? It is like climbing a mountain with a guide who has never left their front room.'

'But won't you be the main guide, Joseph?' asks Austell boldly. 'You will be the guy up the mountain leading the patient on their journey while I stay at base camp and hold the fort. Won't that work best? I represent temperance, a bedrock of stability, while you scale the dizzy heights of inner space with our patients.'

Langley stops his brush stroke and stares at Austell. This was not part of his plan.

'Are you scared?' he asks. 'Because if so then don't worry, my friend. You would be a fool if you were not fearful. I respect your trepidation; it's a sign that you'll be a fine psychedelic explorer.'

'Well, yes, I am scared. But there is more to it than that. I accept the mission, Joseph. I can see exactly what you are trying to do.

108

But I think the project will work better if I remain outside the trodden path. Countless millions have taken hallucinogenic drugs and pontificated endlessly about their experiences. I've seen it for myself with all those trippers in San Francisco. I have heard and read their stories but I want to approach this project without that first hand knowledge. You said you wanted an everyday jobbing psychiatrist at the helm; well that's me. Do you not agree it would be best if I remain in this state of ignorant curiosity for the duration of the study? That way I can look at our patients' progress simply from the point of view of a curious psychiatrist. I don't need to dose myself to see the effects, do I? If there are real positive effects with this medicine then I want to measure them in my patients with a clear mind. Do you see?'

'Yes. It does make sense,' but Langley is puzzled. 'Does this mean you have no interest in *ever* glimpsing these magical realms?'

'Of course I do!' laughs Austell. 'But only when this project is over. Believe me, *then* I will be ready for the experience - with you as my guide. Until then I will remain outside it, safe within the sanctuary of my medical journals, amongst the evidence-based graphs and statistics of my over-prescribed profession. I do not want to be just another faithful believer, Joseph. I want to be an objective cruncher of data. I want to be the man on the outside.'

The pair paint, carpet and plaster through spring. The rooms they create take on special meaning as the trans-galactic routing stations from which all their test subjects will begin their cosmic journeys. The quality, nature and degree of the psychedelic experience are dependent upon the conditions under which the drug is taken and the variability of effects of psychedelic drugs can only be controlled if certain factors are kept as constant as possible. Of course the dose and choice of drug are also big factors – be it LSD, Psilocybin, Ketamine, DMT, MDMA, Mescaline, Cannabis, Ibogaine or any one of many other hundreds of active chemicals found throughout nature or synthesised artificially. But it is the control of the mental *set* and the environmental *setting* that really determines the outcome of the experience.

'We, the guides, are responsible for the mind-set,' says Langley as they walk along lanes heavy with cowslip. From behind hedgerows sheep murmur contentedly to their young. Their eyes are on the sky where clouds roll in, swollen with rain. England's response to global warming has been an excess of summer rain. The seasons, which used to be beautifully demarcated, are now merged into one consistent homogenous warm drizzle lasting from April to November with only brief windows of mild summer and winter variance. A shower lashes their faces as they trot and Austell grumbles. But Langley allows the water to run over him contentedly. Having lived in the deserts of the world he appreciates the sheer luxury of liquid pouring right out of the atmosphere into one's mouth. Langley is a visionary sponge for the earth's energy in whatever forms it presents itself. The vibrational vigour of love is contained in all elements, he says, to which Austell simply grunts in return. Death stalks Langley, so for now he intends to live.

'Psychedelic chemicals are not drugs in the traditional sense of the word,' he cries, his arms outstretched to the rain. 'There is no specific reaction, no expected sequence of events, somatic or psychological. But we must nevertheless do our best to educate our patients about what they are taking; where it comes from, what the effects will be, how long it will last, what are the risks, the benefits and the history of its use. We need to create a positive mind-set so there are no surprises.'

'None at all?' asks Austell, turning his collar.

'Well, there will be some surprises – that's inevitable. We want to create an atmosphere of informed knowledge. But if you take LSD and *expect* to go mad or die then you will!'

'Not actually *die*?' asks Austell. 'You told me LSD is practically physiologically inert.'

'Yes, yes it is,' says Langley. 'I don't mean *literally* die – that would never happen. No one has *ever* died from the physiological effects of taking LSD. Indeed, there are recorded instances of people accidentally snorting lines of crystal LSD thinking it is cocaine and ending up consuming tens of thousands of doses in a single hit. Sure, they have an intense psychological experience but do not come to any physical harm. Watch out!' cries Langley as two large tractors driven by farm hands high on cider grind past them.

'To prepare our patients' mind-sets we must diligently prepare the psychedelic session. If the patient is too rigid or inflexible they will fight against the drug. Which will create a hellish experience for them; they will become overwhelmed.'

'Right.'

'Anxious patients will understandably try and control everything. We need to create an atmosphere of trust where the experience can flow over them and take them wherever they need to go. Knowledge is power. Say know to drugs!'

'OK,' says Austell, anxious to start recruiting for the study. 'So to whom are we going to offer this treatment?'

'That is a good question, Bob. And this is where you come in. Your major role is to choose the patients. You, the jobbing psychiatrist, have a caseload of patients for whom traditional psychiatric methods have failed to work.'

'I sure do,' laughs Austell.

'We are talking neuroses only, mind. We can't offer this new treatment to people with psychosis. Drugs like LSD tend to shift people with psychosis into a more florid state – which, personally, I don't think is such a bad thing in a controlled environment, from a psychotherapeutic point of view, but I don't think the authorities would let us do that.'

'I'm sure you're right.'

'If I had my way I would give LSD to schizophrenics to shift the fossilisation of their negative symptoms - and also to children with autism. These people could do with some *oomph* to move them on.'

'Maybe. But perhaps let's not go there right now.'

'Agreed. That is for a future project. For now what we need are neurotic patients, not psychotics. Do you have anyone with anxiety disorders on your books?'

'Of course. Hundreds. Anxiety is rampant.'

'Good. So get thinking about which patients you want to use. That's your task. Give me the patients and I'll give you the right drug for the job!'

Gladly abandoning his purposeless one bedroom flat in Taunton Austell moves into the farmhouse. Langley, who wants to be even closer to nature, sets up an on-site caravan in the meadow. Working night and day the doctors transform their farm into a setting fit for internal exploration.

'We must dismantle the 'patient game',' says Langley. 'Remove them from the stresses of their everyday world and provide a blank slate onto which they can project their inner psychic material – their demons as well as their angels. There must be no distractions. No telephones. No knocks at the door. We need total removal from the outside world. And plenty of time is also important. Sessions require a 48-hour window with no meetings or appointments; nothing. Coming down from LSD can be painful enough. But coming down whilst having to deliver pizzas or speak to the mother-in-law is impossible. Our patients will have a slow and gradual return to the world of their usual behaviours. It simply will not do to be thrown straight back in.'

They go to the nearby town of Glastonbury, with its peculiar mixture of tourist crowds and wholemeal mothers breastfeeding twelve-year-olds. Langley buys Indian drapes and a low table of heavy wood to decorate their clinic. They find incense and burners and some large prints of Hindu and Buddhist images for the walls.

'Nothing too distracting,' he says, as they peruse the market. Austell remarks how upbeat and positive Langley appears today – which Langley puts down to having positioned his caravan on a ley line, but Austell attributes to a resolution of the terrible cough that has plagued his colleague since he arrived in England. 'And fresh flowers are essential. On LSD one can become lost in the petals of a rose! And that's another thing: we need a nurse.'

'A *nurse*? Where are we going to find a nurse? You can't just pick one up in a crystal shop.'

'Yes, I meant to tell you. We have to find an experienced nurse for the clinic. The sessions will be lengthy and we need someone with a calming influence, a constant figure to be with the patient throughout. A feminine, maternal presence is important. In the midst of a harrowing trip nothing holds one's fears like a heaving, scented bosom.'

Austell's developmental trajectory, in terms of intimacy, has not taken him close to girls or women of any kind. His utter lack of interest in such things has paradoxically endeared him to many women in the workplace, where his inauspicious attitude has resulted in most female colleagues assuming he is gay; a misunderstanding that removes him from the usual awkward obligations of social intimacy and suits him fine.

British Association
For Researching
Drugs Of Odyssey

'Bob,' says Langley, beckoning him to come and greet a new arrival.
Austell has an indistinct recognition of the beaming woman before
him but cannot place her. 'This is Betsy.'

'Betsy!' exclaims Austell realising who she is. 'I know Betsy!
We met in San Francisco.'

Betina Kowalski Zahradnik heralds from Bohemia,
Czechoslovakia. In her present bodily incarnation she is in her late-
sixties and occupies the husk of a flowering hippie lady. But like
everyone else her worldly departure will culminate in a field of
untainted energy, spiraling off through an intergalactic wormhole to
re-emerge on earth in a different human shape. She floats forward
beneath shape-obscuring layers of printed cloth and greets Austell
with a gripping handshake that merges effortlessly into a hug.

'Dr Austell, I am pleased to see you again. I thought our paths
might cross once more.'

She has the face of someone who has spent many years staring
into the meditative inner space of fiery neural activity. The lines
emanating from the corners of her eyes betray laughter. Her voice,
which Austell remembers from the conference as distinctive, is an
exotic twinge of Eastern Europe and Californian.

'When Joe described you,' she says, 'I immediately remembered
our encounter in San Francisco: Dr Austell - The everyday jobbing

psychiatrist.'

'Yes, that's me.'

She continues to hold Austell's hand, squeezing, using the interface of touch to download information from his brain, and then turns back to Langley, 'And to see *you* again, Joe…such a long time that we have known each other! How long I do not care to guess. My brain is not capable of computing such figures! I would rather think in light years and the distances between stars - such numbers are of greater interest to me than your earthly statistics.'

Austell, unable to contain his broad smile, remembers how struck he had been by Betsy's serene calmness. And here she is now in Somerset. Langley has come up trumps with the nurse. They walk out into the countryside and climb a pre-historic barrow. The aerial view across the Somerset levels is that of the circuit board of ancient civilization's giant supercomputer. Studded with cattle and sheep, field-upon-field stretch unbroken in all directions. The barrow stands erect in the middle of this luscious plane as it has done for thousands of years.

'This place is magical,' says Langley. 'Built, of course, by ancient people who worshiped hallucinogenic mushrooms.'

'Really? I have spent all my life here and never known that. To me it is just rainy old Somerset.'

'Yes, truly. From this pre-historic mound of earth the universe curves away at the edges, falling into the void and dissolving in white light flowing as energy radiating through the fungi's pores and spores.'

Betsy smiles, her eyes closed. She is all too familiar with Langley's psychedelic pontifications.

'Those ancient Britons knew the score, as did the Greeks,

116

Romans, Aztecs, Mayans, Bwiti, Australian Aboriginals and the highly intelligent purple-green liquid-based organisms from the twin moons of planet Lysergicus who first visited this planet to propagate life throughout our galaxy. They all knew that within the quarks of the psychedelic infrastructure of the mushroom lie a wealth of healing potential.'

'Joe tells me you wish to discharge the power of the sacraments upon your patients,' says Betsy to Austell, taking his hands in hers again.

'Yes, yes. That's the plan.'

'Good,' whispers Betsy. 'The time is right.'

They stumble back down the bank with jellied knees to find a pub. Langley needs to take his daily apple-brew medicine and Betsy wants to drink unimaginably strong coffee.

In the early eighties Betina Zahradnik was heralded with a bright future when she started her first nursing post. She had excelled throughout her training and could have easily gone on to Prague's best teaching hospital but she ignored the offers and opted instead for an obscure clinic at a sanatorium outside the small eastern Czech town of Olomouc. She knew exactly what she was doing. The Olomouc clinic was a place with which she was already very familiar. There in the 1950s Betsy's parents had led a group of revolutionary Czech psychiatrists on a pioneering project of psychedelic drug treatments. For a brief moment in history their work put Olomouc at the centre of the world's LSD scene.

In a bold move that went much further than any other use of the drug at that time the Czechoslovakian project used infrequent but very high doses of LSD; up to 800 micrograms. Betsy's parents guided their intrepid patients into deeply spiritual states in which

117

there was a total loss of sensory integration. The boundaries between self, world and time dissolve entirely at that dose until one is left stripped and naked of selfness, floating free of all physical shackles.

By the time the youthful Betsy entered Olomouc in the early eighties, however, a lot of the light of those pioneering years thirty years earlier had faded. Her parents had passed away and LSD had become considered, as it is now, a public enemy. But she labored hard, carrying her parents' legacy and was soon embraced by the small community. Working her way up the ranks, she became senior nurse, ward sister and matron until she eventually sat on the executive board of the hospital, all the while promoting a re-visiting of the out-of-fashion psychedelic drug therapeutic programme.

Having grown up in her parents' psychedelic clinic Betsy has a deep understanding of what it is to guide an anxious patient through the process of consciousness dissolution. As a tiny infant her parents took her in their arms into clinical psychedelic sessions and laid her little hands on the trembling bodies of patients as they lay foetal-like, laughing, weeping and screaming with the existential joy and panic of men and women coming face-to-face with their fundamental existential selves.

As she grew and mastered the art of psychedelic therapy for herself she learned how anxiety, addictions and psychoses were all amenable to treatment with LSD. She worked with her patients alongside their friends and families, nursing them back to health through their own inner-mechanisms of self-realisation. By the time the clinic folded in the late eighties it was the longest running psychedelic centre in the world – having managed to stay in continuous operation behind the iron curtain for almost forty years. But with glasnost and the eyes of the world looking on, the authorities discarded psychedelic therapy.

In Czechoslovakia, as in the West, the growing industry of antipsychotics and antidepressants became the Eastern Bloc's drug-area of choice. The pioneering work at Olomouc fell into obscurity and became the target of baseless criticism from authorities seeking financial gain by jumping on the media bandwagon against the work of psychedelic therapists. So Betsy fled to the States and sought refuge amongst the underground psychedelic culture she found there.

'I spent some nomadic years drifting,' she tells Austell, while Langley stands at the bar. 'I was living in progressive communes up and down the West coast. Then after doing that for a while I got bored of the States and my travels took me to South America, to Ayahuasca tribes and the mountains of Peru and beyond. What a time that was! It was in Peru that I developed an interest in the healing potentials of high dose tobacco leaves mixed with bat guano. What I found was that when this heady mixture was ingested in the correct manner, with care and attention paid to creating the right psycho-spiritual environment, the user experienced deep trance states. Oh boy! I was living in a state of utopian bliss amongst the hill tribes of Peru for three years.'

'Acting as resident lover to at least three different tribal elders and countless visiting statesmen,' added Langley with a sassy laugh, 'according to the local custom - or so she was told!'

'Oh, ignore him! I was using my well-honed technique of bat-shit powered mind expansion to communicate with the dead - and I became something of a local celebrity! I was happy there and could have easily stayed with that tribe till my dying days. But then I contracted *Cryptococcus neoforman*, which was inevitable eventually, given my chosen medium for intoxication. So I moved on again, returning to the non-civilisation of the Western world.

'And it was whilst recuperating in Mexico City that I first met this fine man here, Dr Joseph Langley. He was almost twenty years my junior but this did not quell the immediate passion between us. After a brief but passionate affair we travelled to the East together and deepened our shared interest in psychedelic experimentation, living together as part of a newly formed community of disaffected flower-children in an ashram in Nepal.'

'Yes, I remember,' says Langley. 'We offered our services to the rest of the ashram as co-therapists for those seeking enlightenment through hallucinogens. But this did not last long. There were a lot of twisted Westerners reaching for the stars at that place. It all folded, rather messily if I remember rightly?'

'There was a lot of love in that Nepalese ashram, Joe.'

'And acid.'

'After peaceful non-verbal negotiations the community dispersed due to irresolvable differences about the distribution rights of communal astral planes.'

'Something like that,' slurred Langley, tucking into another warm pint of scrumpy. 'I then returned to America where I resumed an old contact with the Navajo and Betsy, I think you disappeared from view for some years. God knows where you went.'

'Well, I am not at liberty to tell the next bit of my story in its entirety,' the Czech nurse smiles. 'The rumors are that I was in the Soviet Republic working with the KGB on the development of psychedelics as truth serums for the military. According to acid folklore, so I am told, I was actually a double agent, using these government connections to develop my own highly profitable

120

export business. It has even been alleged that for some years I was personally responsible for the worldwide distribution of some thirty million doses of weapons-grade LSD during this time. Of course, I could not possibly comment!'

Whatever the stories of the past, Langley is immensely pleased to have her on board with this project, feeling as he does a swollen sense of achievement from his own small part in her life. And Betsy is equally pleased to be here.

'I am truly grateful for your call, Joe. This project sounds like just what I need. I feel now, as I approach my seventieth year, that I am only just starting my work. The Czech Republic is in a state of flux and I hope your plans will catch the attention of the world so one day I can return LSD back to my beloved Olomouc.'

Robert Austell does not mind that he is the outsider in this emerging Somerset project. Just to be part of something new, which is, to some small degree, his own creation is inclusion enough. And as far as he can tell, with his limited experience of mental states, he is feeling happy.

'So when do we start? I cannot wait to begin!' he asks the eccentric nurse and doctor. With everything in place he is eager to get back to work. It is a feeling he has not experienced for a very long time. Langley fills their glasses and gets to his feet.

'Bob, I like your spirit. It's time to re-introduce contemporary medicine to a therapy that has been shamelessly lost in the mists of time! Dr Joseph Langley, Dr Robert Austell and Betsy Zahradnik, clinicians of the hallucinogenic hinterlands, we are now bringing it all back home! *This* is the point when modern medicine has its eyes opened to the glorious possibilities of Psychedelic Therapy. Here is to the beginning of the future! Cheers!'

'Cheers!' shouts Austell.

'Na zdraví!' calls Betsy and they smash their drinks home.

We need a name - a name for our clinic,' says Austell. 'What are we going to call this project?'

'Yes, you are quite right, Bob,' agrees Langley. 'It needs an identity. Leary had the *League for Spiritual Discovery*. We have to find a name that is serious and respectable as well as catchy and memorable.'

The three of them spend some time brain-storming, scratching down acronyms and playing with ideas, before Betsy cracks it: 'What about *The British Association for Researching Drugs of Odyssey*?'

'It's a bit of a mouthful...'

'BARDO for short. What do you think?'

'Bardo? Odyssey? I love it!' exclaims Langley.

'I don't get it,' says Austell.

'*Bardo* incorporates the Tibetan concept of soul transcendence,' Langley replies, 'and an odyssey is a journey into the unknown where the brave of spirit encounter adventures and return home armed with wisdom. It's perfect!'

THE THIRD
MOST IMPORTANT DAY OF
YOUR LIFE

John Patterson, who rarely sees the light of day, has emerged from his Taunton bedsit and made his way to the isolated farmhouse. He looks anxious as he crunches up the path towards Austell who is standing in the doorway to greet him with an outstretched hand. The patient looks as shocking as ever, with a stench of new whisky hanging on his old breath. Austell takes his coat and leads him into the stone building. Patterson scans the room uneasily. It does not look like a psychiatrist's office. Gone are the hospital paraphernalia, no filing cabinets, clinical examination couch, sink or walls plastered with trademark peeled paint and dated NHS health and safety posters. Not even a desk and computer.

Austell motions him to sit down on a beanbag beside a low table with a bowl of fresh fruit and a smoldering incense stick. Indian drapes adorn the walls and sitar music gently tinkers. The atmosphere is otherworldly and certainly a world away from Taunton.

'To be honest, it's not really my cup of tea, Dr Austell.'

Austell laughs. 'Nor me, Mr Patterson. But it sort of goes with the territory apparently. Let me explain why I have called you in here today. It's all part of the experiment.'

'Experiment?'

John Patterson's obsessive-compulsive disorder does not leave a lot of room for experimentation. Routines and order are the name of the game so perhaps this was the wrong choice of word to describe the project.

'As you know I have left the clinic in Taunton where we used to meet and I am now working here with another doctor – a man called Dr Joseph Langley – who you will meet in a moment. We want to know whether you are interested in taking part in a new type of therapy. Did you read the letter Sylvia sent?'

'Yes, yes I did. So Sylvia is with you here too?'

All of Austell's patients are familiar with Sylvia. He has enlisted her help with the new clinic because good administration is hard to find. A decent medical secretary can be involved in all aspects of the clinical program as well as having a containing impact on patients, which is an important part of the overall holistic effect. Sylvia jumped at the chance to join Austell again. Since he left the Taunton clinic, life under Maurice Hunter had become intolerable.

'Oh, yes, Sylvia is here too. She is helping us out. What we have planned, John, is a new kind of therapy; a form of psychotherapy that works in a different way to anything you've ever tried before. It is, we think, going to be a lot better than anything you've ever tried before. It really gets to the heart of the problem.'

Patterson is immediately acquiescent. 'Dr Austell, if you think it will help I will try it. But I thought you said there was nothing else left that could help me?'

Austell proceeds to tell Mr Patterson about psychedelic therapy. He describes the history, how hallucinogens work and the risks and benefits. All the while trying to engender a positive mindset in his patient. And then, just as he mentions the inimitable Dr Langley, there is a knock at the door.

'Ah, here he is now!'

124

Langley enters, beaming with excitable tranquility. Making the prayer gesture he sinks to the floor into the lotus position, closes his eyes and begins humming. Austell, sensing this is likely to freak out Mr Patterson, beckons Langley to explain to John some more about psychedelics as healing agents. Langley does so, illustrating his talk with pictures of Buddhist Mandalas and Sanskrit writings. Patterson is surprisingly interested in the proposal. They drink tea and are soon discussing the practicalities of a psychedelic session. Langley hands Patterson a reading list and runs through what he must do to prepare for his first session, which includes stopping all of his current medications, giving up coffee, avoiding meat and studying cloud formations.

'So,' smiles Austell anxiously, unable to read the puzzled expression on his patient's face, 'how about it, John? Are you in?'

Mr Patterson sits on his beanbag, clearly bemused, chewing on a slice of mango (having passed on the kumquats). Langley had lost him at the point about re-entry into Samsara. By now, however, Betsy has joined them. A calming and serene presence beside the two psychiatrists.

'To be honest, Mr Langley, I don't understand any of this. But I do know that I am unwell. And I do want to do something about it. All this…"cosmic reality" stuff…' He turns to Austell. 'Dr Austell, what shall I do?'

'You need to go away and think about it, John.'

'No, I want you to tell me. What shall I do? I want your opinion. You know I've never been great at making decisions.'

'John, this must be your decision and yours alone. But what I can assure you is that Dr Langley here has many years of experience. He is an expert in this field. And I, personally, feel confident about the project. This treatment could be the next big thing in psychiatry and a great step forward for you.'

Patterson thinks for a moment. He glances around the room and takes a long look at Langley.

'Dr Austell, you have cared for me all these years and I trust you. I always take your advice about my treatment – even though most of what you have prescribed for me over the years has been useless. But if you are saying this will be good for me then I will do it.'

Austell is moved by Patterson's loyalty. Here is a vulnerable man who is prepared to put his trust in, and hand over his sanity to, an alien team based on nothing but the prior relationship with his psychiatrist; a relationship which has produced little more than well-meaning but less-than-perfect medical interventions. Austell suddenly feels terribly responsible. He knows he must do the right thing for John Patterson.

'Look, John, the truth is I'm also new to this. But I am absolutely convinced by what I've seen and heard from Joseph. This sort of work is still experimental. But there is a great wealth of anecdotal evidence about these drugs, which have been used by humans for thousands of years. I fully support this project and will make sure you are well looked after. I promise it, John.'

Patterson looks at them all. Three eager clinicians chomping at the bit - they clearly cannot wait to get their hands on his ailing brain. To be honest, he thinks, my brain is pretty much open to offers from just about anyone who reckons they can do a better job with it than I have for the last 60 years. He really doesn't have anything else to lose.

'OK,' he smiles. 'You can count me in.'

'Bravo!' nods Langley. 'Ladies and Gentlemen, we have our

first patient!'

'So what will be our first drug, Joseph?' asks Austell. Langley does not need to give this too much thought. 'I think we start at the beginning with the mother of them all, Bob. LSD. And at a good dose too. Let's not be shy.'

Psychedelic research, like all research, but more so than most conventional studies, suffers from all the inevitable delays and complexities that surround giving humans controlled drugs in a non-recreational setting. This is most irritating for professionals involved in such research – especially when all of the psychedelic drugs are so freely available, without regulation, safeguards or experience on every street corner of every town.

The weeks drag into months and summer is over before anyone has taken anything more mind-expanding than a cup of lapsang. For Austell, Langley and Betsy it is an anxious waiting game. The clinic building is finished and their first patient, John Patterson, is prepared and ready to go. He has adopted all the groundwork regimes dictated by Langley, most of which have been easily manageable. Coming off his medication didn't cause any significant symptom relapse - a sign of the uselessness of the stuff in the first place. He is even coping with his prescribed diet of tofu and brown rice.

Then some good news: Langley reports excitedly that the Home Office ethics committee has fully approved the study. At Betsy's insistence the LSD is coming from a company based in Czechoslovakia, *Paradigm Shift Inc*, expertly synthesised and produced in tablet form at a purity of 99.97%. After all these years the Czechs still make the best acid by far – something to do with the soil and quality of potatoes according to Betsy. *PSI* produces its experimental drugs at astronomical prices, but the ethics board insists they use a bona fide chemical production company, which is understandable. However, given that Betsy owns *PSI*, everyone's a winner.

'John,' Langley addresses the patient. 'This is a very important day. Taking a psychedelic drug for the first time is the third most important day of your life. The first is being born and the second is the day you die.' On saying this a shiver courses through Langley's body. Death sits on his shoulder.

One thing the *Bardo* team has decided not to do in preparation is conduct endless personality questionnaires and psychological rating scales. After years of strangling bureaucracy Austell is relieved by this omission. The only outcome they are measuring in this non-blinded, open-label, non placebo-controlled study is *how is the patient feeling, by their own qualitative admission, after the treatment compared to before.*

Mr Patterson is led through to the treatment room and takes his place on the low couch beside Langley. Betsy disappears next door to prepare the medicine while Austell lights a candle and some incense then chooses a CD of Tibetan throat chanting.

'Good choice!' chimes Langley. 'Tibetan chanting sets the brain into theta rhythm and prepares the neurons for the passage of the sacrament.' Austell is not sure he believes this but is willing to go along with it. This is after all the spirit in which they intend to run these studies.

Ethereal theta-genic warbling drifts through the room and Betsy returns with a modestly sized pink tablet and a glass of water.

'Right, John, are we comfortable? Joe? Bob? Make a note of the time please. It is exactly 9.42am and I am administering a 300 microgram dose of LSD.'

128

John sits up from the couch and swallows the tablet, thanking Betsy who shuffles out of the room. He is then encouraged to settle back on the couch and don the eyeshades. As soon as he is in this position Austell and Langley, sitting on low chairs either side of the couch, exchange glances. It is a whopping dose but Langley has assured Austell it is essential for the first trip. Once a voyager is used to the LSD experience they can take much lower doses and still quickly orientate themselves therapeutically to the unique mental space. But for the first time one needs a sufficient boost – a leg up – to scale the wall of ego-resistance and drop down the other side into the garden of delights.

Betsy returns and hands out another LSD tablet; this time a small blue one for Langley to swallow. Langley is going to simultaneously take a dose of 75 micrograms, a reasonable pick-me-up, so he can psychically energise and effectively steer Patterson on his journey. This is a well-practiced technique for psychedelic guides. It allows them to be with the patient in a similar state of mind but not so overwhelmed that they are unable to keep a foot firmly planted in the external world. Now all they have to do is wait.

O, NOBLY BORN, THE TIME HAS COME

Forty minutes have passed. John wonders if the drug is going to work. *I must be immune.* The Tibetan chanting seems to have gone away (*How come I didn't notice them changing the CD?*) and now Bach carries him onwards, its meandering mathematical rhythms picking him up and placing him on celestial shoulders.

There is nothing to be afraid of. After all, where are the demons? Are there really demons inside that little pink tablet? That's not feasible is it? How can a tablet contain anything bad? How can it produce demons out of thin air? So, if there are demons they must already be inside my head. And if they are in there anyway then what's the harm in simply meeting them face to face? Nothing... think about nothing...Langley said to think about nothing...but then he also said nothing can hurt me...

Langley, leaning back in his chair, is beginning to feel the tingling edges of reality waver in his peripheral vision. He takes up a book and starts slowly reading out loud – ever so slowly – for Patterson's benefit, from Leary's *The Psychedelic Experience*, the prototypical trip guide:

'*O, John, Nobly Born,*
The time has come for you to seek new levels of reality.
Your ego and the John game are about to cease.
You are about to be set face-to-face with the Clear Light.
You are about to experience it in its reality.

131

In the ego-free state, wherein all things are like the void and the cloudless sky,

And the naked spotless intellect is like a transparent vacuum;

At this moment, know yourself and abide in that state.'

The psychiatrist then slowly...*ever...so...slowly*...lowers the book and hands it over to Austell, who takes up the monologue while Langley sinks further into his own chair. Meanwhile, quietly and with no movement from behind his eyeshades, Patterson lies still. Ever so still. Stretching out from him in all directions is the stillness of a glassy lake. Not a ripple. Not a sound.

What was that? Is that supposed to be funny?...I don't get it... did he say something about the sky?...Why is he talking about the weather?...Am I...falling?...falling. Such stillness...Why is everything so...so...So? Why is it so light in here...behind these eyeshades?

At this point Betsy enters and puts a blood pressure cuff onto John's arm – an annoying distraction, but unavoidable as it is one of the unfortunate stipulations of the ethics committee that they measure the subject's physiological response to the drug's administration. She pumps the bulb and inflates then deflates the cuff, letting out the hiss of air and listening for the thump-thump-thump of his returning venous flow.

'Don't worry, John. All part of the procedure'

Blood pressure, yes, I remember...Betsy...Ah! Betsy... She is outside. I am on the inside and she is on the outside. Not just underneath the corner from around the edge...but... COMPLETELY...outside the other side of the edge...yes, that's it!... But no...I think I know I mean a yes but it's all wrong. That is I think

132

I disagree…

'Dr Austell…Robert? Dr Aus…'

'Yes, John,' comes a voice from a billion light years away. It is a voice sliding and slithering through a hole in the sky. *Is that normal?* Light rain trickles down from somewhere. Everywhere. *It must be raining now. It was lovely this morning when I arrived.* John is now sitting on the floor.

'I am here with you, John. We are here. Myself, Dr Langley – Joseph – and Betsy. This is where you are. We are all sitting on the floor.' And now a warm hand is holding him. So warm.

He, John, is fine. My very John-ness is fine. I, John, am fine: I am John and I am fine. Hello, I am John and I am fine. How are you? This is OK. This is perfectly normal. Nothing. Think about nothing. "Nothing can harm you." QED: Everything I think about can harm me. No! Everything is fine. It is the drug. LSD. Everything is perfectly OK. After all, Dr Austell is here. He is a good man. He gave me LSD. That's what it is. Micrograms. Three Hundred.

'Good, fine. Great, thanks Dr Langley,' says the patient.

I am the patient. This is their experiment.

'Yes, John,' comes a voice from a billion light years away. A voice sliding and slithering through a hole in the sky…*hang on, I've already thought that*…Light rain rains down from everywhere. Langley is talking. Slowly and gently. It is Langley's hand that is holding John's.

He is a good man, this professor. He is here to help me. He knows what he is doing. And Dr Austell is a good man.

From the chair where Langley is reclined at the other end of the room - about twenty million miles away, give or take a few light years (it is difficult to tell in this fog) – the psychiatrist says

133

something, in an ever so containing voice.

There he goes, talking about the weather again…

'Is it raining, Dr Austell?' asks John, clear as a bell.

'Is it raining? Is that what you said, John? No John, it's clear. It's a lovely day actually. Bit windy though. They'll probably be a drop later…'

I knew they were talking about the weather! But then why is it so LIGHT behind these eye-shades!

Langley is now crawling over the floor to join the patient, who is curled up beside the couch. *Inside. Outside. Inside. Outside. Inside. Outside. Is it Ok if I just repeat this for a while? An hour, say? Is that OK with you? Inside. Outside. Inside. Outside. Inside. Outside.*

'Do you want to go outside, John? Have a stroll and take a look at the trees?'

OK…Sure. Why not.

John took the LSD two-and-a-half hours ago and has had the eyeshades removed for almost an hour, but it doesn't make a great deal of difference to what he is seeing. He rocks gently. He does not look scared as Langley approaches, crawling over the carpet on all fours. *It's a long, long way!* Padding softly with those lion paws across that vast expanse of savannah. He is not cowering or flinching. John is being born. In his eyes there is depth, warmth, an almost humorous light pulling Langley in towards him. He is unfurling into the light. His whole body is reaching in through the gap between his eyes and his brain and…and…and he has become his own mothership. He is literally *out of his head.*

'How are you feeling, John?'

I can't really blame her, my mother, can I?

This is a moment of relative calmness. Quite suddenly John feels

134

almost completely straight. He looks up, quite lucidly. 'What is it now, doctor? Two hours in? Three?' The waves of swirling colorful confusion have passed and he is here, simply here, sitting, lying, curled, somewhat incongruously maybe, on the floor. Never mind. He is holding one of the Indian drapes against his body. Langley is holding him. Betsy is there too. She is holding him. His face is wet with tears. He has been crying. Weeping, screaming at times, he thinks, for what must have been over an hour.

Betsy is here, everything is going to be fine. It is over. The trip has finished. That's it! Phew! Jesus Christ that was amazing! I have never experienced anything like that before. Incredible! And now it's done. Phew. Thank God. All finished. No more of that. The LSD has worn off completely now. Finished. Caput. Wow, thank you Dr Langley. That was amazing!

John has taken off his shirt and now sits only in his vest. He says he is comfortable like this, so Langley has done the same. Everything is perfectly normal. Nothing could be more normal than this. This is just another perfectly normal day at the office...*Ha, Ha, Ha!* 'A typical day at work for you lot!' laughs Paterson. Laughing, laughing, laughing! The tears are streaming down his face. How ridiculous! 'Just a normal day at work for you, is it doctor? Ha, ha, ha! This is your day job!'

Austell comes and sits with them on the floor, his back against the radiator. It is warm. Positively cozy. Three men lying on the carpet. Betsy is hovering. Outside, the promised rain lashes the windows as the afternoon wears on. The sound of a distant train and intermittent birdsong is exquisitely beautiful. Unfathomably so.

'I suppose it is, John, for us. A normal day at work. All in a day's work at *Bardo*.'

It is over. Thank God for Jesus Christ it is over.

'How you feeling now, John?'

'Good, fine.'

John laughs some more. And some more. And some more. And some more. But it is not normal laughter. There is no reason for it. It is a painful, encompassing laughter. Awkward gut wrenching laughter. Tears pour from his eyes, they fluctuate between laughter and deepest despair. It is not joyful laughter. It is a purging, agonizing spew of laughter. Then the cackling, weeping cry stops suddenly and John looks out intensely. His mind is captured by something else. He has lost the meaning of the conversation, if that is what it was. He is off again. That brief window of normality is somewhere else now. He is outside looking in.

Oh look! There he is again…it's Bach!

RAIN. And LIGHT. It's not over. RAIN. No, it's not over! RAIN…No John, it is *not anywhere near* over. *God I need a drink.* Is that rain, Dr Austell? Yes John, it is raining. Do you want to go outside, John? No John. Yes, John. Rain, John. 'What time is it?'

What does that mean? It doesn't matter anyway…IT IS NOT OVER…IT HAS BARELY BEGUN. It is still…yet also moving…it is dark…but also not…another hour…maybe two passes…they go outside and laugh at the cars…they come back in…someone passes around blissful strawberries. The peel of an orange and the peal of a bell, carry the calling of painted birds away; over the drabness of the hills beyond this Taunton towards another.

I wish I could bring back that laughter…That laughter, John?… Don't wish for anything, John…just wait and see what happens… what will be will be…'You OK John?'

'Good, fine. Great, thanks Dr Langley,' says the patient. *That's me isn't it? The Patient...* 'Yes, you can hear the church bells from here, John.' *Just like when I was child...*

Betsy has crawled closer. *I love you.* Childhood. *She is holding my head in her arms. She is cradling me. Oh, Betsy! Mother. She is holding my head in her arms. She is cradling me. Oh, Betsy! Mother.* My darling child. *You worthless piece of shit.*

Yes, John, go there. Tell me, John.

You worthless piece of shit. Mother. RAIN. *You piece of shit.*

It is not over. Look, he's peaking.

'Yes, John,' comes a voice from a billion light years away, sliding and slithering through a hole in the sky. Light rain rains down raining light lightly down from everywhere. It hurts...THE LIGHT. *Stop it John! Stop it Daddy! Stop it John. YOU NAUGHTY BOY! Take that! Fucking piece of useless shit! Of course it hurts... someone just stuck a bloody needle in me! Ow! Oh, it's OK. It's just Dr Austell. He said he'd do that...* Remember, John? Just a wee drop of blood...

'OK, John? Just a little blood test.'

'Good, fine. Great, thanks Dr Langley,' says the patient. I'm here with Dr Austell. I've taken LSD, I'm not really mad.

Yes you are.

It has barely even begun.

No it's not...it's almost over. God I need a drink. Who told you that John?

Langley gets up and goes next door. Patterson knows he is on the phone to the Prime Minister. He can hear their conversation because he has extra sensory powers.

'Yes, that's right, sir...yes, Prime Minister...about six hours ago...LSD, I gather, sir...yes, I can spell it out to you if you want:

*L.S.D...*Yes, it is that dangerous mind drug, sir...difficult to say, sir...another ten hours perhaps, sir?...oh, very well...no, I mean yes, I agree...we told him not to take it, sir...they made him do it...of course not your highness...give my regards to the Seraphim.'

Is it over yet?

The rain, John?

'Dr Austell?'

'Yes, John...'

'Is it still raining outside?'

'Er...yes, John, it is. It's slowed down a bit though. Do you want to go outside and have another look?'

'No...no, I don't think so...' *God I need a drink. It is her fault – more than his even. But I have to look after little Emily. It is definitely not her fault. But as long as I keep repeating the same routine over and over and over and over and over again...I will be fine. Tears, flowing, raining tears of hatred and hatred for the bastard son of a bitch, mother-beating, cunt, mother-beating, bitch, fuck, PAIN. Oh sister! Oh mother. Oh why was everything always my fault? God I need a drink.*

'Where are you, John? How are you feeling now?'

It is too much: The carpet. The floor. The wall. The fireplace. The sister. The lampshade. The floor. The carpet. The wall. The sister. The floor. The wall. The carpet. The chair. The fireplace. The sister. The lampshade. The floor. The chair. The carpet. The wall. The sister. Dr Austell calls wildly: 'Joseph, Betsy! I need your help!' John Patterson is acting uncontrollably. He wants to find Langley's car keys.

'It's alright, John. It's OK. Look, it's me, Dr Austell – Robert. I'm here with you. So is Joseph. It's all OK. You are safe here with

138

us. Everything is fine. Look, there's Betsy! Come on, let's have a stroll outside…look at the trees…you liked that earlier…'

They lead the vacant figure outside. Dribble, laughter and distance in his eyes. Round and round the farmyard. They trudge down the drive and back up to the house several times. The rain has stopped and the autumn trees drip with transcendently beautiful crystal jewels. Patterson chuckles as they walk. A depth of what some people call normality returns to his gaze. Almost eight hours have passed since he took the 300 micrograms of LSD.

They go back inside to the warmth and sit on the floor. There is a fire in the hearth. Logs crackle providing that elemental animalistic sense of containment. Sitting in the mouth of a cave, safe within the protective arms of the tribe. People have been doing this since time immemorial.

'It's a drug, isn't it, Dr Austell? Or maybe it's not the drug. Is it me? It's me isn't it?'

'Yes, John. It's LSD. And it's also you. You have taken LSD. Everything is fine. You took 300 micrograms of LSD about…oh, nine hours ago. How are you doing?'

'Surprisingly well, actually, doctor. I am OK aren't I, Dr Austell?'

'Yes you are, John. You are doing brilliantly. Everything is brilliant. You are doing really well.'

'Oh, thank God for that, Dr Austell. I just wanted to check… you know, make sure I'm…behaving OK…you know, for your experiment…'

'You are doing just fine, John,' smiles Austell warmly. 'Don't you worry about a thing.'

'Thank God for that, Dr Austell. And tell me…'

'Yes, John?'

'Where's your friend, Dr Langley? And Betsy?'

'Oh, they are right here with us, John. Look, Betsy is holding you. She's sitting right behind you. You are cradled in her arms, John.'

'Goodness, sorry Betsy!' looking up, 'I didn't see you there…'

'Hello John, O noble wanderer!' says Betsy, stroking his head tenderly.

But it's not really over yet at all, is it, Dr Austell?

'Shall I read to you, John?' asks Austell.

'Please, I'd like that.'

'OK. You OK, John?'

God I need a drink

'Read from the Second Bardo, Bob,' says Langley. '*Let us be reminded that Voidness cannot injure Voidness…*'

Austell finds the passage and begins to read. (Somewhere in the dark wilderness a cold coyote calls…)

'O nobly born; listen carefully;

Your own thought-forms are becoming visible and audible.

They are the products of your own mind with its back against the wall.

They indicate that you are close to liberation.

Do not fear them.

No harm can come to you from these hallucinations.

They are your own thoughts in frightening aspect.

They are old friends.

Lose yourself in them.

Welcome them. Merge with them. Join them.

They are yours, John.

Whatever you see, no matter how strange and terrifying,
Remember above all that it comes from inside you.
Hold onto that knowledge.
As soon as you recognize that you will obtain liberation.
Voidness cannot injure voidness.
Exist in reality.
Only within your own skull.
This will dissipate the fear. Remember it well.
Ommmmm'

Mr Patterson has never experienced anything quite like this before. No one ever has until they do. A high dose LSD session is like nothing else on this or any other planet. He is aware that the voice has stopped. The darkness from behind the shades affords him a sense of disconnection as if transparent or invisible. It doesn't make much difference if the shades are on or not, he realises that much now. His eyes are X-ray tubes and his bones are transparent. He has no bones. He has no shape or form or body at all.

'John,' says Langley. 'Maybe put the eye shades back on and lie down?'

They can't see me. I'm not here. And I thought it was all over!

It's barely started, John

'What?' *I said it's barely even started, John! The doctors have disappeared. The darkness that has filled my world is creeping away from me, away with me and into my head and through my brain and from behind my eyes it fills my nostrils and seeps down my neck into my spinal cord where it feeds from my chest and fills my lungs with darkness and blackness and heavy rain and rain and rain and blackness and everything is blackness and all at once it is...*

'Is it raining, Dr Austell?'

'Yes, John, it is. Shall we go outside into the rain?'

'Yes, yes,' answers John quite clearly.

The patient starts chuckling and then suddenly pulls off the eye shades and looks out, his gaze fixing absent-mindedly on the carpet and the edge of the chair and the couch where the carpet meets the chair leg and where the corner of the wall meets the chair and carpet touches the edge of the table and next to the carpet near the chair where the table and the chair adjoin the wall and the wall meets the edge of the carpet and the wall and the carpet touch the table leg and the chair and the wall are beside the carpet...*Fuck that!* He pulls the shades back on.

Tears are streaming, like a growing sneeze, and his body starts to wind up towards a convulsive laughter. He sits up again.

'Do you want to get up, John?' asks Austell gently. He glances across at Langley, who is fully reclined as far as he can get in his chair, with his eyes closed. There is a serene lightness in his facial expression. 'Joseph?'

'You may get up, John,' smiles Langley, opening his eyes and nodding gently in Austell's direction by way of approval. 'John may now wish to partake in the ceremony. The ancient rites of the people of Eleusis are with us. This is the moment of your triumphant implosion, John, your chance for ecstatic fusion with the ethno-pharmacological galactic vision. Come, sit up and listen to the textures of the light entering your fingertips.'

John looks anxiously at Austell. 'Am I alright, Dr Austell? What is he talking about?'

'You are terrific, John!' Austell wishes Langley wouldn't say things like that, but supposes he knows what he is doing.

Mr Patterson slowly pulls himself into a sitting position and Betsy, who has been diligently standing in the corner of the room, keeping guard, the sentinel, steps forward and removes John's eye shades again. *This time I have formal permission to see. Everything will be OK.* Blinking, as his eyes adjust with their normal physiological response to light but also blinded with thrill and wonder, as if he is witnessing the birth of a thousand universes. He is Adam on that first day of creation. He is the egg hatching and he is the spring air that dries the fluid from the stretching wings of the newborn fledgling eagle. His eyes scan the room in awe at the incredible sight of conjecture before him.

God I need a drink.

'John, do not feel alarmed. Betsy needs to take your blood pressure again. Is that OK? Just like we discussed. We need to measure your blood pressure once every hour. OK?' *Every hour… what is an hour? Wait, I think I have one here in my pocket. I was saving that for later.*

Betsy applies the blood pressure cuff and takes her reading before filling the details of Mr Patterson's cardiovascular state in her ledger.

What characters are these? Here…all over the floor…here? What is this? Why are there…

'But…Why are there?…Why are there?…' stutters John.

'Yes John, this is all happening,' says Langley gently. A warm smile holding John within his embrace.

'It…it's a beautiful…castle. A castle, a princess fairy castle! Yes, that's what it is!' says the patient.

He starts to stand up and the two doctors do not intervene to stop him. Now he is back down again, lowering himself gently onto all fours and crawling over the carpet. The patient has stopped climbing.

'Robert.'

'Yes, John?'

'Is it the Prime Minister again?'

'Sorry, John, I didn't catch that?'

'Was that the Prime Minister on the phone again, Dr Austell? Just now?'

John, you're embarrassing yourself again…why do you always do this?

'It's OK, John. You are doing fine. Do you want to lie back again? Or you can sit up if you prefer…'

A bear. A snake. A dog. Mr Patterson carries on crawling, prowling around the room. His shirt cuffs drag behind him as he gracefully slides across the thick warm *jungle floor. Such beauty. Everything is aglow! All shining…so…much…passion…so…much…LOVE! Articulation, they ask me. Articulation! What a silly word…and there on the mantelpiece is the clock giving me the time. What is this time they talk of? I have no need for this time. I am time. I am outside time and space. Here, glittering in hyperspace, beyond the stars. A bear…that is what I am, a bear in hyperspace sliding through the void…what is a day or a night or an hour? BOOZE. How funny! What is this BOOZE?*

'Dr Langley, what is your take on all this?' answers Patterson quite clearly and coherently. So much so that he surprises even himself.

'Yes, O voyager, whose taste of honey from mother is not quenched further by the smell of whisky or wine or urine,' answers Langley, the mind-smelter. 'O, nobly born; meditate tranquilly

144

upon the protective figure of the John game. John is the reflection of the moon in water. He is apparent yet non-existent. Leave him to wallow and float and leave his booze behind him on that water's edge. Like illusion produced by magic. Cause the visualized form of your protective ideal to melt away from the extremities. Yours, John, is a very profound art. By virtue of its re-birth it is inevitable. A more illuminated future is assured.'

'Yes…yes…doctor…only I've forgotten what it was I was going to ask now…' *God I need a drink.*

'Don't worry,' laughs Austell. 'Let it pass…'

'Dr Austell…'

'Yes, John?'

'Nothing, Dr Langley,' says the patient. 'But…wait a sec…Can you see that?'

'What, John?'

'Can you see…the air?…Over there…can you see it?'

'Can you, John? What does it look like?'

'Oh, Dr Austell! It is *so* beautiful! So full of colour…'

'OK, John, O noble one. Then fuse into the halo of rainbow light and let the core of pure Buddhahood take you in,' says Langley. 'Merge into it, John…become it, John…'

Thirteen hours have passed. And now it really does seem to be reducing. John is finding he can control the visions, the endless stream of thoughts. Yet, from time to time, when he takes his mind's eye off the ball…

…this isn't happening. You did not actually come here today, John. You are not alive. This is what death feels like. You have gone insane. You will never recover. This is what it is to die. You will stay like this forever. I should know, John, I am a doctor. This is my job.

I am employed by the state to poison people, tear out their eyes and feed them to the stars. We haven't started yet. I am about to give you the drug. Bend over now, take it like a man…

But then he can grapple control back again and engage with the process. It's fascinating. Beautiful even. But above all else fascinating…

By the time the session peters to a close the patient, the doctors and the nurse have utilized every bit of space in the clinical room. Charcoal and sketching paper litter the floor. A bowl of fruit has been explored, climbed through as if each bunch of grapes represents a million pounds of diamonds from the ceiling of a gold-walled mansion; each apple and strawberry a gift from the gods, an offering from ethereal forces grown in the Hanging Gardens of Babylon. Austell and Betsy – both sober – represent a solid stage, containment for the slippery chaos of their partners' meandering. Langley and Patterson continue to dance their cosmic games, weaving through one another's neural circuits high above the soil of Somerset's green land. From up there in the West Country vapours they can see everything.

Austell is proud of his patient. John Patterson is a man who has been crippled with self-doubt and internal terrors of demons for all of his adult life. Here is a man who has not set foot outside his house in the light of day for decades for fear of humiliation from social interaction; a deeply obsessional, and emotionally bland man. Yet here he is now! He is alive in a way Austell has never witnessed. And it is more than mere intoxication, rather this has been a genuine *waking*. Realness like never before. What Austell has seen today is the most sincere mental state that John Patterson has ever shown him. This is the real John. The Iron John.

146

'Oh, doctor, oh doctor! Look at me! I am…I am…', laughs John, his eyes like headlights blazing, shining, filling the room with torrents of blinding white energy. 'I am…'

Langley, who is lying face down on the carpet in the corner under the low table with the lava lamp, creases up with laughter and rolls himself across the floor to join the giggling Patterson.

'Yes, it is funny! It's *ludicrous*!' laughs the experienced old psychiatrist, his forty-so years ripped through with smiles and cosmic mirth. He carries stories from beyond the grave, from generation to generation inside the cells of his body. 'But it is also so very…serious.'

'It is?'

'It is,' repeats Langley. 'It is time, John, to take us back, to carry us with your thoughts to another time. Perhaps it is time to relax with the eyeshades again? I think the visions are less intense now, yes? Are you ready to do some work?'

'Yes, yes, of course,' says John, ever so earnestly. 'Of course. Serious stuff, doc. To the couch!'

And laughing, all of them, Langley, with Austell at his side, take Mr Patterson back, way back. Back to the Neanderthals. Back to where the first breath of life entered his cells and first gave meaning to his inner soul, back to where his OCD began. And now the patient tells his story. He speaks fluently and spontaneously about the time his mother hung him up and his father let him bleed and his classmates bullied him sexually and his first wife left and his children – except for Charles, his second child (ah, Charles the Second!) who *died* – left him and then came back and then the drinking started and has never stopped.

'That's when I first met you, Dr Austell. That's when you came

147

on the scene…'

John tells them everything between the tears and senseless laughter. And he means it. Every last word is as sincere and real as he has ever spoken before. He is weeping and Betsy holds him; crushed with the power of generations of abusive men inflicting themselves upon weak and desperate women. Patterson has crept through these shadows alone for too long.

'Thing is, Dr Austell, Betsy, Joseph, I've…I've never been able to talk about these things before…not with anyone…ever…but… you know, now…it sort of…it sort of makes sense to tell you…do you know what I mean? And…am I…am I…Am I doing okay, Dr Austell?…For your experiment?'

'Yes, you're doing fine, John,' all three therapists say together, almost in unison, which makes everyone laugh.

'That's right, John,' says Langley. 'They are still here. All your children are here with you John. It is not them that ever went anyway, is it, John?'

No. It's not. This Langley is an old medicine man. A witchdoctor. The Mother Crow. The ancient mother of my children and his children before that and the grandparents of those children are all from this same man. This spirit. And that is why I choose the drink, your honour, Dr Langley, sir. Dr Austell knows all about it. The binds. The ties. The thoughts. The endless thoughts. They have so bound me and held me and…but my father and my mother…the emptiness and the hunger and the wealthy silken waste of time that has been my life…

This is incredible, thinks Austell, holding John's hand. The patient is crouched now. He is spasmodically retching though nothing is in his stomach. The vomiting is a psychic symptom, a purging of memories, an upsurge from his unconscious, his forgotten childhood events. The emotional conflicts of youth are being relived. Toilet training, weaning – even birth itself. All of this is spewing forth. It is truly amazing. Months – maybe years of psychotherapeutic results are pouring out of this man in what has so far been a truly spectacular sixteen-hour session of kaleidoscopic revelation.

'Does that make sense?' John is saying. 'Only I can't really tell how much I am telling you and how much I am just thinking. It all sort of makes sense to me.'

'Yes, it's fine, John,' says Langley. 'It all makes perfect sense to us. I'm glad it does to you too. How does it feel?'

'Good, fine. Great, thanks Dr Langley,' says the patient.

...my infant rage...my dependent infant rage is boiling! Such anger and pain and regret and guilt. But is was not my fault! It was not my fault!

'It was not your fault, John,' says Langley, pushing back the stray and wild hair from the patient's face. John lifts his head and looks the old psychiatrist in the eyes. Their gaze meeting full on and burning deep welts into the violent magnetic fields flowing through their dissociated bodies.

'It was not your fault,' repeats Langley.

'I know, I know! I can see that now! It is all...love. It is all bright. So, bright, so clean. I can see it all so clearly now. Every molecule in my body is filled with such a glorious and soothing sense of love and peace. I love her, I do, I love her...'

'And she loves you, John.'

'She did! I know that now. I love you mother. I love you. Father, I love you too...I can't believe I just said that.'

Mr Patterson is getting up now. There is still a burning fire in his eyes but his movements have taken on a sense of urgency, a missionary zeal.

'I need to tell her…tell someone! I must take this message out of here and into the world!' he starts to make for the door. But Betsy, with nothing more than a gentle hand on shoulder dissolves this physical energy and he flops down onto the couch. That is the touch of a true expert, an angel. She has tens of thousands of flight hours to her name. She knows all the moves.

'Yes, John,' she says softly. 'Let us sit.'

Light rain trickles down from somewhere. Everywhere.

'I am here with you John. We are here. Myself, Dr Langley – Joseph – and Betsy. This is where you are.'

That phrase again. It's obviously not all over yet. But it is easing off.

'It's easing off, doctor. It's getting easier.'

'Yes, John, I know, I know. It's fine. You are doing brilliantly. You really are.'

'I am?'

'Yes.'

'Love sees behind the laughter and the tears, doesn't it?' asks John.

'Yes, of course, John,' replies Betsy in her Eastern European enunciation. 'Love sees beauty in the faces of those whose eyes are sparkling bright. Love knows the pain and torture you have had to endure, John. Yes, it does. And love sees the man John and we do too. We all do. That is what you are, John. You don't need to tell anyone else this. They all know it. We all know it. Everyone has seen it in you.'

150

John smiles and the tension falls away from his shoulders. He lies down onto the bed and closes his eyes.

'Have you really seen it, Betsy?' he murmurs, taking her hand and squeezing gently, as if he is falling asleep.

'I have John,' she says, mimicking his voice pattern and tone exactly, as if her voice were an exact internal answer of his own questioning conscience. 'She is so beautiful. She is you, John. You are inside her and she is part of you. We all are. Everything is one. One vibration. Everything is pure energy. That's what it is and you have to call that love, John.'

'That's what it is?'

'That's what it is, John.'

'It's love, John.'

'Love?'

'Love.'

'Love...yes it is...'

'It's love, John. That's what it is. That's all it ever was.'

'Love...yes, love...'

And over the course of the next two hours the theme of love persists. Love is everyone and everywhere. Love is everything. The visions fade and dissolve and the energy slowly creeps back to where it lies dormant, where it belongs, waiting in the flow between objects and people; back up to the stars and the clouds and the moon. The trip fades. And in its place there burns a soft orange light, the post-hallucinatory afterglow. Where all other things in the universe used to be there is now only love filling every nook and cranny because, at the end of the day, that's really all there is.

'Love, John. That's what it is, John,' Betsy repeats, stroking his head. The skies are darkened now. Presently John opens his eyes and sits up. It is almost one o'clock in the morning. Getting on for seventeen hours since John took the LSD. Langley puts a warm dressing gown around John's shoulders and he goes next door and takes a bath before emerging to drink tea and eat soup. Austell has stoked up the fire and they stretch out and chat. All is aglow. They drink some wine, it softens the edges, beckons warm sleep. So warm. So soft. So lovely. Sleep.

PART 3

THE PLATEAU

DYING IS NOT
SUCH A BAD THING

Austell lies on his camp bed made up in the barn. He is completely unable to sleep (unlike his patient; the peaceful post-acid Mr Patterson, who is snoring away next door like the most contented baby imaginable. He has, after all, just been born). What Austell had witnessed at today's LSD session was nothing short of a man going mad. Mr. Patterson literally did *lose* his mind. But crucially he lost his *old* mind. And the hope, at least, is that he will wake up tomorrow with a new one.

'But in fact, Bob, the psychedelic experience is far from the dangers of madness,' Langley reminds him the next morning over a breakfast of fresh eggs bought from a nearby smallholding. 'It is a perfectly safe, controlled state and doesn't fit the description of psychosis at all well. Even in the most profound moments of John's mental unravelling he knew he had taken LSD all along and that his was in a self-induced, temporary intoxication. That level of insight is not analogous with psychosis.'

'Yes, I suppose that is true,' agrees Austell. 'The psychotic patient cannot, by definition, be reasoned into understanding his experiences are delusional.'

'Precisely,' nods the Californian, loading his plate with fresh bread. 'So rather than thinking of the LSD state as being a foreign, external state of mind, it is actually an intense form of authenticity, a true glimpse of *super-reality*. Taking LSD is actually the very furthest from being mad that one could ever get

155

in one's life. And the very closest to being utterly grounded. The psychedelic experience unlocks the unconscious mind and provides an outpouring of repressed material. Although this flood of id, this primordial avalanche of repressed psychic material, is short-lived, it is *remembered*. With expert guidance – as we gave your man Mr. Patterson – the patient can draw upon and benefit from it. Inaccessible parts of the personality can be resolved.'

Austell had come to these same profound conclusions about Patterson's session the night before when he went to bed, which is what kept him awake. He had lain there reflecting with insomniac hunger on how these drugs, LSD and the like, appear to be nature's 'reset buttons'.

'It really is a lot to take in, Joseph,' he says. 'My immersion into the world of psychedelics has been an unbelievably steep learning curve. Ever since my first glimpse in San Francisco I have been eager to discover more. What is more, I am now more enthusiastic about the subject of medicine than I have been for years. I feel re-energised and thrilled to be part of the new post-sixties psychedelic movement, especially with you as my guide.'

Langley settles back into his chair. Breakfasting in the sun surrounded by the Somerset countryside of his dreams is as close to heaven as he can get right now.

'Well it is kind of you to say such a thing, Bob. And hearing that makes me realise that dying is really not such a bad thing. Not so bad at all,' and he drops a wee tad of whisky from a hip flask into his morning coffee.

Austell looks up from his breakfast.

'What do you mean by that, Joseph?'

'The point is, Bob, that the successful LSD experience cannot

156

fail to induce weighty change. And once glimpsed those visions will alter the user permanently. Their world will never be the same again. The new insights learned are irreversible, forever tainting the outlook on life. Lurking around every corner, popping up again and again until the day one dies. Clouds will forever be greater in depth, flowers will exude more perfume and everything will sing its colours.'

'Hmmm,' muses Austell. 'If that really is the case then is there not something slightly horrific about such a prospect? I think that humans fear the irrevocable. There is nothing worse than finding oneself lumbered with irreversible memories. The capacity to forget, to erase, is a fundamental gift of the passage of time. So if, as you say, an LSD trip is an irreversible experience does this not throw up all kinds of nightmarish outcomes that almost don't bear thinking about?'

Langley laughs, 'Well, yes, perhaps, for some people. If a trip is allowed to run havoc, uncontrolled, one can easily be left asking questions like: *What if I've permanently broken my brain?* Or *What if I never come down and stay like this forever?* These are common concerns during that first LSD trip – tremblingly, reflected in the bathroom when one has broken away from the partying throng of friends for a moment of solitude (even though they warned you not to spend too long staring into the mirror), one can be left believing one has damaged one's brain. One hasn't, of course, but it can feel like it sometimes.'

'Well, sounds pretty scary to me,' says Austell. 'I know all about brain damage. I have spent the last twenty-five years subtly tweaking the mental states of my patients; watching them stumble and fall, unable to resolve the hidden aspects of their lives. I know

157

better than most the impact of repressed childhood memories on everyday consciousness and how it produces lifelong functional decay. Childhood corrodes insidious tunnels through life, burning everything in its path with sulphuric erosion. Traumatic incidents are carried in the skull as an ever-present trickle of negative thoughts. Impossible to escape their powerful control over self-esteem, they undermine confidence, a daily reminder of one's uselessness.

'I have worked with patients aged ninety-nine who still spout the same opinions handed to them as a vulnerable toddler. Even after a lifetime of treatments with clinical, chemical and psychological tricks of the mind these self-induced narratives continue to eat away at reason, leaving the recipient twisted and detached, with an ingrained core personality incapable of closeness with other humans.'

Langley is impressed by Austell's narrative. 'I knew I'd found the right man for this job, Bob. We share the same belief that it is psychotherapy – not maintenance drug therapies – that provides a trusting platform whereby patients can explore repressed memories, bring them to the surface and stare them in the eye.'

'That has always been what I think, Joseph, but in my experience this technique often doesn't work. People are just too well defended, too robust and well practiced at dodging attempts to uncover their past. They don't want to give up their precious defences when their sanity depends on staying repressed. This is how the brain works. Sigmund Freud knew it – as did Plato and Shakespeare. And by the turn of the twentieth century science consistently validated it. Defences are the cause of useful misery. They are the brain's autoimmune reaction and psychiatry has never had a decent suppressant.'

158

'Until now, Bob, until now. And the way you describe this concept of *the permanency of experience* brought on by childhood is fascinating. Indeed, if LSD really *can* alter the brain, modify one's already deleterious blueprint then this is of immense and profound importance. It means personality change – a true fundamental shift in outlook – *is* possible. One can retune the system back to default factory settings. What an incredible, perhaps the *ultimate*, opportunity for clinical intervention! Do you see?'

'Yes, yes…'

'It does in fact,' says Langley, 'render all other psychiatric treatments – such as paltry CBT and the transient effects of maintenance medications completely insignificant in comparison. Permanent change is not something to be feared, it is truly desirable. LSD is surely the Holy Grail of psychiatry.'

'So what's next, Joseph?'

'Well, Patterson will need to continue his non-drug psychotherapy sessions. A single LSD experience is not a panacea. He has only just begun his journey and will need more sessions before he gets to know LSD, learns the contours of its mental spaces and develops internal maps to navigate its territories. But he has blown out the cobwebs and started towards integration. The material that emerged during his first drug-assisted session is not simply random. One person who takes LSD sees a flower and another sees a snake. All the symbolic visions experienced have personal meaning. But just like analysing dreams, the latent material released requires a skilled psychotherapist to sift through the waking dreams so the patient can interpret the meaning of his experience. Now he has taken LSD John does not need anyone else to tell him he has just had the most meaningful experience of his life. This he knows with absolute certainty and self-validated conviction.'

John Patterson's transformation in the days after the trip is little short of miraculous. This is not a word doctors tend to use but on this occasion it fits. Gone is the man whose bitten fingers wring themselves in knots. On his return to *Bardo* Patterson stands tall, walking with an assured stride into the farmhouse and leaning nonchalantly against the reception desk, dressed in new, flattering clothes, bought in daylight from the high street rather than rummaged at night from skips.

THEY DON'T CALL HER ECSTASY FOR NOTHING

Robert Austell looks through his cloudy pint of cider and squints at the setting sun. 'I'm amazed, Joseph, I really am, I have to be honest, I had no idea it would be this dramatic.'

It's been three weeks since Patterson underwent his first psychedelic psychotherapy session and he continues to show sustained functional improvements. 'I mean, even if John relapses again – which I don't think he will – the therapy has given him a valuable opportunity to enjoy his life. It's truly amazing. I am humbled by the effects of your LSD.'

'Not *my* LSD, Bob. And it wasn't only the drug that did this. You've played a role too. Let's not forget John trusts you. The years of your care for him have contributed to his success.'

'I don't know about that. I've been struggling with this guy for decades. It wasn't until you came along that anything like this has happened. It's nothing to do with me.'

'You need to start believing in yourself,' says Langley. 'It is you, the therapist, the *doctor* who gets the patients better. Sure, catalysts like LSD are helpful, but life is beautiful, Bob, it really is. We are very lucky to be part of it, so snap out of this nihilism, man! It's time to find a new volunteer.'

'OK. I'm keen to see it work again on someone else. John was one of my most resistant patients. If LSD can work with him then it'll work on anyone.'

Langley downs his pint – his third compared to Austell's first –

and stands up, knees starting to go slightly for a second. 'Right, Bob, another drink? But next time we're not using LSD. We're using a chemical called 3,4-methylenedioxymethamphetamine – MDMA – or, as it sometimes gets called: Ecstasy. For this we need someone with a traumatic past, with the core symptoms of Post Traumatic Stress Disorder.'

Austell has so many patients who fit the bill.

'They must have failed to respond to previous treatments and never completed a course of psychotherapy because of the severity of their traumatic memories. Someone who has tried to focus on their past abuse but is always overwhelmed by it. Does that remind you of anyone?'

There is one name that pops immediately into Austell's head: a patient whose life experience is so dreadful as to be near irredeemable.

'I know *exactly* the right patient for your ecstasy treatment.'

When Langley toddles back with his drink Austell tells him Claire Castle's shocking story, wincing as he describes her full gamut of PTSD symptoms. Langley sips his pint and shells pistachios as he listens to Austell recounting the tale of her childhood experiences of physical, emotional and sexual abuse, her multiple admissions to secure units up and down the country, the episodes of sexual violence in forensic units and an ever-flowing regimen of prescription drugs. Claire has known a string of foster carers, children's homes, half-way houses, warden controlled flats, failed college places, exclusions, arrests, detentions, custodial sentences, intravenous drugs, exploited sex, pornography, crime, pregnancies, abortions, social services interventions, failures, disappointments and broken promises. Her life is a catalogue of shattered dreams and wasted chances.

'Bob, you're a good man,' says Langley. 'All of my professional life I have been gallivanting around pleasuring myself in the name of scientific progress. I envy your clinical experience. I don't know how you do it. You are truly a saint working with these poor people. It's very noble.'

These words, which just a few months ago would have skimmed off Austell's impassive brain without registering any emotional impact now stare him in the face. 'I'm just doing my job. I feel close to my patients, you know. I have a certain responsibility for them.' *At least when I'm not fantasising about murdering them.*

Langley smiles and puts his arm around Austell. 'Bob, I promise you we will look after her. Your Claire will be safe in the hands of *Bardo*. Don't you worry, man. MDMA is a gentle mistress. They don't call her ecstasy for nothing.'

As a child in the mid-seventies Langley was in California when therapists were experimenting with a little known legal compound called MDMA or what they called 'Adam'. It was only recognized by a small handful of doctors, a few courageous therapists, who at the end of the sixties when LSD had been made illegal discovered that MDMA possessed the ideal qualities for enhancing psychotherapy. In fact, as they said at the time, if one were to invent a hypothetical drug designed for psychotherapy it would be MDMA.

After his infant migration from Somerset to California Langley grew up amongst a select group of West Coast pioneers, vicariously immersed in a scene where the boundaries between patient and therapist were blurred by the Western sun. By the mid-eighties, when MDMA followed a similar trajectory as LSD, leaking from the medical community, banned by the authorities and exploding into massive widespread recreational use popularized by rave parties, Langley had moved away and was in medical school working his way through the mainstream pharmacopeia. He then travelled to India, Kathmandu, Mexico, Zaire, and just about anywhere he could follow the hippie trail – still aglow from two decades earlier - in his search for marijuana, sex and parties.

So don't bother telling Langley drugs are bad – he won't believe you. It's like saying knives are bad and then try cutting a loaf of bread without one. Langley believes drugs of all kinds are essential psychic pick-me-ups to enhance and enrich the lives of millions. He will also tell you that drugs need to be treated with respect and understanding. But since meeting Austell, Langley has learned a little about discretion. There is a welcome sensibility about Austell that appeals to him. Austell's commitment to his patients has rubbed off on him and is beginning to colour the edges of his peripheral vision. This next chapter in Langley's life will be his last and he intends to make the most of it. He may even cut his hair.

On their way home Langley is half plastered as usual. He often insists on dragging a flagon of scrumpy along from the beginning, and Austell has become used to his companion's *joie de vivre*, finding his drunkenness a tolerable accompaniment most of the time. But despite Langley's substantial substance history today he rarely takes drugs other than alcohol – except for the small dose of whatever agent he is administering to patients in the context of a session. But that's different, that's work. There is a difficult to understand vein of self-destruction about Langley.

'The truth is,' slurs Langley, panting up the home incline to the farm as heavy clouds muster, the flagon of cider swashing at his waist, 'if we can show that psychedelic therapy works this could

164

have tremendous implications for a health care system already buckling under strain. We are at the earliest stage of this new development, but if what we are doing here at *Bardo* brings in good anecdotal data then the world will *have* to look at it.'

He thrusts the bottle skyward and Austell reaches for it and shares a swig. 'I'll drink to that.' Austell is faithful to the mission. And as a paid-up member of the psychedelic club he realises he can do a lot worse than join Langley in his relentless celebration of fermented apples.

NOT A BROWN RICE KIND OF GIRL

Austell sits nervously in the waiting room for Claire. Despite his initial enthusiasm about her joining the project he is now having doubts. Is it wise to be blowing the mind of someone whose mind is already so far gone? He is supposed to be her doctor not her dealer. Langley senses his anxiety but remains typically nonchalant.

'Don't worry, Robert. Honestly, she sounds perfect. PTSD, a lifetime of abuse, unable to engage with psychotherapy. She's textbook. I'm looking forward to working with her.'

'I don't know,' muses Austell. 'You haven't met her yet. It's not just PTSD. She is *very* borderline. She has no meaningful attachments whatsoever and a very distorted sense of self. She can split staff and be manipulative. I'm worried we may be biting off more than we can chew.'

'Look, it'll be OK. How long have you known her?'

'Oh, I don't know. Ten years? I inherited her from the Child and Adolescent Services. She's been with me ever since.'

'And she keeps coming back?'

'Just about. She has a chaotic lifestyle. Always in hospital, being arrested; prostitution, drugs, violent boyfriends, that kind of thing.'

'But if she's stuck with you for ten years then it's not true she has no meaningful relationships. She's got you. Give yourself some credit, Bob. She likes you. You must be doing something right.'

Austell shakes his head. 'I don't think Claire Castle likes anyone. I've never done much good for her. I keep her on my caseload because no one else will have her. But if you think she'll benefit from MDMA then I suppose we have nothing to lose. However, don't say I didn't warn you!'

An hour late Claire Castle arrives. She stands in the doorway, and Austell beckons her into a seat but she doesn't move, just stands in the threshold eyeing the two men suspiciously. She lights a fag and eventually speaks, not caring if anyone is listening.

'It fucking stinks around here.'

The obvious response would be, 'It's a farm, Claire', but Austell and Langley don't say anything. The number one rule of psychotherapy: *Don't just do something. Sit there.*

Silence ensues and Claire finishes her cigarette, flicking it out into the yard. She could have dropped it in the doorway where she stands but chose not to. This small piece of courtesy means progress.

'It was a fucking hassle getting here.' She flicks her hair and looks indignantly at Langley. 'And who the fuck is this?'

'Why don't you come inside? You can leave the door open if you want. Take a seat. This is Dr Langley…'

'Joe,' says Langley warmly. 'Pleased to meet you, Miss Castle.'

Claire's barriers are immediately raised under the threat of Langley's kindness. *Fucking rapist.*

'Look, mate, I don't know what this is all about. So let's just get on with it. Why have you asked me here? I've got a lot on. Darren is waiting for me and he's not a patient man. He's got business. Got to get the car back by two.'

Austell and Langley glance beyond Claire and see a thin man in a tracksuit, heavily tattooed with a shaved head, texting on his phone, pulling hard on a stub of cigarette and pacing anxiously. They have a narrow window of opportunity. She turns her nose up and looks past the pair, viewing the inside of the room. Austell can tell she is interested.

'OK, fine,' says Austell. 'We'll come straight to the point. I want to offer you a new treatment, an experimental therapy. This sort of thing doesn't come along very often and it could be a good opportunity for you to make some progress.'

Patients like Claire are surplus to requirements in the medical profession and she knows it. Psychiatry is the Cinderella of the NHS, lacking the status of other services, with none of the political kudos or media interest showered upon those vote-winning babies in Great Ormond Street. The public – and sadly many doctors too – consider people like Claire an embarrassing blight on society. They regard her troubles as self-inflicted: *She asked for it. It's her fault. The slut. She chooses to drink, take drugs and cut herself like that. She could sort herself out if she tried. She just doesn't want to. She'd rather sponge off the state. Cut her welfare benefits, that's the best thing to do. Then she'd learn to stand on her own two feet.* Claire has come to expect this attitude from everyone. She still doesn't see why she should trust these men.

Langley talks to her about MDMA. She has heard of it, of course, in the form of ecstasy, but despite her immersion in the culture of recreational drug taking it is not the sort of thing she has much time for.

'Eh? Yeah, of course I fucking knows it,' she says in her derogatory West Country tone, ''s taken by poofs in fucking gay bars, innit? What good will that do me?'

'It has remarkable qualities, Claire,' says Langley. 'It could be described as the *perfect* drug for psychotherapy – especially for a case such as yours.'

Claire turns to Austell, her psychiatrist, snubbing a pout in the direction of Langley. 'What the fuck does *he* know about *my* 'case'?' she says. 'I thought *you* were my doctor.'

'I am Claire. But listen to what Joseph says. He is an expert in this field. I trust him when he says he thinks MDMA could help.'

Claire darts a look back at Darren. She knows he won't wait much longer. He's on a mission; got to see a man about a dog. He's owed money and he doesn't like hanging around when he's owed money. Darren flicks his fag, snaps an inaudible comment at her and she mouths a 'fuck off' back, before turning back to Austell.

'Look, if you think it's what I need then I'll try it. I mean, let's face it I haven't got much choice. I've tried every other fucking drug known to medical science. None of them work. I don't know why you think giving me a couple of frigging gurners is gonna do any good. But if you reckon it will then I'll give it a go. Alright?'

'Thank you, Claire, that's great.'

The two doctors let her go, loaded with armfuls of literature and instructions about how to prepare herself for the therapy. But neither Langley nor Austell believes she will manage to fulfil the pre-session arrangements. They have little confidence in her engaging in the project at all. She is just not a brown rice kind of girl.

...but she does engage. Over the next few weeks Austell and Langley meet with her regularly and go through the procedure in detail. She meets Betsy, signs the consent forms and has all the necessary tests. With no difficulty she comes off her medication and abstains from all illicit drugs for a month, passing the urine tests every time. Surprising everyone, patient number two is soon fully prepped and ready to go. Meanwhile Langley and his apprentice continue to learn from one another. Austell is continually amazed

170

to hear how far from the mainstream medical path one can wander and still consider oneself a doctor. It is a credit to the profession, he supposes, that Langley's story is as tangled as his hair.

Places You Usually Cannot Visit

Exactly as they did with John, the staff at *Bardo* work on Claire's mindset in preparation for her session with MDMA. They use optimism as an active therapeutic tool – it is not merely a passive placebo effect. They instil it into her alongside all the necessary background information about the substance. She needs to know how the drug works, how long the experience will last and what to expect. In non-drug therapy sessions she has begun exploring what kind of issues from her past she would like delve into whilst under the influence of the MDMA. And above all, the back and forth visits to *Bardo* act to build up a relationship between her and her guides. Langley, Austell and Betsy have noticed she is more engaged and slightly less defensive than before, but has thankfully lost none of her idiosyncratic charm. 'You're still a bunch of dicks,' she lovingly reminds them whenever she feels things are getting a bit lovey-dovey.

On the day of the drug session she is late as usual. She bursts through the door, flicks her cigarette and coughs. 'That fucking bastard Darren. He was supposed bring me in today. He knew all about it. I've been talking about it all week. And then he goes out on a bender last night. Fuck knows where he is this morning. Took me three buses to get here. *Wanker.*'

Hearing her arrival Austell comes through to the reception and passes her a cup of coffee and a plastic specimen pot. 'Well done for making it, Claire. Have you got an empty stomach?'

'Yes. And I've got drug free piss. You can fucking test it if you don't believe me!'

'OK, fine, thank you, we will. It's not that we don't believe you, Claire. But it's part of the protocol, so if you could fill this and pass it to Betsy that would be great.'

She shuffles off to the bathroom, cursing. Austell and Betsy exchange an affectionate smile. They have all warmed to Claire. Her brashness is so honest that it betrays a hidden agenda, one of subversive cloaking. Everybody wants to trust her but they are all sufficiently experienced in recognising the typical phenomena of splitting, seduction and rejection. There is no charm like that of a Borderline or Psychopathic patient. Such fundamental damage to the personality often expresses itself in flawlessly sophisticated defence mechanisms, which is not meant as insulting or stigmatizing. Rather it is flattery.

Langley comes into the room, dressed in a long white caftan, his flowing hair neatly washed and brushed out of its ponytail, hanging down his back like Gandalf.

'Morning all. I see Claire is here,' motioning to the cigarette smouldering in the bowl of potpourris by the door. 'How is she today? You look worried, Bob.'

Austell cannot hide the fact that Claire is one of his 'special' patients; no matter how much he tries not to label her. He cares about her and wants this to succeed, perhaps excessively so. However, firm boundaries are essential. He knows he must detach from personal issues but can't help feeling a strong sense of responsibility to make sure she comes to no harm and, crucially, that she benefits from this session.

Langley senses his friend's nerves. 'You mustn't worry, Bob.

174

It'll be fine. MDMA is forgiving, and completely different from LSD, even at high doses. The principle effect is euphoria. Believe me, it is almost impossible to not have a pleasurable experience with MDMA.'

Betsy chips in, scientific and matter of fact as always, 'It is also shorter acting than LSD, taking five or six hours for the drug to wear off completely. It possesses a unique psychological profile characterized by a specificity to act over the human emotional sphere without notably affecting other psychological functions. And it is less perceptually distorting than LSD. Don't worry, Robert, we will look after her. She will not come to harm.'

'But she *will* be challenged,' adds Langley, looking sternly at Austell. 'There would be no point in doing this otherwise.'

'Yes, I realise that. Don't worry. I am sure she will be fine. Tough as old boots is Claire. And don't worry about me either. I'm perfectly on top of it.'

Claire returns and they settle into the session room. They have discussed which music she will listen to. Claire said there is no way she is having anything poncy like Bach. She wants 'UK grime' but after further discussion from the guides she is able to temper her choice. The compromise is 'ambient chill'. The tide of electronic beeps sweep over them as Claire lies back on the couch. Betsy enters with a small white capsule containing 125mg of pure MDMA, produced in California in the ramshackle garden laboratory of a brilliant chemist.

'Thank you, Betsy,' says Claire with an uncharacteristic smile, due more to nerves than delight, then swallows down the cap with some water. 'Down the hatch! Sure I can't tempt any of you into joining me?'

They had already discussed that on this occasion it would not be necessary for any of the guides to be under the influence of the sacrament. They all know they have a lot of hard work to do over the next six hours. The plan for this session is to keep Claire on track and focused on addressing her traumatic memories. They must make her feel safe, contained and trusting of the process as it unfolds.

Thirty minutes post ingestion. Time ticks on with unavoidable precision as the creaking barn warms with the day and relaxes around the small group of humans whose atoms settle, like cornflakes in a box, to their lowest state of entropy. The branches of an elm creep over the farm buildings and tap gently on the window as they wait. It takes Claire a while to notice the developing effects of the drug. The main reason for the delay is that it is a feeling so utterly unknown to her; *peace*. She is not expecting it so she hardly recognises when it happens.

'I...I feel...' she murmurs from behind the eyeshades, 'I feel... *relaxed*.'

The two doctors look at one another and Langley smiles a nod of approval at his colleague.

'Good, Claire. Just settle into it and let it start to work. Let this relaxation wash over you and grow. This is a peaceful and relaxing place.'

It almost looks as if Claire is asleep behind those eyeshades. But then fifteen minutes later she has begun moving in a gentle undulating rhythm to the music. She starts to let out a soft murmuring, almost a song. 'It is so...so...*soft*. I am so...peaceful. Like a...like a wave. A wave of...softness. It is...so...' Then she lapses into silence again. The hour mark is approaching.

'Claire, it's Joe speaking. Do you want to sit up and remove the eyeshades? Or are you happy lying where you are? I am here, with Bob and Betsy. This is a gentle place where you will come to no harm and can think safely about difficult things. Even scary and frightening things. This is a relaxing and peaceful place. A beautiful place.'

Under normal circumstances someone speaking in this way to the heavily tattooed Claire Castle would have been thumped. Claire does not suffer fools gladly (except in the form of those bastard abusive men, but that's different, that's a relationship), so she would not normally tolerate Langley's soothing whispering in her ear like this. But on this occasion she offers no protest.

'Mmmmmmmmmmmmmmm...' she says, letting out a long and gentle moan. 'I am so floaty! Like walking on a cloud! It's...it's like...it's like...no, it's *not* like gear...it's more...floaty, a *bit* like heroin, but it's also more...more...more rounded...not like the gear...it's more...it's more sort of...*real*...is that the right word? I'm more awake...'

'It is real, Claire. It's very real. And it's coming from you. The drug is just a catalyst. The reality, the softness, the *floatiness* and the *beauty* of it are coming from you,' says Langley. 'They are *your* feelings. You have these feelings inside you. You are capable of these feelings all on your own.'

Claire writhes as she groans. A huge beaming smile, almost a maniacal grimace, is plastered over her face. She motions that she wants to sit up and gently pulls off the blindfold. Her eyes flash with expanded pupils and she holds a contorted expression, her jaw protruding. Sitting on the edge of the couch she gently swings her legs to the swirling music. Looking at the two doctors with depth and understanding her eyeballs roll back in her sockets

177

as a tremendous rush comes on. She draws in a deep breath and exhales slowly, blowing out through her expanded nostrils, her eyes disappearing into the back of their sockets. Betsy sits down beside her and Langley moves off to the edge of the room. Then she sits up, quite abruptly, looking suddenly very pale.

'*Ugh*...I feel...a bit...' Quickly thrusting a hand to her mouth she retches dryly. Betsy reaches down and holds a cardboard dish under her chin and with the other hand rubs Claire's back. 'It's OK, Claire. Do you need to be sick?'

Claire, her eyes watering, fixed firmly on the floor, swallows and then retches again.

'Let it out if you need to be sick.'

Betsy rubs between her shoulder blades. Eventually Claire closes her eyes again and then slowly settles back. Her eyes roll back in their sockets again and she breathes heavily.

'It's OK now,' she groans, a contorted smile spreading broadly across her face again, her jaw grinding away like a ruminating cow. 'I feel fine. I just felt really sick suddenly...but it's OK now...it's beautiful now...it's *so* beautiful now.'

Betsy holds the bowl close by Claire's face for a while longer and then silently motions to Austell who treads over and removes it. 'She'll be fine now,' she whispers. 'Sometimes that initial rush can be quite intense. She'll be all right now.'

The three therapists have discussed and rehearsed this session carefully with Claire during the preparatory work. They all understand how to proceed. Claire will lead the agenda. Austell will act as the primary therapist and Betsy will assist. The combination of a male and female therapist provides a positive therapeutic triad. Langley's role will be one more of an observer.

178

Claire's shoulder blades tense together; the whole rush gripping her from head to toes, pulling her into a tight ball, crunching, growing, spreading through every vessel, bone and muscle; then reaching the climax, peaking, peaking, peaking…then gushing out of her…exploding, EXPLODING, E X P L O D I N G, E X P L O D I N G in an endless wave of energy, crashing over the rocks, breaking over the shoreline. Coursing waves of intense ecstasy, torrents of beautiful, gorgeous warm light-as-a-feather loveliness bursting…

'How are you feeling Claire?'

'Oh! So floaty…soooooo floaty. I want to…to *touch*…'

She opens her eyes and they roll slowly forward to settle on Betsy's face and a great knowing twisted smile is shared between them. Claire reaches out a hand to the old woman and Betsy takes it in hers. As their skin meets a jolt of electricity shoots through Claire and she jerks back taking in a sharp intake of breath, closing her eyes, which roll away back into the depths of their sockets again. She lets out another long and sustained groan and starts rubbing and massaging Betsy's hand furiously. Betsy takes control of the rubbing, slowing it down to a gentle circular pace.

Langley motions to Austell to let the massaging continue and the men move away from the women and position themselves at the other end of the room. The guides are keeping strict boundaries, providing a safe and breathable space in which Claire can acknowledge and explore the need for tactile sensation. One of the principle components of the MDMA experience is that it boosts physical touch to astronomical levels. It is not called the hug drug for nothing.

As the two women caress one another's hands, in the background Langley whispers to Austell, 'It is important to draw a distinction between the sensuality of MDMA and frank sexual feelings. These feelings of Claire's are undoubtedly close to orgasmic, sexual feelings but they are not the same thing. The MDMA experience is like having an intense sexual orgasm that lasts for hours – which therefore means it is very *unlike* a sexual orgasm – which is necessarily episodic.'

'Yes, of course,' whispers Austell, as if he, of all people, has any deep personal understanding of sexual experience.

'The purpose of this session is to get in touch with *emotional*, not sexual issues. In some respects what we are looking for is the antithesis of sex. What we want is for Claire to take us into the difficult forbidden past, her hidden painful memories. We are using MDMA as a buffer, an emotional cushion to delve into the parts of her life that she would normally not want to go near. MDMA is a breathing apparatus, an inflation device, an arm-band, or a bullet-proof vest.'

Langley leads Austell back over to the patient and talks softly to her as Betsy continues the massaging.

'Claire, do you remember what we have talked about for this session? Do you want to take us to where your feelings are at this point? Remember this is a place where you can explore those feelings. This is a safe and beautiful place. Where are you now?'

Claire opens her eyes, which are wavering slightly as if in a waking REM sleep. Her eyeballs shudder in a fast vibrational frequency. A distorted frown continues across her face, her teeth chattering rapidly in synchronicity with her eyes. There are a host of phrases used by clubbers and ravers to describe this state. Out of her tree. Smashed. Mullered. Hammered. Munted. Wasted. Boxed. Fucked. Whatever; her gaze weaves softly around the room, smirking more than smiling, her eyes rolling uncontrollably. She licks her lips and swallows preparing to speak.

'I know….I know…I do *want* to talk…I know what we are here for…I feel…stronger…not just detached…not just numbed but…but…*protected*…I feel as if I can…go there.'

She closes her eyes and starts drifting away again, falling swiftly into a waking-sleep of deep eiderdown blanket cotton-wool candy-floss inebriation. Langley coughs, and covering his mouth with a fist, signals a gesture for Austell's benefit to bring Claire back, back to the session. The real trick here, the job of the guides, is to keep her engaged, to explore her traumatic childhood memories, but done in such a way as to not be overly directive. It is essential to not be suggestive. The therapists are not there to tell the patient what to think. The nature of the MDMA experience is that it has the capacity to totally envelope her, so it does need some direction. Otherwise left to her own devices Claire will simply waste the day away staring at the ceiling, which, whilst undoubtedly pleasant for her, might not be the best use of this magical mental space in which she now dwells.

But Langley's coughing only increases further as he tries to suppress it. Taking a handkerchief from his pocket and covering his mouth he launches into a violent paroxysmal spasm, whilst waving his free hand, gesturing for Austell to continue. Austell is shocked by the creased-over figure of Langley. He looks drawn and worn out, in stark contrast to the blissed-out recumbent Claire. He struggles for breath and his uncontrollable hacking eventually interrupts Claire's serenity. She mumbles and writhes, sitting up and opening her eyes, which roll back in their sockets making it impossible for her to focus on the commotion of Langley's making.

The doctor, looking worn out from his coughing, stands up and again beckons to Austell to continue, as he shuffles quickly from the room. From out in the corridor the coughing crescendos into a series of painful-sounding and hideous outbursts. Austell composes himself and lays a gentle hand on Claire's shoulder, easing her back to her lying position. She quickly settles into a more relaxed and serene state, with her eyes closed and her limbs gently undulating to the electronic peaks and troughs of the music.

When Langley re-enters the room he is somewhat calmer, albeit now drenched with sweat. Before resuming his place on the other side of the couch he stoops to pick up the handkerchief that he had dropped when rushing from the room. Austell cannot help noticing that the handkerchief is stained with blood-streaked mucous. He looks up at his colleague in shock and opens his mouth to speak, but Langley cuts him off, stuffing the handkerchief back into his pocket and beckoning Austell to attend to Claire.

'Claire,' says Austell, and her eyes pop open again. 'Claire, I want you to take me there. Let me go there with you. Do you remember what we wanted to talk about, to think about while you have the MDMA within you? Let's use this space...let's see what we can achieve while we have MDMA's beautiful protection over us...can you feel how gentle she is? How protected you feel? She will look after you and not let you come to harm...tell me, where is 'there' and what is going on? Tell me where you can go, places you cannot usually visit.'

A frown comes over Claire's features and for the first time since the drug took effect Austell is reminded of the look that Claire usually wears; that look of fear, one of panic, with an undercurrent of anger and spitting rage. His heart rate quickens when he sees that

182

typical Claire-face and with it comes a stirring emotion of violence. A fantasy emerges whereby Austell pulls the pillow forcefully from under Claire's head and thrusts it over her face, pushing down and smothering the last breath of life from her lungs. But then Claire raises her eyebrows, the MDMA visage of peace returns, banishing the look of fear and back comes that serene smile again. With this flashing change Austell's fantasy also dissolves and he feels an intense rush of warmth, love even, for his patient.

Langley notices immediately that Austell is experiencing a contact high. And when Austell instinctively reaches out a hand, catching Langley's eye, he receives a gentle nod of approval from the experienced guide, and so proceeds to place his hand on the patient's shoulder, absorbing the electrical flow of energy emanating from Claire into his own body. There is a sense of physical healing between them of a quality and intensity such that Austell has never experienced before. Everything around him radiates goodness.

Claire sits up. The rush passes and a look of painful sobriety washes over her again. Then with another deep breath the eyes are off and she returns to the MDMA cloud. But determined to work, she sits up again, composing herself.

'That's right,' says Austell. 'We can do this. We can talk now.'

'Good, good,' whispers Langley, encouraging Austell to carry on the flow.

'Yes…' she says, looking at him seriously. The gurning eyes are still there but underneath is a mature and reflective Claire, ready to work. 'Yes, yes, I can…I *can* talk about it, Dr Austell…it is…it is almost *funny* to imagine it…but I can think about it and talk about it…it is actually possible…'

'OK, Claire. Let's go there together. Tell me where it is we are

183

going.'

Sitting forward, Claire swallows and takes stock. When she breathes in deeply the rushes wash over her again, but with composure she is learning to hold them back, just managing to keep the overly distracting effects of the drug at bay so she can talk. And think.

'It's like I can think about stuff that normally I wouldn't be able to think about. I can think about what it was like when I was young, when I was a little girl...I *am* a little girl...I am a *good* girl...but there are so many things I have seen, and so many *painful* things.'

The frown comes back and the eyes look straight ahead. There is a shuddering in her arms and Austell sees that she starts to reach for her forearm as if to begin scratching, digging at the wounds on her arm. This is her reflex gesture whenever faced with the intrusive memories of her abuse; memories that drag her back to those dark places. This is usually the point where she enters into a dissociative episode.

'Claire, I want you to stay with me. I want you to talk to me about where you are and what is happening right now. You have nothing to fear...'

'I know, I know!' she laughs, lifting her fingers away from her scarred arm. Tears are welling in her eyes. 'It's...it's amazing! I can think about my dad...my mum...even my dad! I can see him...I can see him...I'm looking at him now...he's just my dad...that's what he is. He's just a sad man. I'm a little girl...I've...never been able to have this memory before.'

There are tears rolling down her cheeks. 'He is just so...' she says, the smile returning, '....he is just so...I mean...he is *my dad*...I hate him and I hate him and I hate him...because of my mum and my sisters…they can't help it…*I* can't help it. How can it be my fault? I am just a little girl. I know he says it's all because of me but how can you say that to someone this young? I mean… not *now*…not when everything feels so…so…*lovely*…I know that sounds crazy…but it is! Everything is so beautiful and soft and… and I know that *I* must be beautiful too…'

Austell wants to take her deeper. The MDMA is reducing her anxiety but this will return again soon. He wants her to use this temporary state of power to gain access to her emotions and internal conflicts without the overwhelming fear that is normally associated with such memories. She has already said more to him in the last few moments than she has uttered in all the years they have worked together. He wants to work with her to go deeper into her experience of sexual abuse and see if she can to put it into words.

'Claire I need you to keep this experience here in the room. I know you want to drift, and this is OK, but can you tell me more about your father?'

And she does. Claire Castle, for the first time in her life sits and faces her psychiatrist and talks. She composes herself, weeps and between tears, laughter and embraces, with a chattering and slurred speech, she talks and talks and talks.

'I'm not really a woman at all, am I Dr Austell?'

'How so?'

'I was never really a child in the first place I have always only been a monster. I am an object, a non-person. An abomination.'

Austell holds her hand and Betsy cuddles her as Claire spills forth years' worth of material. The weight is lifting as she speaks. A whole new person is emerging from behind the exterior of the fearful and frightening Claire she has projected up till now. On the outside, and intellectually, of course, once one gets beyond the obligatory trophies; the amateur tattoos etched into her skin in Youth Offenders Institutes, the scars and piercings that accompany immersion in a violent sub-culture of drugs and sexual exploitation, Claire looks normal. It has always only ever been her *mental* make-up, the core features of her personality – and especially her incapacity for seeking and maintaining emotional relationships that is most warped. Exploring these issues in therapy in the past Claire has never got beyond the superficial. There was no way she could ever return to those painful memories, even if by some miraculous act of impetus she chose to do so.

But now for the first time in her life she can share her version of her history, the only true version, with Austell. Under the containment of MDMA she lives out these sequences from her past with vivid reality, whilst remaining somehow shielded from the most acute pain of the memories, she is able to talk and reflect and heal as she goes.

'I'm a shit, a terrible shit!' she cries. 'That's what he told me.' Identifying with her drunken father squeezing the life out of her when she was a terrified trembling child following his brutal acts of sexual violence. He has fallen on his knees and is pleading forgiveness from his daughter. Claire, six, looks at him through her tears, rigid with fear. Pain and shame. 'Why are you calling me a slag, dad? Am I really such a fucking bitch? But if I am, then I ask you, dad, who or what the fuck are *you*?'

A pitiful bastard, a drunken broken man playing out the trans-generational pattern of abuse, drenched in maudlin self-regret for the vicious re-enactment of his own shattered childhood and repeated buggery at the hands of *his* father - her grandfather, who also abused

186

her. That's what he is. A damaged, frightened little boy. And the saddest truth of all is that no one in her life ever loved Claire more deeply than her post-ejaculatory father. She has held this horrific image in her mind's-eye for twenty years; images of this circus, not only from her long-deceased father, but from many others too.

'I used to wet the bed; I used to do it on purpose! I thought if I pissed the bed then they wouldn't want to get in there with me and...when I heard my grandfather was coming over I would wet the bed...I was only six! I did it to stop him...stop him doing...'

As she grew up and left home, fostered and then left to rot in multiple children's home, she learned to replace her father's exploitation with a succession of abusive relationships that began in her late childhood. She flees into the open arms of one violent man after another; each of them fucked up in their own unique way; all of them misogynistic abusers; little boys repeating their own pain inflicted by rejecting mothers and violent fathers. Claire has been their emotional and physical punch-bag all her life. She has thrown her projections at these men; her need for violent affection tinged with infantile care and they have lapped it up and beaten the shit out of her in punishment for asking for something that reminds them of their own desperate mothers.

The hours under the influence of MDMA pass and as she becomes more accustomed to the landscape in which this magical drug has placed her she is less overwhelmed by its foreignness and she can sit within it feeling protected whilst she talks.

'It is so amazing!' she cries, surprised and delighted at her own ability to feel. She cannot believe she is able to do this. The whole experience is utterly validating in a wholly positive way. 'I am talking, Dr Austell! Listen to me! I am talking! Thank you...thank

187

you so much…thank you for showing me I can do this!' She says through tears.

But Austell plays only a minimal part. His role is not to ask direct questions. And once she is underway there is little need for him to talk. She is not under the spell of the director's suggestions; a mere passive observer receiving commands from a therapist. This is radically different. Under MDMA Claire is in a steady state of mildly clouded consciousness but she is very much awake, she is alert to the session. She can choose what she wants to talk about, she can get up and wander round the room, change the music on the CD player, even make a cup of tea if she wants; *she can do anything*.

'I just want to talk!' she says, now four hours into the session and even more in control of the overwhelming effects. 'This is incredible…it feels *safe*…safe to talk. All these years I've been *trapped*…but now it seems so ridiculous to feel so stuck'

Another hour passes and the tears return and with it the frowning increases. She says the loveliness of the MDMA is fading. She is feeling more and more negative or spending longer periods lying back with her eyes closed in silence. The smile is falling away from her face and that familiar look of waking terror is flickering in the wings again.

Langley motions to Betsy to prepare the booster dose. 'Claire, would you like to take more MDMA like we discussed? This is the point where you can do that. You know that this MDMA feeling cannot last forever – that is not the purpose of the session. But we want to give you as much time as possible to explore the past whilst you are under the drug's effects. I'd like to give you another capsule but I want you to stay with me and focus again on the thoughts and memories of the past. Shall we do that, Claire?

188

She takes the booster dose, another 62.5mg, and within half an hour she has got back into the therapeutic space again. This time she is faster and better at staying on focus. It comes on quickly again, with intense rushing and eye rolling. She feels sick again and retches a little, then lies back and lets the drug carry her away again to that salutary space.

'Are you ready?' asks Austell after another twenty minutes. She is and this time she has an agenda. Thanks to the preparatory sessions Claire knows exactly what she wants to achieve. She has work to do and now is the time to do it. She describes how since the moment of her unplanned and brutal conception she became a veteran of the mental health services. Untold opportunities to rescue her and her siblings from their childhood hell were missed. One systemic blunder followed another and all the children stayed in the care of their parents, who continued to abuse drugs and expose the children to an ever-increasing battery of assault. No doctors or social workers could ever help her. But now she utterly, totally, trusts her psychiatrist. She feels that he *wants* her, understands her and is able to carry her through this process.

By the time the booster dose is wearing off Claire has been talking for almost seven hours. She has covered areas of thought and feeling that she did not know existed within her. She has been back to the site of her abuse, described the noxious smell, the texture of her rapes and the intense pain and humiliation, the utter shame and feelings of guilt, responsibility and searing, scorching agony. But with MDMA as her guide she has stared these memories in the face, conjured up these moments from her childhood and they could not hurt her.

Eventually the session winds down and Claire feels increasingly part of the everyday waking consciousness that is enjoyed by the others in the room. But the difference about this state for her now compared to before taking the MDMA is that she feels *comfortable* in it. As the intoxication recedes she does not feel an immediate return of her familiar pain. There is something different about her.

'It is still *so* lovely,' she smiles warmly to her three companions, who are now sitting on the couch sipping hot chocolate with her. Betsy has opened the windows wide and they are looking out over the starry fields.

'The effect is definitely still there but I quite suddenly feel sort of...really quite 'back' with you all...although it's not like I ever really left, is it? I was always here. I was just...being looked after.'

'How does it feel to be sober?' asks Langley.

Claire sips her drink. 'Great!' she says.

'Do you want to go back there again?' asks Austell. 'Do you want more MDMA?'

'What now? No, not at all!' she says adamantly. 'I feel as if I've done something important, and now...well now it's like I've done the work...the world really can be a lovely place...a peaceful place. I don't need the drug to tell me that. I've seen it for myself. So, no thanks.'

Langley settles back with a look of satisfaction at a job well done. He smiles warmly to Austell who exhales deeply and politely returns the look. But all Austell can think about is the sight of Langley's blood-stained handkerchief.

Spiritual Emergency
Of Epic Proportions

Since his first session John has had a further two LSD experiences and he continues to make great progress. He remains largely symptom free and is making great improvements in function, particularly in terms of relationships with his family. He has also started work again – something he has been unable to do for years. Admittedly his first new job as a plumber was mending the sink in Langley's caravan, which sits in the field behind the orchard at the back of the farm, but it's a start.

Austell is won over. 'I have to say I'm surprised by our results. And I want to see more. I want to get more of my patients into the program so we can introduce them to psychedelic therapy. I'm convinced it could work for them.'

'I like your attitude, Bob, but don't get too carried away. Stay objective and focused. Let me be the crazy one! But you're right; we do need more patients, someone for Ketamine and someone for Psilocybin. Do you have any other good cases?'

Austell laughs. 'I have plenty of cases. What sort of diagnoses do you need?'

'For the Ketamine it must be a patient with alcohol or opiate addiction, someone who has tried everything but can't get out of the rut of addiction? Ketamine, which is a truly bizarre compound, is perfect for that.'

'And what about the psilocybin?'

'Ah, the sacred magic mushroom! We should try that on

someone with a good case of religious guilt, someone tortured into an oppressive spiral of guilt-ridden angst.'

Austell immediately has a patient in mind. 'A Catholic lady perhaps?' he asks.

'Perfect,' Langley chuckles. 'Is she hopelessly neurotic? Entangled irrevocably in a spiritual emergency of epic proportions? Must be if Catholic. With Psilocybin it's all about journeying into the archaic past. Magic mushrooms are proper caveman fodder.'

'Oh, I know someone who fits the description of existential angst perfectly. A sweet little lady called Kathleen Rattick. She is the sort of patient who I have often thought would benefit from a stick of psychic dynamite; in the nicest possible way of course.'

There is a knock at the door and John Patterson pokes his head around ready for another of his non-drug follow-up sessions. Coffee is served and they sit on beanbags. He starts by showing the doctors a series of photographs taken with his newly purchased camera; all bright outdoors shots of flowers and sunsets. He tells them he used to be a keen photographer when he was young. He has not taken a picture for years until now.

'I have become obsessed with nature,' he says. 'Since the LSD I feel more in touch with the planet; the flowers, the earth, that kind of thing, you know how it is. It's all been going on around me but I hadn't noticed it before. It's stunning.'

Langley nods knowingly. 'People often say this about LSD. Even long after the trip has worn off they feel permanently changed for the better. Acid gives them new eyes to see old things.'

'And my kids laugh at me now,' says John, 'but in a good way. They think it's funny that the shape of clouds or the sound of the birds can excite me. But I've gained a new sense, as if I've awoken from my blindness. I have always been running from myself, you see doctor; that's the problem. I've never been able to get away. But when I thought I had died and then came out into the light, well, I don't know…it's like at that point I was free, I guess. I broke free.'

Tears are welling up. He wipes his eyes. 'I broke at that point and I still feel that way now. I am part of the universe now. I can *see* the universe in everything I do. There's a macro-universe and a micro-universe; they are one and the same thing. There is a perfect unity in all things and I am part of it.'

'How do you know this, John?' asks Austell. 'How do you know this is real and not just your mind playing tricks on you?'

'This is not a delusion, doctor. I know what I saw with my own eyes! Call it faith, or spirituality or whatever. I have intuitive knowledge of the universe. I have transcended normal time and space. I know that sounds crazy, but this is the most real, the *sanest*, I have ever felt about anything. It's difficult to explain.'

Austell looks across at Langley. Normally whenever he hears this kind of talk he reaches for his section papers and prescription pad. But there is no accompanying ego-dystopia. John presents as a sane and rational man with a renewed sense of peace and joy in his life. And Austell has to admit that functionally his patient has changed beyond all recognition.

'Look, Dr Austell, I am not sitting here telling you that everything is perfect in my life now. Far from it. I still live in a crummy bedsit, I have no employment and the issues with my family are not yet resolved. But I feel I have made some really important first steps. The LSD experience has at least pointed me in the right direction. Do you see that?'

Later that night Langley and Austell sit on the hill above the

193

farm under the black starry sky.

'Bob, I was impressed by how you handled that situation with John this afternoon. It takes a sensitive doctor to accept such profound changes in his patient. You are the expert here. You know how your patients feel and it's your long-standing relationship with these people that makes this project a success. Please do hold onto the values you have brought to this project and don't worry; you are right to be cautious. These drugs question the universal truths about reality, humanity and consciousness but that does not necessarily make them worthwhile medicines for all patients. You are the one who makes the decision about whether they work as psychiatric treatments or not. I want you to be convinced by the results.'

These are comforting words. Austell is here as a scientific observer, and he is genuinely intrigued and positive about what he has seen so far at *Bardo*. He just wants to be sure before they announce it to anyone. He is still to make up his mind.

'Yes, what I am seeing with John and Claire is very weird for me. These are my most hardcore, untreatable patients. I have worked with them for years and seen nothing like this. So I can't help being sceptical. Before we can tell the world about *Bardo* we need more positive data.'

'Exactly, I agree,' nods Langley. 'We want reproducible and consistently positive results. There are no quick fixes.'

The following day, the two friends sit in a flowery pasture behind the farm where a small stream trickles between sheep fields. They are taking in the swirl of Somerset hills and discussing Claire's session. Austell, who is convinced of the efficacy of MDMA for his patient, nevertheless represents the voice of reason and caution.

'It is all very well to be intoxicated by the effects of a pleasurable

194

drug, but does it really have any meaning in terms of psychotherapy? I was completely convinced by John's use of LSD, which was so awesome that it *must* have had an effect on his long-term thinking. But I cannot help feeling suspicious about MDMA. It just seems too easy. John had to really fight, to battle with demons, to reach his conclusions. But Claire had a mere drug high. I mean, give her a half bottle of whisky and she'd feel equally liberated from her past – for a while at least.'

Langley grins. 'It's a good point. And I suppose time will be the ultimate decider. Maybe whisky *could* do it equally as well. It certainly does it for me! But despite the popularity of self-medication with alcohol I don't think it's a useful mental state liberator. It's not nearly as good as MDMA as a tool for psychotherapy. Too toxic, it causes brain damage, far more so than MDMA or LSD. Alcohol has too narrow a therapeutic index and overdose on booze is a serious risk. It also has long-term toxicity issues that far outstrip those of the psychedelic drugs. So no, I don't rate alcohol as a useful medical tool. Basically, it's too dangerous.

'However, with MDMA Claire has had a really good glimpse of alternative mental strategies, even new personality possibilities. I think this could have lifelong effects on her if she continues to nurture her experience into a healthy lifestyle. She has had an experience of permissible love. We'll have to wait and see how it pans out.'

But Austell has not listened to his friend's reply. He loves Langley. Not on a physical level – though the touch of their hugs does provide a level of entactogenic quality he has never previously enjoyed – but more so on a mental level. It is ironic therefore that alcohol, which the adopted-American psychiatrist swigs away at now as ever, is a barrier to their intimacy, which is ironic given Langley's frequent statements about its toxicity and harm. What is more, Langley's drinking, and coughing, is getting worse.

When the moon had risen and Langley had slinked back off to his den, wheezing and hacking, Austell's pensive silence is interrupted by a ringing telephone. He was greatly surprised to hear an equally breathless Hunter on the other end.

'What-ho, Robert, Maurice Hunter here. Thought I'd drop you a bell to check in and see how you're getting on with your…what shall we call it…little experiment? How's it all going?'

'Well, er, Maurice. Fine, thank you. And how are you? How's Taunton?'

'Oh, same old, same old. Not there much these days actually. Got my fingers in a few other pies as it were. I was just wanting to check in with you about your little project.'

'Which aspect in particular are you interested in, Maurice?'

'You said you were setting about giving some bunch of unfortunate souls magic mushrooms and the like, are you not, Robert? Just wondering if, well, you know, whether it *works*? Have you had any interesting results yet?'

'I didn't think you had any interest in this field, Maurice,' replied Austell. 'I was under the impression that you considered it "a load of old mumbo jumbo." I think those were the words you used when I last talked to you about my plans. What's changed your mind to want to know about it now?'

'Oh, come on old chap. You know me. Always keeping a keen eye on the latest developments.'

Austell did know Hunter. And he knew that the man had no interest in new developments of any sort except those that served his own needs. There must be something more to this than a genuine desire to learn about psychedelics. But nevertheless, Austell recognised this as an opportunity to educate Hunter in some ground-breaking research.

'Well, since you ask, Maurice, it's all going very well, thank you. We have seen several patients treated most effectively with a variety of different drugs. We have been extremely pleased with the results so far as a matter of fact.'

'Splendid, splendid! Which drugs?' Hunter blurts.

'LSD.'

'Right, LSD! Anything else?'

'MDMA, and next we are going to try…'

'Wonderful. Ecstasy, eh? And, well, do they work?'

'Yes, yes they do,' says Austell, relishing this opportunity to impart knowledge to a non-believer. 'It appears to be the case that these drugs facilitate a remarkable ability to help patients engage with hidden, repressed parts of their psyches. Under the influence of drugs like LSD I have seen my patients embrace and challenge…'

Hunter cuts him off and jumps in. 'So, do you see these mushrooms and their like eventually replacing the drugs we currently use, Robert? Will we some day be giving our patients LSD and MDMA? They are, by the way, off patent and therefore provide only minimal potential revenue for the pharmaceutical industry, rather than the hugely useful and, frankly, under-prescribed antidepressants and antipsychotics that we use presently? Can you really see that happening?'

'Well, yes, I think so,' answers Austell. 'I don't see why not. I think these psychedelic therapy treatments could be the next big thing for psychiatry actually. Let's hope so, eh?'

197

'Yes, yes, of course. Well, thanks Robert. That is most interesting. Most interesting indeed. Anyway, mustn't keep you, old chap. Toodle pip!'

THE DARK SIDE: NON-HIGH PEOPLE

Over the course of the autumn and right into the winter Austell and Langley see Claire and John for continued drug and non-drug follow-up sessions. They see them individually and also together. And then Austell introduces a third patient into the mix, Kathleen Rattick, with her life-long affliction of Catholic guilt; tormented by celestial pressure she has become avoidant of modern life.

Ms Rattick is keen to try anything that might lift her out of her pit of despair so she joins the group meetings as part of the preparations for her first drug session. By witnessing Claire and John's transformative changes Ms Rattick is slowly immersed into the project. However, at first, she feels somewhat out of kilter in the group sessions, which always begin with, at Langley's insistence, all the members lying down surrounded by candles listening to white noise. Kathleen shifts uncomfortably on her beanbag. Claire's tattoos and Patterson's faraway look unnerve her, the incense irritates her nostrils and she always needs the loo. So it takes some time, but after several sessions, over a period of weeks, Kathleen begins to unwind and eventually contribute to the group.

'I knows it's not my fault and I'm not to blame. But I can't get this niggling thought out of my 'ead that I am guilty 'bout something. It's just the way I was brought up. As a child I was always apologising for something, always saying sorry. There was just no...no *joy* in my child'ood. Everything was all wrong. So's I went to church to pray for forgiveness. But I's never really know what for!'

John Patterson feels immediately connected with her experience and is a great support to her in the group. 'My upbringing was similar,' he says, 'I always felt guilty, like I'd done something wrong. I was always saying sorry for just being alive.'

'Yes, that is how it was,' agrees Kathleen, dabbing an eye, 'always feeling guilty. Always on the back foot.'

Dr Langley talks to the group about Ms Rattick's sacred psilocybin mushroom session she is due to have next week. He reassures her that psychedelic plants have been used as sacramental tools by non-Western cultures for thousands of years. He wants Kathleen to understand how much these drugs have helped ancient people to communicate with their gods.

'You are not the first person in an existential crisis of Biblical aetiology, Kathleen,' he says. 'It's been happening for millennia.'

Kathleen looks anxious. 'But that's what I'm scared of. I mean, what if I don't like it? What if I experience hell and then I get stuck there and never return to sanity?'

'Who says any of us are sane?' contributes Patterson. 'I know I wasn't. At least not until I took LSD. I have no doubt that LSD has saved my life, not ruined it. I feel saner now than ever.'

'Also, Kathleen,' adds Langley. 'The psychedelic experience only exists in your head. If you see demons then that is what is in there. You won't learn anything about yourself that you didn't already know. But the difference with psychedelics is that you have to look at it. All over the world people use magic mushrooms, *psilocybin*, the drug you will be taking on Tuesday night. So you will not be alone when you imbibe this magical sacrament.'

'I have just never understood why people want to take these

drugs,' she says. 'You know, why do kids take them? It doesn't look to me as if *they* are taking them for spiritual or religious reasons.'

'Of course psychedelics can certainly be taken only for kicks, Kathleen,' says Langley. 'But when it comes to drugs it is all about *context*. Besides, young people have a greater spirit of adventure than us boring adults. Maybe there is something we can learn from them when they take LSD? Even if they do it just for fun.'

'Kathleen,' says John Patterson warmly towards the new group member, 'you will be fine. Many cultures use psychedelics as part of a religious ceremony led by a Shaman. A respected elder of the tribe who holds the role of both doctor and priest. They use hallucinogenic plants and fungi, together with drumming and chanting to alter consciousness, to induce a dreamlike state and communicate with the spirit world. The ceremonies have a cohesive effect on the whole community. You will be carrying out a well-practiced form of religious healing.'

Kathleen nods in understanding.

'And it is not only humans that want to alter their state of consciousness,' continues John, the ex-plumber-turned-armchair-guru, 'many animals – fish, insects and mammals – are attracted to hallucinogenic plants and fungi. The reindeer of Siberia drink the urine of those animals that have eaten the Amanita muscaria mushroom – well known to the local shamans to be excreted as an active compound. They press their fleshy reindeer lips right up against the urethral opening of other reindeer in order to drink the potion directly as it is pissed out.'

The group sits and meditates on this image for a while. Langley smiles. He is pleased to hear how far Patterson has come, who since his LSD ingestions has embraced psychedelic culture

201

wholeheartedly and has been reading the various psychedelic books he left lying around *Bardo*. With little trace of his Taunton-bred roots he is keen to impart his new-found wisdom to this new group member. John's impressive background reading is testament to his willingness to embrace the psychedelic experience in its entirety. And his tendency to waffle would fit in well at the next Opening Minds conference.

'Thank you for that, John. Kathleen, I think you will find the mushrooms a much more effective tool at connecting with God than all of those years you have spent under the spell of the Catholic Church.'

'I hope so, Dr Langley. God knows I need to do something about it.'

They bring the session to an end. Austell and Claire shuffle away to discuss her forthcoming session arrangements and Langley sits and meditates for a while longer. He watches as John takes Kathleen by the arm for a tour around the farm. There is a definite chemistry between Patterson and Rattick. It can only be good for the group as a whole.

Kathleen's pertinent question about why young people choose to take drugs recreationally ignites precious memories of his own experimentation with LSD as a teenager. There is something about those early days that stays with one. Psychedelics are something of a rite of passage during adolescence. And Langley, like most kids, was careful when he carried out his early investigations. Older teenagers in his gang acting as guides for the younger, talking them through it and seeing that preparations were in place and safety is adhered to.

Langley has fond memories of that elusive first moment; that feeling when the acid starts to work with tingling warmth in the stomach and then spreads through the limbs to the extremities. Things will appear to be slightly out of place. The group of friends slowly develops into a shared togetherness. Banal and innocuous comments suddenly become funny. Laughter ensues, concepts and ideas become tangential and then wildly fantastic and the friends alternate between interacting with one another in weird exploratory social activities and taking oneself off to a quiet corner to delve into one's head, walk around the corridors of the mind and peek into cupboards and mysterious corners that haven't been accessed for a while.

Langley remembers those teenage parties continuing throughout the night and into the morning. At first everyone is hanging onto their seats as the LSD effect climbs; getting higher and higher then peaking for an endless number of hours. Perceptual alterations are a delightful wonderment, either in solitude or as part of the group:

'Hey, wow! Look at how the patterns on the curtains move! Woah! Have you checked out the carpet in the hallway?...No way, man!...Cool!...Hey, man, let's go outside...Woah! Look at the clouds!...Hey, try this...what is it?...*Strawberries*!...No way, are those strawberries?...*I...I think so*...Really?...No, man!...ugh!... *What is it?*...Hang on a second, let me see that?...Ha ha ha! That's *soap*!...*No way, is it? Soap*?...Yeah! Where did you find it?...*over there, in the bathroom*...ha ha ha ha!...cool!...No, hang on...*it is a strawberry!* Woah, man, have you seen your skin?...It's all...it's all...*My skin, what's wrong with it?*...Woah, it's all sort of...What? What?!...it's all sort of *aglow*...all green and blotchy and...'

And so on, and so on, and so on, and so on. As the experience progresses the teenagers are carried further away until, depending on the drug, the dose, the set and setting, they lose track of time altogether. They are floating freely in a void where edges no longer meet, where the body does not happen except as a mere thought existing only in one's imagination. But even throughout these perilous moments there is always interaction; laughter, chatting, drifting in and out of people's scenarios and always in a state of hyper-realised distance from the normal waking condition. As long as the users feel safe, fed with appropriate stimulation (or lack of, if preferred) this plateau can go on and on. But then it will eventually, one is relieved to know, start to fade. And once one begins the descent, the shadows and colours that previously had been unfathomable and kept the group in concentrated rapture for hours, recede back to their usual forms and make sense.

As the trip declines the everyday social games, the rules of ordinary existence take back their place from the idiosyncratic boundaries set up by transient immersion in aromatic baths of infinite possibilities. The psychedelic experience slowly fades away as gradually as it had started. Then there is the come down. Hours of sitting around whilst the laundered brain puts its pieces back together, looks for logical connections between things and works out how to use language. It will be some time before the grinding stimulation of the LSD rattling in the system subsides enough for sleep. In the meantime all there is to do is to lie around in the developing daylight with blankets over the windows, listening to music playing gently from a dark corner of the room, cannabis circulating for those in need of a softening of the edges, warm conversation edging back into the group. And drinking tea. Endless rounds of tea.

Sometimes people will get up and wander off to bed prematurely and then return, wrapped in blankets with the realisation that if one is going to have to sit there staring at a wall its probably better to do it in the company of other speechless zombies rather than alone in the cold stark reality of one's bedroom. Attempts are made to bring back the buzz, to re-visit the mad scenarios that six hours earlier had everyone rolling on the floor. But now tiredness has set in and the same illogical funny jokes sound empty. Friends exchange smiles and grunt to one another, passing spliffs in silence, draped over the living room floor. The come down just has to be sat out, endured. This is the body and mind's reimbursement, the built in regulator; a safety mechanism to prevent excessive use of these magical sacraments. It is the unavoidable payback but it needn't be all bad, as long as no one has anything to do the next day. Simply remain locked-up in forced penance, in solitude, before daring to interact with the outside world. Stay away from the daylight. Do not under any circumstances answer the phone! It will be a message from The Dark Side, from *non-high people*.

Sleep severs the bondage and releases the repetitive thoughts, the obsessions of madness that lurk behind the eyelids. But that is all it takes, one decent night's sleep to sort everything out and reboot the brain. And when it is all over, for maybe a day or two, Langley remembers how he and his friends were left feeling warmed, shaken and refreshed. Colonic irrigation for the brain, that's what it is. It can be messy at the time but well worth it.

And that, thinks Langley, in response to Kathleen Rattick's (or anyone else's) question as to why people take drugs, is the answer. The psychedelic experience is an intensely fascinating, intellectually curious and highly entertaining thing to do. Maybe the reason kids do it is simply for the kicks, and maybe the lofty existential realisations only come later. But to not take LSD at all;

or worse still, to demonize it *without ever even trying* it, to criticize and deny the potential value of such an important experience seems, to Langley, and the tens of millions of other people who have benefitted from psychedelics, to be folly in the extreme.

GENTLE BUT FIRM HAND
ON THE TILLER

'I *do* want to speak to God, but just not for too long,' she said. 'And I don't want none of this creeping up all subtle, I want Him to appear to me suddenly and powerfully. That's how I've been expecting Him all my life and it's never happened. I want my Lord to come bursting in, all guns blazing, just as it happened for the Holy Saints of the Catholic Church.'

'Psilocybin is the perfect choice for you then, Kathleen,' says Langley. 'All of the classical psychedelic drugs have the ability to trigger spontaneous spiritual feelings. This is a tried and tested phenomenon. They induce a Peak Experience, which, like discovering God, can be life-changing and intensely healing.'

'Oh, Dr Langley, I really could do with that. I feel like He has let me down all these years. I do hope He doesn't disappoint today.'

'Oh, don't worry, Kathleen, I think *She* will certainly not disappoint you. In fact, the reason I say tried and tested is because one of the most famous historical psychedelic experiments of them all involved giving a bunch of theologians taking psilocybin whilst they listened to a Good Friday Catholic mass.'

'Oh dear God, poor buggers!'

'Well, yes,' laughs Langley. 'Indeed, dear God! Trust me, it certainly worked that time for Walter Pahnke's experiment back in 1963 and I get the feeling it will work for you today.'

Intravenous psilocybin, however, has more in common with DMT than with magic mushrooms. It is unusual for a user of psychedelics to be catapulted from sober baseline to the peak experience within a matter of seconds, but that is what is about to happen to Ms Rattick. She will not get the insidious shifting in consciousness that occurs when one has ingested LSD or mushrooms by mouth. Kathleen is a timeworn woman from the working class of Taunton. She is keen to emphasise that this is not a mere teenage kick. Rather she is seeking a dramatic shift from her stagnation, a firing into the cosmos from a powerful cannon. It will not do to have her climb there on an arduous ladder, merely to suffer the consequences of having to carefully pick her way back down again.

There are only a tiny handful of people in the world who can say they have had intravenous psilocybin and Ms Rattick, a cleaner from Taunton, is about to become one of them.

Betsy returns with the syringe containing 3 mg of synthetic psilocybin mixed in a 10ml saline solution. With a nod from Austell she injects Kathleen.

'OK Kathleen, here we go. Hold on tight.'

The drug immediately enters the brain and floods the 5-HT$_{2A}$ receptors on the pyramidal cells in Layer V of the cerebral cortex, causing an instant decoupling of her pathways. One minute Ms Rattick is lying there sober as a judge, telling Langley that Primark in Taunton have a sale on with men's polo shirts selling at £6 for a pack of three, then the next minute she is soaring on the most intense psilocybin trip imaginable. At first all is darkness for Kathleen behind the eyeshades; then abruptly all is light. From out of nowhere comes a rumbling, glowing, heavenly blur. It advances, picking up speed, then explodes into her visual and auditory fields with orange and red checkerboard patterns, fractals and Celtic symbols, spinning, arching, falling over themselves, charging in from the periphery of the darkness. And then all of a sudden there she is: catapulted straight to the heart of the highest mystico-spiritual realm.

Kathleen Rattick has left the building.

She is kneeling in a white room in front of a cross, but she's not some Lilliputian figure looking down on herself in an out-of-body experience. She has no body. She does not exist. There are no edges, no dimensions of physical space. And nor is she dreaming. She is still Kathleen Rattick, but just *more so*. She has lost the Kathleen Game entirely and is now simply a notion. She is not dead either. She is more alive than ever. She will remember every part of this experience as if it is real, because it is real. Before her there is a cross. Not a crucifix, she is surprised to see; there is nothing Christian about the image. This cross is a simple reference point, a symbol on a map. A plain cross; thin, like a crosshair gun-sight hovering before her. And she knows this is a judgment – but not before *God* – because *she* is God.

This is the source of everything in the universe. God is a minor figure next to this! She is intensely scared, terrified beyond imagination. But this is a fear unlike any other; she knows she is so utterly abandoned to fate that the fear is strangely bearable – almost comical. She has been obliterated so completely and helplessly that what is there to fear? It's game over anyway. But what she cannot figure out at this stage is whether she has lost or won.

Coming from somewhere in the room – or *space* rather (to be a room it would have to be made of something, be part of physical matter, which this is not, it is far too intensely white to be made of mere matter), there is a pounding, screeching, almighty loud sound. Yet, curiously, she is also in perfect peace.

Time has ceased to be, yet she knows with complete certainty that she has been here forever. In some respects she has never been more sober, never been more natural. This white room is a world of paradoxes. For every realization Kathleen has about what is happening she is also aware that the complete opposite is simultaneously true. Her bodiless mind is filled, quite suddenly, with an intense feeling of bliss. Kneeling in space before that non-Christian cross, floating in the whiteness, feeling an emanation of concentrated passionate energy radiating into her she now realises what this is: it is a true representation of pure *love*. Love is all around. It protects her and is within her. *She knows she has not done anything wrong.* There is no such thing as wrongness. There is only love.

At the two minute mark on Austell's stopwatch Kathleen starts shaking. Langley, who stands beside the bed takes her hand and begins reciting from memory a passage from the *Tibetan Book of the Dead*, just as they had rehearsed together in the preparatory sessions of the previous weeks. Kathleen's shuddering slows and she lapses further into a deeply contented state of blessedness. She is nine years old, climbing upwards through the sunlit branches of a magnificent tree that grows at the bottom of her garden; that place where she enjoys rare moments of escape from childhood sorrow in her secret green shelter, now illuminated to the point of total white-out in the searing light of love.

'Kathleen…Kathleen…can you speak?'

From her cavernous white space amongst the branches Kathleen finds she can speak. But it is simpler just to think whatever it is she wishes to communicate. The ether, the vapours in which her bodiless soul will transmit any message that needs to be said.

'Yes…I…I have arrived…I am here.'

Langley says, in a scarcely audible whisper: 'Kathleen, float downstream and let the river carry you...we will take care of your husk, your shell, your fallible body....all you have to do is... journey...'

His voice drifts away to nothing. Kathleen begins shuddering again; spasmodic jerks firing through her recumbent frame, prompting Austell, for the first time since starting this crazy venture with this beautifully eccentric Joseph Langley, to worry whether they ought to be calling for an ambulance. But no need to fret. Betsy has a firm but gentle hand on the tiller. Let's face it, she has seen this a thousand times (though granted, not so often with intravenous psilocybin). She calmly takes the blood pressure of her subject. All normal. Heart rate up a little, at around 110 bpm, but of no great concern. She motions silently for Austell to relax. The participant is doing fine. Leave her be. Let her soar. She will return. After all, to break down is to break through, as Ronnie Laing said.

Kathleen is beaming now. She lifts an arm and gently pulls the eye patches away, yet her gaze remains fixed on distant visionary sights. She is, it appears, with her God.

'You are so...*beautiful*?' she says, or asks, not quite sure which, in a drawl exemplifying a paltry capacity to verbalise the beatific vision. On a tiny galaxy her mind hangs in oblivion, carrying with it insignificant and meaningless cares through endless cycles of birth and reincarnation. Her body, useless, idles serenely in a neighbouring galactic cluster. After all, she asks herself, what is a body other than a mere stinking hunk of dirty meat kept barely above room temperature by a friable series of electrochemical organic processes for a few short moments? Despite this she is acutely aware that on top of her head she cradles a brain of immeasurable power.

211

Even now, while her physical casing is in a state of shutdown her motherboard is rapidly upgrading new software. The system will need to be restarted before the new updates can take effect. In the meantime it is best not to unplug the device. Rather just let it get on with it. It will reboot automatically when the download is complete.

We are now beginning our descent.

Within half an hour Ms Rattick commences the return to the routine shifting patterns of everyday reality. The rudiments of human language return. She slowly remembers some of the popularly used words and then figures out how to order and categorise them according to learned procedures.

Ah yes, that's it: vision and speech. Language is what they apparently call this phenomenon on earth.

And with this comprehension there comes the power of speech again and soon after this she is able to sit up and see. She rubs her face and smiles heartily at Austell – much to his relief. As he helps her up she gives him and Langley a warm a hug.

'It is a miracle, Dr Austell,' she says, the tears pouring down her face. 'Nothing short of a miracle, I tell you!'

These doctors are the Edmund Hillary and Sherpa Tenzing of the hallucinogenic world. They embrace their patient lovingly on her return to base camp, all of them basking in the shadow of the majestic mountain peaks around them.

Before the hour is out coffee is passed round, and some wine for Langley, and they all sit and watch the day drift languidly into a luscious wet evening, one immersed in the dripping fecundity of the enveloping countryside. Afterglow is an understatement.

PART 4

THE COME DOWN

STATE OF
EXCITED NONCHALANCE

During this gradual phase of cosmic re-entry Kathleen is invited to stay at the farm. The *Bardo* premises have grown into a site for tranquil reflection and she wants to feel part of the zeitgeist. Austell and Langley have opened up further buildings, including a small cottage into which John Patterson has now moved, leaving behind his grimy bedsit. Claire too is now living on site, in a yurt pitched in the far corner of the apple orchard, and in the mounting cold of winter, while she continues to negotiate her MDMA landscapes, she stays snug in her tent with a log burner and piles of Tibetan yak blankets supplied by Betsy. Many evenings are spent in the yurt, with the *Bardo* staff and patients together. It becomes an important place for the patients to unpick their therapeutic psychedelic experiences, and the boundaries between patient and staff begin to blur.

'All my life I have had other people telling me about God,' says Kathleen. 'But for all the churches, sermons and masses that I have sat in – been *made* to sit through as a child – for all those hours I have put in, I don't think, until now, I have ever *experienced* God for myself.'

Langley laughs. 'Kathleen, There is a famous saying by the nineteenth century Native American, Quanah Parker, referring to the Indian use of the psychedelic Peyote cactus: *The White man goes into his church house and talks about Jesus. The Indian goes into his tepee and talks to Jesus.* It frustrates me to see how often the contemporary Christeo-centric approach to spirituality gets it so wrong. For all the hours put in by Christians they rarely *experience* God themselves. The congregation in the pews are maintained as mere passive observers, being told about the spiritual experience by the priest. The flock is rarely offered the opportunity to actually experience the spirit themselves. When we use psychedelic drugs we offer exactly that.'

Claire is pensive. Subsequent MDMA sessions have been even more revealing. She has effectively completed ten years of traditional psychotherapy in as many weeks. And with these new personal insights the realisation that she is good person has left her feeling bolstered. She is keen to get more involved in the *Bardo* project, wanting to give something back to the people who have given her this new opening. But there is no spiritual component to her enlightenment. Rather she is on a mission to rid herself entirely of the material trappings of her former life. This means above all her use of all drugs, including alcohol, which she is beginning to see are impediments to enlightenment.

'When I take MDMA I don't feel God. But I do feel... *connected*...connected with *myself* more than with anyone else. That is enough for me.'

'That is fine. It is all you need, Claire,' reassures Langley. 'Once you have stepped through that door you will never be the same again.'

'Amen,' says John, who has also transformed considerably from his original presentation. He sits cross-legged in a kaftan plucking amateur melodies on a guitar. Reaching awkwardly down the fret board where his beaded mala dangles over the strings, his eyes closed, and his playing excruciating for anyone within earshot. The sentiment, however, is noble.

216

Kathleen regards the group of figures, whose shadows shift and dart in the flickering fire light. She has reached what she refers to as her 'own state of excited nonchalance'. No one quite understands what she means by this but no one questions it. That, she feels, is enough.

'What I have is better than God,' she says. 'But the drug thing still bothers me. I was always brought up to think of drinks and drugs as a false paradise - the idea that drugs are not *real*, they offer only illusions - that when it comes to seeking God one must be sober. One can only find God with a clear head.'

'Oh, Kathleen!' Langley smiles, hiccoughing as he steadies the cider bottle back down on the table. 'How effective this Christian church brainwashing has been! Psychedelic drugs simply alter your consciousness. They do not add or take away *anything* from what is already out there or *in here*,' he smiles, tapping his temple. 'Religious enlightenment is all about stepping outside one's everyday experience of the world and seeing things differently. The church knows this. That is why they use their spooky ethereal choral music, stained glass windows and big booming voices to impress the vulnerable. The intention is to put the receivers into an *altered state of consciousness.* That way they are more suggestive to spontaneously look at themselves. These techniques are not qualitatively different from using psychedelic drugs; just quantitatively so.'

'Maybe, but I can see Kathleen's point,' adds Claire. 'I agree there are many paths to God, and that these psychedelic drugs are as meaningful as any other non-drug ways in. But surely, once one has glimpsed the numinous, as you so often say, one need not keep topping up over and over again…'

'Perhaps, Claire, perhaps…' answers Langley, reaching again for the bottle.

'...just like you keep on doing with all of that booze, Dr Langley,' finishes Claire boldly. 'Do you not think there is a slight smidgen of inconsistency, Joseph, in your heavy drinking? I mean, it doesn't fit well with the concept of clean living you are always encouraging us to follow.'

'Well, yes, ha ha!' Langley stumbles. 'Nothing like a bit of the old 'grape and grain' to, you know, wet the whistle!' He looks around for approval from the group, but their attention is on the tremor in his hand as he pours. 'No harm in a bit of social lubrication, Claire!'

'If that is all it is,' she brazenly replies. 'And let's face it, you don't need a fucked-up patient like *me* to be lecturing *you*, a renowned psychiatrist, on the hidden meanings behind drug and alcohol abuse, but, as far as I can tell...'

'Well, Claire,' interjects Austell. 'We have come far enough along this road to know that the finger of blame plays no part in our understanding of such dynamics.' He puts a sympathetic arm around Langley, who has now started coughing, and rubs his back. 'We need to look after each other. We are all in this together.' Turning to Langley, 'Joseph, it is obvious that Claire cares about you deeply. We all do. I think that is what is going on here.'

'Yes,' smiles Claire – a rare expression from her indeed. 'I am worried.'

'And for that I thank you,' splutters Langley, composing himself. 'But really, you have nothing to worry about. None of you do. And I take your point about the drinking. I will try, I will endeavour to be less of a menace to sobriety.'

'Amen,' adds Patterson again. Group therapy provides fertile ground for the outpouring of the 'experienced'. The fledgling

218

psychonauts are getting to know their compounds better; learning to navigate their drugs' terrains, gaining personal insights as they journey. The same is true of the doctors leading them on this journey. And it was clearly a relief to everyone to hear this confession from Langley. None less so than Austell.

Over time more patients are recruited, joining Claire, John and Kathleen. They complete their preparation sessions and then take their own cosmic plunges into the celestial void. The farm-dwellers grow in number with each newly recruited patient because no one wants to leave *Bardo*. They cook and eat collectively as a group, and together with the two doctors and Betsy spend their evenings sitting huddled in the yurt when the wind is high or out under the stars around a fire when nights are clear. A lot of watching of the extra-terrestrial heavens goes on.

Langley and Austell exchange smiling glances as they sit and watch their patients discuss their wonderful integration of their drug experiences. Once touched by the psychedelic experience people often feel obliged to spout forth pseudo-scientific claptrap; talking about the 'infinite universe' and that kind of thing. And for Austell this is sometimes difficult to stomach. Who says the universe is infinite? All the latest evidence from theoretical physics says otherwise.

But the chaos in these people's minds; fluidly falling over itself with senseless interpretations, are part of the great uselessness of explanation; totally pointless but such an important component of psychedelic assimilation. All of the recruits need to go through these phases of growth. But once they have talked themselves into silence they will, of course, realise that he who talks does not know and he who knows does not talk. And if there is one person who knows more than others when it comes to secrets and silence it is Langley.

Lately, his blood-streaked sputum and hacking cough have been further augmented by intense headaches, pains that can last for days, accompanied by a peculiar bodily weakness that defies his medical explanation. He is experiencing rapid mood swings and is also losing weight. He bulks himself up to hide the physical changes but his moodiness and preference to self-isolate are harder to keep veiled. Langley is also on a journey. He has endured, and like his patients, will carry his own visions with him into the nothingness. Behind that mischievous smile of his there hides an encyclopaedia of meaning. It is later than he thinks. He intends to enjoy himself.

REIGNING IN THE CIRCUS

December hits *Bardo* hard. The warm winters of recent years are finally eclipsed by near arctic weather. Rain drives incessantly into the West Country from warm Atlantic fronts and collides head-on with north-westerly's sweeping across from Russia, giving Somerset a heavy pounding of snow on the Sunday before Christmas.

Austell wakes to find the landscape under a good ten inches of drift. It obscures the lanes and erases the detail of trees and gateways. Paths are buried, bushes, hedges and cars are homogenised under snowy dunes. It is extraordinarily beautiful in the early morning with the first sunrays cutting halogen light across the glare. And like the wintery blanket, the *Bardo* bubble itself has enclosed its cast members into a fully blown therapeutic community. They are now in a movie where people watch the edges of their twenty-first century lives merge into antediluvian bliss. A myriad of substances have removed the defining traits between personalities, highlighting animal uniformity and human distinctions alike.

Once the veil of psychedelic vision has descended all objects in one's life appear blurred by the blizzard, everything part of the same universal whole. Community rule and the distinctions between healer and patient, sky and hills, dissolve gently into a white noise of frozen tranquillity. Everyone is snowed in together. But it's not all about the drugs. There are issues for this quasi-society. This Cosmic New Town must work out. Rebuilding the population with new rules that apply to citizens whose appreciation of reality will not allow them to be fobbed off by mind games relying on the aggressive patriarchal logic of the medical model. Nothing will work here unless it obeys the principles of psychedelic non-reasoning.

Austell dons his coat and ties up his boots as the farm collies, Dropper and Blotter, jump around eagerly at his feet, desperate to get out into the snow. He trudges to the far end of the meadow and waves.

'Lovely morning, Claire!'

'Isn't it beautiful!' From her yurt a thin plume of smoke rises into the frozen air. 'We had some new arrivals late last night,' she says, beckoning his gaze towards the far end of the meadow. 'And it looks like they are stuck here now!' Two unfamiliar live-in vehicles; one an old 1970s touring coach and the other a converted horsebox trailer, adorned with the obligatory 'om' symbols and boarded windows, have turned off the lane and taken a place in the corner of the lower field, their tracks eradicated by last night's fall of fresh snow.

'Right, I can see that,' says Austell. 'I suppose we had better go and say hello and give them a cuppa. You got your fire going? Hard to believe we'd be this popular out here in the middle of nowhere!'

Claire laughs, 'I don't know about that,' she says, 'wherever we go we are always exactly the same distance from the centre of the earth. I'm sure that's the sort of New Age reasoning they'd give you for deciding to centre their transient existence on *Bardo* farm for the time being.'

'Yes, probably! Come, let's go and say hello. Whoever they are they are going to need warm fires and some hot water. It is certainly going to be a developmental challenge for all of us this winter.'

Austell takes Claire's hand to steady her as they traipse towards the vehicles. He is aware that apart from restraining her from killing herself with a broken bottle many years ago and more recently suturing her wrist lacerations this is the first time he has held her in

222

this way. Their boots crunch deliciously in the firm snow.

Knocking on the window of the large coach, a child's face immediately parts the curtains of the cab and peers out. Followed by another one. Inside they can hear a smaller baby crying. The door swings open and a tall hairy gentleman with a kindly face, wonky teeth and an enormous spliff beckons them in. Before long the kettle is on and hot-knives are warming whilst Claire and Austell are clambered over by bright-eyed children in baggy jumpers. The interior of the bus exudes an atmosphere of family warmth and lived-in necessity. Everything has its place, with dark aromas of incense and diesel, decorated by mandalas, dream-catchers and UV light free-party banners. Outside the farm dogs circle the bus dogs; sniffing one another's genitals in a manner of cementing familiarity that humans have lost in the midst of time, thankfully.

Austell helps the bus people (Dave Ar'ju, his wife Spira and their children) to feel comfortable then goes back to the farmyard and returns with a wheelbarrow of logs and armfuls of blankets.

'I love it,' he replies when Claire asks him how he feels about the numbers swelling at *Bardo*. 'It's all part of the shared community. And I think our project here is bolstered by a climactic test such as this snow. Thing is, Claire,' he says, with a confidence and fluidity he did not know he possessed, 'I feel like these people are my family now, my children no less. I have never attempted to embrace my cynical psychiatric work colleagues like this in the past, I always felt outside their group - albeit tied into the dogma of their clinical procedure. But this is different. This is the *Bardo* family.'

Leaving Dave to dig out his bus, Austell and Claire trudge back up the field to the cottage to wake Langley and get the fires going. 'Let's wake the old man up,' says Claire. 'Today will bring new sessions and new insights. Let's see how Joseph will feel about his beloved Somerset deep under snow.'

The acidic rays of searing sunlight cut through the eastern clouds and set alight the crystalline sea of ice blue. 'Jesus, Claire. It is unfathomably beautiful!' Claire can connect Austell's high and takes the opportunity to ask, 'So, doc, does your enthusiasm for the *Bardo* community extend to taking the plunge and having a psychedelic experience of your own?'

'No, not yet, Claire,' he laughs. 'I will fulfil my pledge to avoid imbibing the magic medicine for now. I'll keep my palate clean, as promised. In fact, as I watch the months pass and more patients come through the door I feel ever less inclined to take that trip. Not because I fail to see it working – on the contrary I am now convinced it *does work* – but because I made a promise to myself and Langley. I want to appreciate all the beauty going on around me with the same eyes I used to judge so much hopelessness in the past. I will remain a passive scientific observer in order to compare the results as they emerge. Trust me, Claire, it is fascinating enough to simply watch the circus from my ringside seat. I have no desire, at this point at least, to run away with myself and join in!'

'Sounds fair enough to me, doc.'

'But I'll tell you one thing,' adds Austell. 'I do so wish Langley would keep his own palate cleaner. At times he seems to be cracking up. I worry about his late night dosing with cider and apple bitters.'

'Me too,' says Claire. 'His drinking has been on the up. And all that alcohol is bad for the soul.'

As January departs there arrives a thaw and a welcomed milder spell. The inhabitants plant gardens and start keeping pigs and sheep. There are now twelve patients who have successfully completed the whole program, which entails both drug and non-drug mindfulness psychotherapy sessions. The therapeutic courses are running themselves. Many people have begun the tentative journey down the path to recovery and they support one another through the turbulence of sessions, exposing the raw welts of childhood experience as guttural tears emanate from barns all over the farm. John Patterson, six months since his initial drug session, has become a team leader. He and Claire welcome the new recruits and work alongside Betsy and the two psychiatrists to prepare and counsel patients for their flights.

In all weathers, Langley and Austell have their evening stroll through the community smallholding. It is the closest they get to a business meeting. In the area of hilly farmland above *Bardo* Farm there remains a remarkably old plateau from a distant prehistoric age. Rich in quartz and iron mineralisation, the calorific soil provides lush grazing land for wild deer and fat sheep. Cows with feral stares chew the cud in the valleys surrounding a tiny northern Somerset village, providing the milk that gives rise to the world's most famous cheese. (The village of Cheddar is coincidentally also a hot-bed of base amphetamine abuse amongst the local residents for some unknown reason). On the higher ground water-logged acidic soil of Exmoor, far above *Bardo,* where untamed ponies roam, the Dunkery Beacon looks out to the sea and in the distance the South Wales coast sprawls industrially.

'It's really taking off here, Joseph, isn't it?'

'Yes indeed, Bob! Is this how you expected it?'

Austell laughs, a little guardedly. Nowadays it is difficult to predict how Langley might react from one moment to the next.

'When we began all those months ago I never dreamed it would end up like this.'

'I know! Fabulous. It really is.'

'But it'll be getting on for a year soon,' musters Austell. 'How do you feel about the way things are changing around here? You know, with so many new people arriving? Personally, I'm not sure. Do you think all of it is for the better?'

'I guess so, Bob. Don't you?'

'Well, I don't know. And, well, I mean, I am also a bit uneasy about the changes I see in you, Joseph. I mean, you seem to be acting more chaotically than ever.'

'Man, you gotta break down to…'

'…to break through, yes, yes, I know. But sometimes it seems as if your eccentricities – which have always been a welcome part of your character – are becoming, well, how shall I say it, *more exaggerated*? It is as if your entire personality is shifting.'

'It is?' queries Langley nonchalantly.

'Yes, I think so. There is this emergence of impulsivity that makes you edgy around the other inhabitants. Thing is, if I hadn't grown so close to you as I have I wouldn't feel so deeply troubled.'

They trudge together in silence. In the distance on the ridge a tractor pulls a plough through the red clay sod, its wake peppered with birds. Langley says nothing but continues to swig at his flagon.

'I think it's time we took stock of what's going on,' says Austell. 'We need to make sure we continue to operate with a strictly professional code of practice. All these people milling about all day, you know, basking in a hippie commune, it's all very well but it's not going to help us get into mainstream medicine, is it? I mean, if the editors of *The Lancet* came and saw this lot lounging around what are they likely to think? I don't think they'd to be too impressed, do you?'

'I agree, Bob, in part, of course, of course,' replies Langley, his tone rising and falling, manically compared to the laidback soul Austell first laid eyes upon in California. 'On the other hand I don't see that all these lifestyle changes in our patients are such a bad thing. Do you? The post-drug integration of the experience is essential. These people have had new insights and they want to change their lives. *Bardo* can help them to incorporate the psychedelic state into their everyday activities. This is what it's all about, man.'

'Yes, I appreciate that, Joseph. I understand the concept of holistic healing but…'

'No, Bob, you understand nothing!' barks Langley, sending hopping birds to the nearby trees. 'These patients need to go *beyond* their old lives. They need to go without!'

'Go without what?'

'See, see! You *don't* understand! They need to *go without*. Step outside everything they have ever known before. Don't forget, Bob, these are *your* people. They were stuck on the fringes of society having completely failed, mentally and socially, and now look at them! These are not just lay-about hippies. They are essential members of a vibrant group who have made advances because of real brain changes. This lifestyle, this relaxed, accepting and unhurried existence we provide for them is an important part of their recovery. Society at large could take a leaf out of their books! If only everyone was able to live as we have achieved here at *Bardo,* I think Western society could be moved on in ways it desperately needs to achieve.'

'Yes, fine, I can see that. And I think the programme is looking after itself. I love that our post-session patients are sticking around and giving something back to the community. But it's the hangers on, the reams of New Age travellers arriving every week that worries me a little. Don't get me wrong, I love the people, but it's, well, I don't know, I just worry that we may be losing sight of what this project is all about. It is, after all, supposed to be a scientific study. Not a communal free for all.'

Langley stops and they stand looking up into the sky beyond the trees.

'Oh, Bob, I don't know, I feel disappointed to hear you regurgitating this standard medical model. Our patients have made functional changes and improved their quality of life. Isn't that what you wanted? I believe the communal atmosphere at *Bardo* is all part of the package. Don't you?'

'I do, but I'm concerned that your single-minded zeal to create a new society is not necessarily the best way to take our message to the mainstream medical community. Timothy Leary and others tried this way forty years ago and it didn't work. All I know is that the grey-suited types that tread the boards at the Institute of Psychiatry and the Royal College of Psychiatry do not take kindly to words of advice coming from long-hairs in kaftans living in yurts – no matter how sensible they may be.'

Glowering, Austell pulls up a long stem of grass from the hedgerow as they resume their climb up the muddy hill.

'Dangerous words, Bob,' says Langley. 'And hard to believe they are coming from you, after how far you have come in shaking off the trappings of your old ways.'

'Look,' says Austell. 'I share your thoughts about the power of these special medicines. But in order to convince the authorities I believe we need remove ourselves from the ideals of the 1960s. Trust me, the people at the Institute want to see evidenced-based

228

results, not just a bunch of semi-religious lifestyle conversions from drugged-up drop-outs. We were always determined to keep the New Age values out of the treatment manual. For god's sake, it was *you* who told me that, Joseph! So I ask you now, with the greatest respect, as your friend, please reflect upon the current situation. Do you really think it will work this way?'

Langley sighs and stops again to lean against a style. He is breathless and a coughing fit is beginning to emerge. He does, however, have enough insight to recognise his obstinacy.

'Chillax, Bob. This is only the beginning. What we are doing here is just a series of naturalistic case studies to demonstrate the drugs can be taken safely. Trust me, this initial part of the project is going well.'

'Okay, all I'm saying is let's keep going with the great results in the sessions and not let everyone get too carried away with the *lifestyle* aspects.'

'Okay, you're right. I'm being stubborn. You are making sense and I'm all for reigning in the circus a little, if that is what you want to do. I suppose it does seem a bit irregular to have so many people hanging around here. Maybe some of them are now ready to get back to their regular lives and begin re-integrating into society. They have made the necessary mental changes. Cool, in May we hit the 12-month deadline and we publish our results. Then we start the proper double-blind placebo-controlled studies. Okay?'

'Okay, good.' Austell is relieved. Langley is making more sense now.

'Honestly, Bob, you worry too much!' he laughs, patting the pockets of his coat for his hip flask. 'It's all going perfectly to plan. What could possibly go wrong?'

THAT'S NOT THE PATIENT, THAT'S THE PSYCHIATRIST

The Ketamine programme gets underway and produces immediate results for Taunton's entrenched alcoholics. Austell enrols his long-time patient Andy, the traumatised ex-Afghanistan poly-substance addict for a few sessions with Ketamine before his primary post-trauma MDMA therapy starts. Andy is encouraged to come and stay at the farm to carry out the pre-drug preparation sessions but he refuses to reside in the rural setting and subscribe to the hippie way of life like the other participants. That would not be Andy at all. When he pays an early morning visit to see Austell at *Bardo* for one of the preparatory check-ups he finds his psychiatrist holding a clinic in a yurt under an oak tree. Incense and chanting drift lazily from the barn as Andy meanders up the slope with a wide-legged gait, dressed in a tracksuit and bling. Betsy gives him a cup of chai as he enters the tent, which he pours into a plant pot beside where Austell sits.

'Andy, good to see you. How have you been?'

'Sweet as, Doc. But needin' to get my fuckin' swede sorted. Still drinking, and the rest. When do I get to start the treatment, doc? My probation officer is getting proper arsey. He's got me on this course to train as a fuckin' electrician. I'm sick of feeling like such a fuck up all the time.' Then adds, 'Fuckin' hippies everywhere.'

Austell is cheered by Andy's realness. His lack of interest in the stereotypical *Bardo* routine is refreshing. Psychedelics do not push everyone towards macrobiotic tie-dye. Nevertheless, Austell does

231

believe there may be some activities going on at the farm that Andy could benefit from as part of his preparation for his drug sessions.

'Why don't you go and talk to John and Claire about what they are doing here at *Bardo*? We are setting up some workshops for people who have been through the treatment programs. Go and have a chat with them. We really want people to get involved. After all, you lot are the experts here, not us doctors. Just take a wander around. You may find someone you get along with. Give it a chance.'

'All right. I'll have a look. But I'm not making no promises. I couldn't live here in this place. No offence or nothin'. All this shit everywhere. Messes up my trainers.'

Austell directs Andy to the orchard where Claire is managing a team of college students erecting greenhouses as part of the Salvia divinorum project. When Austell returns later he finds that the cocaine-fuelled ex-army burglar has stayed for lunch. He then stays for supper. In fact he blends perfectly into the *Bardo* team; seamlessly bringing his unique personality to the mix. Austell and Langley are keen to ensure the programme is not only confined to the intellectual needs of motivated middle class hippies. Andy represents a distinct new angle for the community, a refreshing development for the *Bardo* group and before long he is part of the furniture.

Summer dries the Somerset earth to Martian red dust and the *Bardosians* learn that where there are farms there are flies. Therapy, integration and culture continue in a productive fashion, and the community soon boasts an arts and crafts centre where locals mix with inhabitants selling their wares. The evenings are given over to musical extravaganzas performed to picnickers who witness the solstice come and go. Autumn winds soon blow in the shorter nights

232

and another season batters the trees, pulling discarded leaves over *Bardo*.

Despite trying to keep the venture low key the farm gets more frequent visitors and before long Environmental Health come poking around, followed by the local council and then the Inland Revenue. But thanks to careful planning and good manners these visits from The Man go smoothly and the project stays on track with all unwanted intrusions kept at arm's length. After all, no one is doing anything illegal. The study has full ethical approval and no illicit drugs are tolerated on site. Furthermore, crucially, the press have not shown an interest. And for now both he and Langley have kept their promise not to give any interviews. Austell is particularly surprised however when he gets a visit from his old colleague Dr Maurice Hunter, who attends the farm on an evening when the inhabitants are having an open day BBQ.

'So this is what all the fuss is about?' sneers Hunter as he treads disapprovingly up the drive, led by Betsy. 'Pretty much what I expected to be honest.'

Stepping clumsily past a group of cross-legged chanting hippies Hunter updates Austell on the old Taunton clinic. Everything is exactly as it was when Austell left it eighteen months ago. Hunter proudly boasts of his affiliations with the bloodthirsty drug companies and his continued practice of buying up their mind-nullifying neuroleptic products as a newly appointed agent for *Arable Pharm Ltd*. Hunter has now progressed into a senior local position representing the pharmaceutical company, which makes his presence at *Bardo* even more incongruous.

Betsy has little truck for the likes of Hunter. Having travelled untold times through the innermost planetary landscapes it takes her just thirteen seconds to recognize him as a man whose opinions are as stiff as his arse cheeks. But Austell, whose belief in the goodness of others has increased since witnessing the successes of *Bardo,* wants to give Hunter a chance. So he leads the cynic over to the barbeque and introduces him to Andy.

'Andy, this is Maurice Hunter, an old colleague of mine. We used to work in the Taunton clinic together. He is visiting us to learn a little about how we work here at *Bardo.*'

'Sick, doc,' says Andy. He is not the least bit interested in social niceties but his powers of instant perception are as finely tuned as Betsy's, only more instinctual. Austell smiles and leaves Hunter standing awkwardly beside the ex-marine. No need to babysit him. Better to let Corporal Andy McGovern make up his own mind about Hunter. Andy used to be a drug dealer in the late eighties before he became a Marine. Then on a single tour of duty his early years of traumatic abuse were reawakened by horrific experiences of murder in Afghanistan. The politicians of the day regret that their war has left poor Andy in this condition. They still need him to be part of their desperate campaign against those violent, ungrateful Arabs, who together with the rising economic success of India and China are denting their post-Imperial ego. With more returning soldiers from Iraq and Afghanistan dying from PTSD suicide than were ever killed in combat, all these body bags are a damned inconvenience. The wars *must* go on, obviously, given the amount of time and money that has been put in over the years developing our great nations' tremendous military machines.

Andy is particularly animated this evening because he has just been given the date for his first MDMA session. His forthright bravado hides an intense fear of counselling. But he is quite at

234

home talking about drugs and pummels Hunter with his voracious experience.

'Yeah, so there you fucking go, doc. Got me gurners coming up, haven't I? I tell you, back in '88 I hitched to Amsterdam. It was the beginning of the early raves and all that. Mate, there was so much demand in London for X and I had the connections, see, through these geezers. So this promoter sent me over to the 'Dam…'

Hunter, the old doctor, looks at Andy in his tracksuit with derision. He is not used to sharing his airspace with such people. Patients are one thing, but one needn't fraternize with them like this. What a dreadful and vulgar tattooed man.

'…so I get there with five grand and come back with five thousand pills, fucking bargain. I mean, I knew I could bang 'em out at fifteen a piece, easy back then. Of course, nowadays the kids are fuckin' givin' 'em away, but back then I was on to a winner. I got 'em in through New'aven. They've only got three staff on customs and if one of 'em's on the sick that only leaves two, and they always have to have at least one in the office manning the phone, which leaves only one geezer out on the fuckin' floor – and his priority is checking the fucking waggons. If you come through as a foot passenger on one of the busy tourist boats no one's gonna stop you. One bloke standing in the fuckin' rain! He's not gonna stop some fuckin' geezer walking in, is he!'

Hunter genuinely fears he is about to be murdered. Or worse.

'So I had the pills stuffed in a fuckin' holdall. Walked right in and no one gave me a second look. Rushin' my tits off, obviously.'

Andy pulls out his cigarettes and offers the pack to Hunter.

'B and H, mate?'

'Erm, no,' snaps the tweed-clad doctor. 'I don't smoke.'

235

'Fair play, doc. Anyway, I got 'em back to London and the fuckin' promoter doesn't want 'em! Said some fuckin' Jamaican geezer got 'em sorted. Anyway, I didn't know what the fuck I was doing. Totally screwed head in those days. Thing is, it's not my scene, mate. I only did it cos I needed the fuckin' money. Back then I was more into the brown.'

Hunter cuts in, having only just understood the topic. 'Am I correct in assuming you are talking about the buying and selling of illegal drugs?'

'Yeah, too right. Keep up, Sherlock!' laughs Andy, glad to see Hunter getting involved at last. 'Fuckin' mental. Anyway, what with this geezer – the promoter – and the fuckin' yardies sniffing around the place I was totally sketched out. Proper psychotic like. I mean, everyone knew who I was and what I had. And it's not like I'm into any of this fuckin' ravin' bollocks anyway. Right. Well, these five thousand Jack and Jills, they were fuckin' kosher. Had a one-fifty mike acid dot in the centre, which hung around for ages after the gurner had passed – seriously trippy come down. I don't think I could handle it now, mate! Anyway, back then I wasn't into all that shite. Fuckin' poof's drug, ecstasy, least that's what I thought. 's'different now, of course, being 'ere. You know, with Dr Langley and Dr Austell and stuff. So anyways I thought what the fuck am I gonna do? Everyone knows they're mine – and I was a right little arrogant shit back then; doing a lot of whizz and charlie. I mean *a lot* of fuckin' speed. I'd been shooting my mouth off about 'avin' these fuckin' biscuits. So I thought, shit, I've gotta sort this.'

'Yes, indeed,' asks Hunter. 'What *did* you do?'

'Well, I did what anyone would've done, doc. I fuckin' split 'em didn't I? All of 'em. Me and my mate cracked the bastards open, took out the LSD. We sold the dots on for a fiver each (it was fuckin' hard getting good dots back then so those bastards shifted no problem.) And the MDMA? Fuckin' capped 'em up into red and white caps banged 'em out as Patriots.'

'Patriots?'

'Yeah, it was the European Championships in '88. Remember? West Germany! The whole nation was on one; everyone bang up for a party. Knocked 'em out at a tenner apiece. Sold the fucking lot in a week. Made…ooh…gettin' on forty grand by the end of it. Patriots! Aw, mate, *those* were the fuckin' days!'

Andy nods furiously to himself and pulls hard repeatedly on the stub of his cigarette. He was very pleased with his performance and quickly downs his glass of John Patterson's alcohol-free dandelion wine. Hunter stands there under the apple trees as cumbersomely as he can manage. He doesn't have to try too hard.

'So you were taking and dealing illegal drugs at this point?' asks Hunter as Andy hands him a paper plate and the men approach the buffet spread.

'Yeah, mate. Was back then, big time. But, you know, left it all behind now. Mate, you must try the mung bean salad. Betsy made it. Fuckin' bute. Goes well with the roasted halloumi. What do'ya fancy, Doc?'

Austell returns and thanking Andy for his time leads the incredulous Hunter away, bombarding him with statistics about the on-going success of Bardo. But the elderly conservative psychiatrist remains uncharacteristically quiet, which provides Austell with a personal victory, seeing his old nemesis reduced to silence. When they reach the main farmhouse, however, their attention is caught by a hullabaloo. Someone is leaning from an upstairs window, waving their hands wildly and shouting to a gathering crowd below in the farmyard. As they get closer it becomes clear that it is Langley. By now any incredulity on Hunter's face has deteriorated into pure horror.

'Holy! Holy! Holy!' screams the hairy psychiatrist. The crowd reply with cheers and whistles. 'Fire sinking into air. Earth sinking into water. Water sinking into fire...yes, my people, we are delivered from the past and the present, and out beyond the future! Look at me...I am naked, naked I tell you!'

'Robert,' comments Hunter, in a bare whisper. 'I don't think that man up there is wearing any clothes.'

Austell loosens his collar and clears his throat politely. 'Er, yes, indeed, Maurice. He does appear to be naked.'

'But how can I be naked,' screams the pot-bellied Langley, dancing with wanton abandon in the window for his guests, 'when I am nothing but a collection of energised particles? I have no body! I exist, of course, but I am undistracted by meaningless concepts like space or time. Is this not true, my friends?'

The crowd jeer and dance below. Langley disappears for a moment then returns, throwing clouds of powder paint into the air from the window. The farmyard is lit by rainbows of colour circling down from the building as Langley hops from foot to foot, scattering the pigment and squealing with joy. 'Rejoice! Rejoice! For death will be painless and ecstatic! Me, you, I, us, we...we will return to a paradise of luscious gardens! A joyful resting place – released from matter and all earthly bondage – to a place of abundance!'

'Are you sure he is all right,' mutters Hunter. 'He is awfully close to the edge. I wonder to what extent such activities conform to health and safety standards, Robert?'

238

The naked Langley is clearly not concerned by such things. But Austell on the other hand is.

'Yes, I agree, Maurice.' Spotting Claire and Betsy he gestures a worried look towards them and they hurry inside and pound up the stairs. Meanwhile Langley continues to spread love.

'We live in a land of fleshlessness where people exist only as spirits! Nothing exists! Me, God, you, us, we create it all! And here we are – on *Bardo* farm – infused, soaked through with love, like a sheet of double-dipped blotter! We are all together in pure unadulterated cosmic unity!'

There are now arms behind Langley in the window; those of Claire and some other helpers, beckoning him back into the room. Langley twists and turns, gaily whistling with laughter as he evades their grasp. Disappearing from view as his assailants attempt to grapple him down.

'Now, I know it is not my place to comment, but this afternoon I witnessed one of your clients talking openly about their illegal drug-based activities and now, now I am seeing one of them behaving in this chaotic manner. Robert, you really need to contain your patients more carefully.'

'Sorry?' asks Austell, tearing his gaze away from the upstairs window. 'Patients? Oh, no, Maurice! That man up there is not one of the patients. That is Dr Joseph Langley, a psychiatrist. He is the lead for this project. He is the man in charge.'

Langley reappears at the window. 'Because you see,' he yells, 'at that exact moment of death there is an extraordinary concentration of energy focused entirely on the pineal gland! And during those final seconds of life the levels of energy within the pineal build up to an unimaginably colossal level! For a small moment in time the pineal gland becomes infinitely dense. The Big Bang in reverse! It is The Mental Singularity! The *Pinealarity*!' At which point he is engulfed by bodies, dragged away from the window and bundled onto his bed with peals of laughter. The crowd let out a final cheer. Eventually Betsy emerges and she and Austell lead Hunter back to his car. As he is strapping himself in, Maurice Hunter looks up at Austell and scoffs through his teeth, 'I don't like it, Austell. I don't like it one little bit.'

'Well, I'm sorry you feel that way, Maurice. But this is it. My project with those dreadful toadstools as your call them has come to fruition, and nothing's going to stop it now.'

'Really?' sneers Hunter. 'We shall see about that.' And the consultant's car grinds dust into the air and high-tails it out of the farm.

DON'T DO COUNSELLING. SO DON'T ASK

They must maintain the credibility of the research program at all cost. Apart from that unfortunate daytime outburst witnessed by Hunter, Langley's unpredictable conduct comes mostly at night. When the sun sinks behind the Blackdown Hills he begins his scurrying, emptying kitchen cupboards for ingredients to make one of his 'magic potions', accompanied by his hacking cough. Langley produces great steaming concoctions of herbs, which he either drinks or smears on his forehead, chattering inanely about 'quelling the fires'. Austell follows him around, through the farm and across fields and stiles trying to reason with his remaining glimmers of insight. These episodes are sometimes amusing, including for Langley, but with the ups come crashing downs and when the mania stops the patient retreats into dark recesses for days at a time.

'Look, I'm fine!' he tells Austell, Betsy and Claire over breakfast one morning. They have a long day ahead, with Marine Andy's first MDMA session for post-combat PTSD scheduled to happen. Austell and Claire look at him warily.

'OK, so I am a bit run down. But aren't we all? I've still got my marbles. Honestly, I'll *know* when I'm on the way out and it's not yet. I'm not going anywhere until the day psychedelic medicines are accepted as mainstream treatments. That is the goal I intend to achieve.'

Everyone is deeply fond of Langley. He is an inspirational guru who has touched all of their lives, and none more so than

Austell. It pains him to see Langley so. But ingrained in him is the founding principle of the *Bardo* therapeutic community, the principle that Langley himself fertilized, that every person is free to grow in whatever way they see fit, and without restraint. Austell is committed to this Kingsley Hall philosophy and has learned enough to know that traditional medical models have little place at *Bardo*. Even though he is convinced Langley is unwell, Austell will not allow such a paternalistic approach to cloud his judgment.

'I want to believe you, Joseph, I really do. However I am biting my tongue. So don't worry. We will persist the *Bardo* way. But there must be some more control on your part. Can you do that? Can you try?'

'Of course. Look, I'm OK. Let me just lie low for a couple of days. I'm clearly in the throes of a spiritual emergency. Don't ask me to try and analyse it, Bob. Let's just see where the vibrational energy takes me.'

'Good idea,' says Betsy. She knows when to fight a battle and when not. 'Come on Joe, why don't you get back up to bed and just sleep it off? Whatever it is.'

'Yes, we can handle the work here,' adds Austell. 'Thanks to your expert training. You just get better.'

'Fine. But are you sure you and Betsy can handle Andy's MDMA session without me today? He's a tough cookie.'

Betsy laughs and she and Austell take Langley up to bed, teasing him about his stubbornness. They tuck him in with a couple of Diazepam and he is soon under a blanket of sedation. Benzodiazepines may be a crude approach to brain chemistry but they have their place.

As they descend the stairs and go to the barn to prepare the session room Betsy asks, 'What do you think is going on?'

'I don't know. Possibly a tumour.'

'I agree...'

'Where?'

'Lung? Although it seems as if it has gone further than that.'

'Are you worried?'

'Of course.'

'Me too,' she says. 'Joe is a tough old bird but he has his vulnerabilities. Don't we all? I have forgotten the number of times I have had to be there to rescue him. Whether it has been from the jaws of existential calamity or from the police, medical authorities or even his parents, on many occasions he has reached out to me and I have been there for him.'

'I don't see much reaching out now, Betsy,' comments Austell. 'He seems like a man with a strong agenda to do things his own way.'

'This is true,' smiles the nurse. 'Perhaps he knows something we don't about the numinous tunnel that awaits him? He has always been flighty – trust me, I have soared with him on the wings many times. I remember one time in Africa when we were researching the psychedelic herbal practices of the local witchdoctors. In the throes of a particularly lengthy datura trip he became convinced he had sold his soul to a bejewelled goddess that inhabited the deepest part of Lake Malawi. He spent the better part of six months living in a cave smoking ganja and casting runes in search of an answer. At the end of it all he came away with malaria and cannabis psychosis, which required treatment with Ibogaine in Gabon. It was a learning experience for us both. But he was different back in those days. He was usually grounded by a greater sense of self-doubt than we are seeing now. There is definitely something more determined about this current episode.'

In the treatment room they scatter cushions and choose some music for the stereo. Austell cannot hide the alarm he feels for his friend. 'I really don't know what to do, Betsy. He stubbornly refuses to see a doctor. He's young. He can't be that ill.'

'This life is short, Robert,' she says, unlocking the medicine cabinet and removing a bottle. 'Death is never far away; be it death of the ego, as we have seen with John Patterson's LSD experience, or the death of contemporary psychiatry, as we will see when our results are published. Material death, the dumping of this physical body, is closer than we all think. The most important lesson is that from death comes re-birth. Death is the beginning of the journey.'

'But I can't buy into that, Betsy!' cries Austell, double-checking the drug off in the ledger and locking the safe. 'These hippie ideals grate with my own personal experience of life, limited though it is. I see no place for re-birth with the death of Joseph. I didn't even feel as if I had been born until he came into my life. Our time together has been so short. I'm not ready to lose him to the other side yet. There is no justice in such a thing.'

'Indeed not, Robert. But come, we must concentrate on the job in hand. We have a patient to guide on a new journey towards recovery. Our ex-Marine Andy should not have seen the things he has,' she says, her voice a soothing vessel of compassion. 'No man should. He is one of that great nation of muted men for whom emotional language is a foreign tongue. *He* has not been allowed to die. They roam the earth communicating as their fathers did through glances and blows. He is solid steel overlying muscle. His body is mined and sniper towers cover all angles. No one gets near, enemies

244

are shot at first sight and no prisoners are taken. Fathers show sons how it is done. Bigger boys push the little boys and mummy is never there to help. That is the order of things.'

'Do you think he will respond to his MDMA session? He is a very well-defended man.'

'Yes, he is. But MDMA is a gentle mistress. Any detritus, and baggage or dumped belongings that have been left lying around will be collected, inspected, bagged and disinfected. She ensures the sorting office is tidied and all of those scattered letters are put back in their rightful places. But first they must be opened.'

A knock at the door heralds the arrival of Sylvia, with Andy in tow. This stimulates the two therapists into action and puts their concerns about Langley firmly to bed. They throw themselves with full respect into the therapy with the battered shell of a man before them.

As the 125mg of MDMA starts to take effect Andy becomes nervous. He disregards the facilitators' advice to lie back with eyeshades and instead paces the room, bothering the fixtures, turning over jars of flowers. Wringing his hands and rubbing his shaved head, he strides as if inspecting his troops, eyeing Austell and the nurse suspiciously, checking out the enemy. Austell uses every ounce of composure to remain calm. Relaxation comes more naturally to Betsy, well accustomed to the outpourings that accompany a chemically loosened brain. She lowers her mudra and rises from lotus to cross the room, where she lays a placid hand on Andy's quivering form. No words are spoken. Her touch transmits her message.

No one is expecting Andy to speak. He made that very clear to them during the preparation sessions. '*I don't do fucking counselling...so don't fucking ask!'* but he does have enough insight to be here at least. He knows this is his last chance at keeping his kids. They, and his battered wife, have had enough of his excuses. Social services are waiting at the door with their child-catching nets and the police and courts stand behind them in the queue, threatening long custodial sentences. He knows it is not acceptable to be pulling people out of cars at traffic lights in Somerset towns because he thought he was at a checkpoint in Kabul. This is the axis of Yeovil, not the Axis of Evil.

Andy shivers the hours away. He digs in, clicking a torch on and off, on and off, and using the soil scooped from the Yucca he smears his face with camouflage streaks. Betsy crawls, commando-like across the desert carpet and approaches his dug out. From a thin slit behind the concrete walls of the Indian drapes he watches her advance. Silent and alert. His eyes darting to-and-fro, like the Action Man from his childhood that he played with in between beatings from his dad. His big strong dad. *Hard as fucking nails. Just like me. Have you got a fucking problem with that?*

Betsy approaches. *She's good this one. Knows her shit. But trust no one.*

'Corporal McGovern,' she whispers. 'I have your reinforcements. Here is the back-up you radioed for.' She passes through a 62.5mg booster capsule of MDMA. 'This is powerful stuff. The Best A Man Can Get. She is strong, MDMA. Ask for her help and she will deliver. Bang on target.'

After another two hours Andy has stopped shivering. Tears on his face have dried into cried out channels. He crawls out of his cocoon like an infant towards Betsy and curls himself into her arms, whimpering, sniffling, snuffling, burrowing. The Eastern Bloc elderly nurse strokes Andy's stubbly face and kisses the tattoo of a snarling British bulldog on the back of his sweaty baldhead.

'She has broken him,' whispers Betsy to Austell as she cradles the patient. 'MDMA has picked our tough Corporal McGovern up by the balls and spread him out into a single layer of primeval cells for all to see. She starts again.'

In the weeks that follow Andy's first MDMA session he barely utters a word and no one pushes him to speak. But there is an inescapable change in his eyes. Where before there was impenetrable emptiness there is now a person. He makes eye contact; even an occasional smile cracks across that lumpy face. And when he smiles he is beautiful, a radiant little boy, just like his mother used to say.

Austell arranges for Andy to stay at the farm and he has another three MDMA sessions. He learns to work alongside his new medicine. He even starts getting involved in yoga sessions. His mantra '*I don't do fucking counselling*' becomes a shared joke around the farm and someone gets the immortal words printed on a T-shirt which he wears with pride as he mucks in with the daily communal activities. Chopping wood, charging the racks of batteries connected to the wind turbines. All is love. All is MDMA. She is strong. She is Ecstasy.

THE BALANCE IS TIPPING

'Welcome back. This is Channel Four News. Coming up later we have a report from Glasgow, where childhood obesity and antisocial behaviour have reached epidemic proportions. And rates of illiteracy are now worse than they were in the seventeenth century. But first we go over to rural Somerset to see a unique medical research project currently underway. Sophie.'

'Thank you, Jon. Yes, I am here 'down on the farm' with psychiatrist Dr Joseph Langley. He is conducting one of the most controversial medical research studies happening anywhere in the UK today. Dr Langley and his colleagues at the British Association for Research into Drugs of Odyssey, *Bardo, have been giving psychiatric patients powerful psychedelic (that is,* hallucinogenic) *drugs. Dr Langley, what exactly is it that you are doing here?'*

'Yes, thank you. Well this kind of treatment – psychedelic psychotherapy – is actually not at all new; it is in fact thousands of years old. We are merely bringing it up to date. We give controlled doses of LSD, MDMA, psilocybin and Ketamine to patients under strictly controlled clinical conditions.'

'Dr Langley, many of our viewers will be alarmed to hear that doctors are giving dangerous drugs, such as ecstasy and LSD, to vulnerable patients. How can you be sure patients won't be harmed by your actions?'

'Well, these drugs are not nearly as dangerous as the media and governments have portrayed them. All of these drugs can be safely administered to humans under controlled conditions without risk of physical harm.'

'What about the risk of people becoming addicted?'

'There is no evidence that psychedelic drugs, given in a clinical setting like this, cause any physical dependence. On the contrary, we are freeing these patients from years of dependence upon prescribed medication; offering them the chance to experience, for the first time in their lives, a course of effective psychotherapy.'

'And what results have you seen so far, doctor?'

'Over the last 12 months our results speak for themselves. Fourteen patients have successfully completed the program and another six are midway through. And don't forget these are some of the toughest, most resistant patients in the region. Since starting the program 70% of our patients are now in full time work; many of them here on the farm. There have been no significant adverse reactions to any of the medicines and all of our participants have remained off their prescription drugs. In short, psychedelic therapy really works!'

'And what would you say to the parents of people who have seen their children die from drug overdoses? Or to those critics who think your work is condoning recreational drug abuse and encouraging people to break the law?'

'Those issues are not relevant to what we are doing here. We do not encourage recreational drug use and there is no possibility our patients could die from the drugs we are giving them. With respect, your questions betray the ignorance many people hold about these marvellous medicines. The psychedelic drugs are certainly powerful substances and must only be used with great respect in a carefully monitored environment. But they need not cause harm, and as we have demonstrated here at Bardo they can be put to positive use to treat severe and unremitting mental disorders. So in answer to

250

your question, I would not say anything to such critics or concerned parents, rather I would listen to them and I would invite them to visit us here, look at our programme and meet the patients who have benefitted from this approach. We can then all move forward with a reflective and enlightened attitude to these fascinating and potentially helpful medical tools.'

'Dr Langley, thank you. Jon, back to the studio.'

'Thank you, Sophie. Well, there you have it. So, Gary, what do you make of that?'

'Hmmm! I don't know about that, Jon. You know where you are with a couple of lagers. Right! OK, on with the sport. Yeovil Town continue to sit comfortably at the top of the Premier League after their four nil win against Manchester United last night...'

The telephone has not stopped ringing since Langley took his unilateral decision to announce to the world that a smallholding in rural Somerset is experimenting with psychedelic drug therapies. As a result *Bardo* suddenly receives massive media exposure. This is exactly the opposite of what they had originally planned.

'Jesus, Joseph, what the hell were you thinking?'

'Oh, come on, Bob, I think it turned out to be a pretty balanced piece of journalism. That reporter got the story spot on. And let's face it, I certainly have a face that deserves to be on TV...'

'This is ridiculous! Betsy, please try and make him see sense!' Betsy's extensive abilities to calm the waters of psychedelic exploration are also well-tuned for disputes in the waking-state.

'Joe, Bob has a point. The plan was to be subtle about how we involved the press. Perhaps what you did was, well, maybe a little... reckless?'

'Oh, rubbish. There was plenty of reck in my actions. Look,

Bob, have faith. I believe that our results at *Bardo* will speak for themselves. The UK tax-paying voters have had enough of modern medicine's ineffective sticking-plaster approach to treating mental illness. They can see the benefit of the *Bardo* programme. Just you wait. I know exactly what I'm doing.'

In the following week Langley and Austell hurriedly write-up their results and fast-track the paper to *The Lancet*, who accept the submission. Langley was right. The medical profession and general public alike recognise in *Bardo*'s academic work an attempt to provide something new. The team find themselves winning support everywhere. When further spin off articles follow in the Sunday papers and lifestyle magazines Austell and Langley are invited to give a speech at the Royal College of Psychiatrists annual meeting – the theme being: *Out of Our Minds – Can Psychedelic Drugs Hold the Key to the Future of Psychiatry?* The doctors seize the opportunity to capitalise on the groundswell of interest in the subject and submit a proposal to the Medical Research Council for major funding for an expansion of the project. Much to everyone's surprise psychedelic therapy has become the government's latest political gamble and money comes pouring in from entrepreneurs eager to get a slice of the pie, with no shortages of patients queuing up to take part.

On the back of public support for the project the government opens negotiations with the justice commission to reconsider the current drug classification scheme with a more evidence-based approach. The pace of change in the air uncontrollably excites Langley. Could it really be that the balance is tipping and the War on Drugs is finally grinding to a halt?

'History will remember this period as the *50 Year War*,' he says,

252

speaking to the crowd at one of the *Bardo's* extended evening soirees by the fire; his flickering figure consumed by a shadowy audience of thirty eager faces. 'We have shown that people can consume these drugs safely. Prohibition funds the wrong sorts of people. Once the authorities realise they can make money if drugs are taxed and available to all they will jump on the bandwagon. So the end of the War on Drugs is a shallow victory for those wanting real freedom. Money continues to drive political decisions but at least we get the right to alter minds without fear of prosecution – whilst we sit and watch humanity falling into the social and cultural abyss that is the end of the world.'

HEAD DOWN!
KEEP LOOKING!

A thin streak of grey in the eastern sky begins beyond the Blackdown Hills and grows imperceptibly through dawn. Austell and Langley pull on their boots and silently close the door of the farmhouse, wrapped against the wind they stir a few of the less sleepy dogs and pick their way across the yard, climbing up into the hills. Grazing sheep look on nonchalantly from the sloping fields as they clamber over styles and ascend into the pinkening sky.

'You know what our trouble is?' remarks Langley, his whisper barely perceptible above the crunch of their boots on the gravel. 'We have become a victim of our own success.'

'Yes, I have to agree, Joseph, despite my initial concern; your outing of our project to the press has resulted in a loosening of restrictions on research and brought us a whole lot more work. Now that we have the double-blind trials underway for MDMA-assisted therapy for PTSD, as well as the psilocybin and LSD-assisted therapy for depression and anxiety – not to mention the Ketamine therapy for alcohol, cocaine and opiate addictions – *Bardo* has developed into something beyond anything I could have predicted.'

The two psychiatrists tread softly in the morning light amongst the fallen apples where pigs snuffle and sheep and cattle shift. Below the ground, deep within that ancient Arthurian soil laid down by consecutive generations of decay and regeneration, there grows a medieval network of cells; a mycelium of gigantic proportions seething like an immense intelligent brain. Its tendrils reach out

255

through the primeval earth and propagate a body of knowledge so old as to be rooted in pre-human times. Awoken by the rain and the darkening evenings the mycelium stretches skyward with its probing fingers, parting the topsoil and pushing into the ether its tiny pointed fruiting bodies. It carries the primeval code of intelligent awareness, a code passed down through generations by the magical medium of psychic transmission between sentient beings. These fruit represent the catalyst by which one age communicates with another – the earliest telephonic system, transmitting genes and memes through its multisensory mystical experience. These tiny fruit are natures macroscopic DNA itself: Liberty Caps – The Great British Magic Mushrooms. Yes, it's that time of year again.

'In order to cope with the new volume of work we will need to recruit more staff,' says Langley. 'We desperately need to take on a clinical psychologist, an occupational therapist and an administration assistant to join the team.'

'I cannot agree more, Joseph. The workload has grown beyond Sylvia's capable hands. This project is no longer simply a scientific study. It is now an ongoing viable business with all the trappings of a modern hospital.'

'Yes. The tide is turning. And it is fantastic to be getting invites to speak at so many mainstream events and conferences, disseminating the results of our project and instructing other teams on how to develop more research. Before we know it Psychedelic Therapy will be a standard part of future national clinical guidelines. It seems that everyone wants a slice of the mushrooming psychedelic renaissance. Indeed, this brings us back to the point of this ridiculously early start: We are out here looking for the Liberty Cap mushroom,' says Langley. '*Psilocybe semilanceata*; a stalwart fungus of the British

Isles since time immemorial. This hardy little mushroom grows all over this isle but particularly in the West Country and Wales. At this time of the year you are almost certainly crushing them under foot without even realising. There are few places it doesn't thrive; meadows, road verges, playing fields, front lawns and low-lying lush grassland are all her home. She grows mostly on north facing slopes, needs plenty of moisture, rich grass and access to a warm daytime sun. She is often found in fields where cows or sheep have grazed, but unlike many other magic mushrooms the Liberty Cap does not grow directly out of dung – but she does like grass that has been enriched by it.

'At night the fruiting bodies burst through the topsoil and reach upwards to drop their spores and propagate their cosmic goodness all over the land for those lucky enough to know their magical properties. Some claim the mushroom was here thousands of years ago; that the Celts, early Britons and druids knew all about them and used them in their religious ceremonies. But if that is so all trace of such use in the UK has been eradicated; systematically demonised by Judeo-Christian generations and replaced by the altogether more sober pursuits of Jesus and his teetotal followers.'

'I doubt very much Jesus was teetotal,' contradicts Austell. 'That long-haired, anti-authoritarian, rebellious, penniless, pagan mystic herbalist from the Holy Land? I'm pretty certain he was well into his hallucinogens.'

'Yes! Well, others believe there are plenty of Biblical references to psychedelics and that conservative writers of the Bible have again attempted to eradicate all direct mention of drugs. Cannabis, *Cubensis,* Datura all grow liberally throughout the Middle East, and are still used popularly to this day by the more enlightened

257

individuals of those lands. You are right, that shaman Jesus may have used them all...eyes down now! Keep looking!'

Heads bent, eyes scanning the ground, they meander systematically across the fields. The shroom itself is a tiny part of the beast, a mere single nerve cell amidst the giant pulsating brain that is the mycelium, some of which can measure acres across, making them by far the largest living organisms on the planet.

'What exactly am I looking for, Joseph?'

'It's small. It is not some saucer-sized edible delicacy you might see in a cookbook. It's tiny. No bigger than one and a half centimetres across. And the cap is distinctive; a pointed nipple, like a witch's hat. This is no coincidence. Witches use mushrooms and toadstools to make their magic potions, which bestow supernatural flight and give them the power to commune with animals and the spirits of dead ancestors. The folklore witch is in fact a psychedelic shaman and her pointed hat symbolises her use of Liberty Cap mushrooms to achieve her powers.'

'Oh, come on, Joseph, please!'

'Head down! Keep looking!'

Many mushrooms pass under Austell's gaze. Stooping to pick them he presents each one to his friend who repeatedly smiles and shakes his head.

'What you are experiencing is the curse of the LBM, the Little Brown Mushroom. These fields are rife with the buggers. Many species of mushroom in every shade of brown and grey grows alongside the Liberty Cap. But these are not the mushrooms we are looking for...keep looking...remember the cap is conical and pointed and it rises on a thin undulating stalk. The gills are black and the spores are dark purple. The stem will blush a soft blue when

258

picked, which is the exposure to the air of psilocin. When they dry, the whole cap colours blue before settling to a lovely pale brown colour. Honestly, you'll know when you see one...keep looking!'

Langley has walked this way over fields, deserts and valleys all over the world, tramping the countryside with the poise of a bloodhound. His instinct carries them over fences, hedges, through brooks and into the deep farmland spreading out unbroken all the way to the far South West of England.

'I sense we are close,' he says. 'I can smell them on the wind. They know we are looking for them. They are playing games with us. We must stay one step ahead. They *want* to be picked; they know we will treat them with respect. When caught and consumed they assimilate into human DNA and communicate their powers and wisdom to the person, who in turn will come looking for more shrooms, imbibe their magic and tell their story. This way legends get passed down through generations and the great interconnected super-brain that straddles the fungal and human world becomes integrated into the cycle of life and death.'

'What a load of complete...'

'Shhh! You need to be in a state of meditation. Pay respect to their magic; ponder their beauty and command. We will soon be guests at their table. They know we are here...keep looking! Keep your head bent low as we walk...you can't see them if you are any more than four feet from the ground...don't take your eyes off the grass...'

The sky lightens and they pass through a wood, wade across a small steam and clamber up the bank, over a barbed wire fence and into a moist cow field where they see a man in the distance.

'Don't worry,' says Langley. 'This is common land. I will handle

259

this. True, it *is* illegal to pick magic mushrooms. But it shouldn't be. Why should it be illegal to simply possess a few mushrooms that grow everywhere at this time of the year? If that were the case then every farmer, park attendant and gardener from Cardiff to Camborne would be considered a drug dealer! Don't worry, I'll handle this.'

'You said that twice. Now I'm worried.'

The figure in the distance approaches. Whether it is illegal or not, muses Austell, we do look most peculiar. Two men walking in circles around a dewy field at six in the morning, heads bent, eyes scanning the ground, stopping periodically to pick.

'Mornin',' says the farmer, looking at them suspiciously from under his cap. 'And what is yous doin'?' His thick accent has never been beyond the confines of the county. No need to go anywhere. This has been his land for generations. His cousin went to London some years ago – didn't recommend it.

'Good morning, sir!' chirps Langley, deferentially tipping his hat. 'We are looking for mushrooms. Seeing what nature provideth on this splendid autumn day.'

'Mushrums, ee says?' smiles the farmer, a mild sigh of recognition in his tone. Austell and Langley are clearly not the first psychonauts to have trodden this way. 'Is that what ee is? We do sees a lot of 'ees out here in d'autumn. I don'ts ne'er sees the fassa-nashan meesel'. But I knows a lot of 'ees does.'

Austell stands there awkwardly, convinced he must have been doing something wrong. He lacks the confidence of the more socially aware Langley. The distinction between legal and illegal may indeed be arbitrarily drawn, but it makes Austell anxious nonetheless. Besides, he doesn't fancy spending the rest of the day in Taunton police station, even if that prospect would be something

Langley might find amusing. So he keeps his distance and leaves the chat to Langley.

'It is the Liberty Cap we're looking for.'

The farmer scratches his head. The eyes and deep carves of his face carry the weather of many seasons. A man like him would never have the luxury of time to spend sixteen hours contemplating nature though a mushroom experience. Rather, he is out here at four o'clock each morning all year round pulling lambs out of ewes and repairing his boundaries. Anyway, his connection to this land goes far deeper than the superficial visions portrayed by a mere drug – apart from, of course, his cider. But he doesn't mind the mushroom pickers. He comes across a lot of hippie types at this time of the year and is sufficiently secure in his own ego to welcome anyone onto his land who is willing to respect where they tread and keep the gates shut.

'If it's the Lib'tee Cap 'ee is seeking then 'ees could do no worse than to carry 'eeself across over ta Jake's lairnd and be inspectin' the cricket pitch out o'er top of moor. She grows a plen'y up there. You sees, tha' land, she's ne'er been ploughed, as she? Aye, yous can count fi'ty generation o' cattle what 'as walked those moor meadows wi'out a single plough bin pulled through em. Fi'ty generations oi says!'

'Splendid! Why thank you, kind sir!' laughs Langley in an altogether too theatrical exchange of colloquial banter. The farmer eyes Austell more charily, picking up an unexplainable morphic field of suspicion arising from the guardedness of one man towards another. And with that transmission the farmer meanders off, striding down towards the wood to check his fences. He lost two sheep yesterday. The doctors stand and watch him go. Then before

261

he reaches the edge of the field he turns around and shouts, 'Watch 'ow ee goes, mind!' he cries. 'I's don't want you's a bothin' my cattle in the next field! And I's 'ave dese prize ewes in the top pasture! Them's have ee's bollocks the size of applewoods and they's must not be doin' no knockin'! You's don't go bothin' 'em, see!'

'Yes of course!' shouts back Austell, feeling a little more confident now that the man is far in the distance. 'We'll be careful!'

So through the next two fields they trudge, careful not to bother the super-fecund sheep whose interest is not in the least bit aroused by the pair of stealthy mushroom hunters.

'Keep looking!' says Langley as they go. 'Little brown pointy-headed love gods! We know you're out there!'

After more stomping and still with not a fungus between them they lapse into silence and take rest on a felled tree. Around them in the mulchy goodness of rotting wood sprout mushrooms of all colours and shapes. Langley pockets a few of them to take home to add to his collection. His personal interest in mycology extends beyond the Psilocybes. He will inspect and catagorise his specimens, examine their tiny spores under his microscope and perform chromatographic tests on their flesh. It has always been his ambition to discover a new species. It is the same for all amateur mycologists; there are still so many undiscovered species of mushroom out there waiting to be named.

They share sandwiches under a few spots of rain blowing down from Exmoor. Austell is pleased to be out here with Langley, whose peculiar and frightening behaviour at the beginning of the summer seems to have levelled off again for the time being. He is back to his old eccentric self. As if reading his mind (or perhaps *actually* reading his mind, knowing Langley) he says, 'I know you have

262

all been talking about me. And I don't blame you.' Austell smiles; always amazed at his friend's psychic ability.

'Yes, we have been worried. Especially me. It's just that…well, I don't know…I was really worried.'

'Look, Bob,' says Langley. 'There is something I need to tell you about my health.' Austell is not an oncologist but he feels he may know what is coming. For solace he fixes his view on the distant clouds gathering across the piercing blue. Eventually Langley speaks again, 'It probably started in the lung, well, that's my bet. I mean, I never had any respiratory symptoms, not really, at least not until lately, apart from coughing up blood…'

'Apart from coughing up blood!'

'But I just put that down to all those years of smoking. Of course I gave up the evil weed – tobacco, that is – when I was cured of the pernicious addiction by the Bwiti twenty years ago, but maybe it was too late for my lungs by then. I don't know. Point is,' continues Langley, 'that the little bastard has now clawed its way into my brain. My God damn brain, would you believe it, my second favourite organ! I suppose if I were a crab I too would want to scuttle to the most auspicious of all the viscera. More fun to be had wreaking havoc in the brain than to remain in the chest and lymph nodes. Yes, I'd definitely head straight to…'

'Joseph, you speak of it as if there is nothing to be done!' interrupts Austell, struggling to connect with Langley's casual manner. He stands up, buttoning up his coat hurriedly. 'Come on, we can deal with this.' After so many months of denying its existence, all that time feeling impotent and unable to help, now Langley's diagnosis is out in the open, there is no time to waste. This is the first opportunity Austell has had to actually engage with his friend's illness. 'Come on, let's head back down to *Bardo* and get you straight down the hospital.'

Langley doesn't move. He stares up at the sky and shuts his eyes, feeling a breeze on his face. The sunlight emerges from behind a cloud and lights his closed-eyed vision, gloriously orange beneath the lids. He remains like this for some time, breathing meditatively. Eventually Austell sits back down and sighs deeply.

'I *am* getting it sorted, Bob,' whispers Langley. 'I am doing exactly what needs to be done. I am being healed as we speak. By sitting here staring at the sun I am downloading the driver for transcendence. The place to be is exactly here. Not hospital. But right here hunting for mushrooms on this glorious autumn morning…but you're right!' he chirps, jumping up with an unrivalled spring. 'We can't be sitting around all day. Daylight is the enemy of the humble shroom. Let's make our catch!'

In mocking delight of the prevailing tone his pace quickens as he leads Austell over the hill and down a muddy bridleway towards their destination: the cricket pitch on the moor. With no further mention of death Langley chats wildly about the natural collage around them, naming every tree, shrub and berry, calling after the birds and describing each breed of cattle and sheep. But by the time they reach the deserted cricket square on the edge of the moor they are again in silence. Langley puts a finger to his lips and crouches behind a low wall as they survey the luminous lush green cricket square.

'Shhh, get down!'

Austell crouches, following Langley's gaze. This is a most irregular place to have a cricket green. The pitch is fringed by a surrounding hamlet of just six or seven houses, perched on top of a hill near an old slate quarry where two ancient roads cross on the edge of the moors. No doubt several centuries ago when the pit was open this place was a hive of activity. Today a few thin plumes of smoke rise from the chimneys of several distant cottages but there is no one to be seen. Nevertheless, Langley's guarded whisper sets Austell racing with anxiety. Then it occurs to him that Langley's crouched vigilance is not because of fear of human interactions but rather in respect of the fungal species.

'I think we have alerted them,' he hisses. 'We must proceed with caution. They had warning of our advance; the mycelia of those lower fields communicated our presence through their network. OK, cover me, I'm going in!'

Playing the game Austell wearily tags along in the wake of his mad friend. Half crouched they step over the wall and trudge cautiously onto the spongy ground. The grass on the cricket square has a different quality to the brashness of the fields. Neatly clipped; a densely packed carpet of short immaculate blades makes it easy to see anything that dares poke through its glassy surface.

'He was right, that farmer. This is virgin ground. Beautiful, it's never been disturbed. If I were a mushroom I would want to live here. Moist all summer, shaded from the frost by those poplars in the winter. This is the place to be. I bet the mycelia under here are the offspring of the same living plant for thousands of years.' Head bent he glides off over the velvety space. '*Yes*!' he shrieks. 'Here we are!'

Austell peers down at the ground where Langley points. Sure enough there is a mushroom. Two mushrooms. In fact as he looks, almost as if by magic, there appear whole clusters of little brown pointy mushrooms exactly as Langley had described them, their sharp nipples reaching up from glossy olive-brown caps. Austell picks one. It is faintly slimy to the touch.

'Careful!' whispers his friend. 'Don't pull them up too forcefully. Try and preserve the body below. And always flick before you pick, to scatter the spores and preserve the patch for next year's cropping. Remember we are only borrowing these children from the mother-plant. We will return them to the energy of the earth later when we commune with their maker.'

Just as Langley said, once one has seen one magic mushroom the rest simply give up. The doctors systematically traverse the luxuriant patch of grass that grows so incongruously on this rain beaten scrap of moorland. All around the isolated pitch are the fierce cow-trodden barrows of the West Country grassland but here is an oasis. Austell trots from patch to patch, flicking, picking and plucking, then depositing the prizes gently in his paper bag. Now he knows what to look for it is effortless. He notices he is even standing on them.

'Are these definitely the right ones? It's just that there are so many of them!'

'Yes, yes. It's a great crop. Oh, joy!' says the eccentric man, checking his watch for opening time and thinking as much about his beloved cider as he is about the sprouting treasure at his feet.

Their pockets bulging with hallucinogens they head home via Wiveliscombe, a quirky orchard village at the gateway to Exmoor, and order double Ploughman's at *The Bear*. Langley spices up his pint with a fistful of cosmic slimy pickings, which congregate in the bottom of the cloudy glass and leave strands of grass floating on the surface; a West Country cocktail. True to form Austell declines the offer to take the mushroom trip. His darkness communicates his sentiment.

'Oh come on, Bob, it's not so bad,' Langley says at last. By the time he's drunk his third pint he is unable to take his partner's silent brooding. 'We are all dying one way or another. Look at the patients you brought to be cured; each one of them hopeless on their pathway to fatality. It's me today but it will be you tomorrow. Birth is our shared existential crisis,' he smiles, 'curable only by death. We've all got to go.'

'Yes, but why *now!*' cries Austell, exasperated by his friend's candour. 'It's easy for you to be so blasé. You've had time to come to terms with this news. I've only just heard. It's a lot to take on board. Just when everything seems to be going so well for us. You don't get it do you, Joseph? What has happened at *Bardo* is the most important – the *only* – important thing that has *ever* happened to me. I'm...I'm...'

But as soon as he has said this Austell realises how selfish it sounds. Nevertheless, it was honest, which is what Langley hears, and he takes Austell's hand, fixing him in the eyes as his recent mouthful of fresh mushrooms begins to take hold. In the face of the worldly psychiatrist burns the volcanic glow of his emerging psychedelic trip. It spreads throughout the cellular matrix of his body; the ancient DNA connecting with an intergalactic wisdom passed on through eons. A broad smile spreads over Langley's face and with this invitation Austell's eyes well-up and a fat tear slides down his cheek.

'You're my...friend,' he says. '*Joe*...my first and only friend.' Such simple words, so easily spoken, yet somehow something denied to Austell throughout his life.

'Fear not,' drawls Langley, his eyes closed, body turning,

soaring through wide, dark, surging corridors. In his mind is the image of a great Sea Eagle, rising from its thorny nest and dropping off the edge of its turbulent cliff; a plummeting missile diving headlong towards the raging ocean. Then at the last second, with two magnificent beats of its titanic wings it pulls up and takes flight, slicing foam off the tips of the breaking waves as it soars towards the horizon. 'I am not going anywhere. It is *you* who is dying. I am being born! I cannot die. My energy merely shifts from one plane to another. Listen to what the mushrooms tell us,' his eyes closing as he submits to the geometry behind the lids.

'The mushrooms, the bloody mushrooms!' exclaims Austell, breaking away from his hold with Langley. 'They are telling us nothing! Drugs, drugs, bloody drugs! That's all you ever think about. That's all this is…'

'But it's much more than just drugs,' smiles Langley, his eyes snapping open. 'It is so much more. it's about communication. Dissemination. That's what you have done here with *Bardo*. You have done this, Bob, not me. Sure, I've shown you the tools, the drugs, but the real *life* of this project, the *guts*, have come from *you*. You have taken the ideals and promises of the psychedelic experience and honed and practiced it with your patients. You have spread the word and turned on the world to this most important of medical advances. *You* are the chosen one to take this further, Robert. I've done my bit…'

'Your bit has not finished, Joe!'

'Not yet, but almost. Now you have to take this project, take the message into mainstream medicine. Present the speech at the Royal College. You can do it.'

'*Me* do the presentation? But…but, I can't…'

'You can, Robert. You have all the resources at your fingertips to do this without me. You are not alone.'

Alone. The single word that sums up all of Austell's life. He has never had a friend until now. But at this moment, with crackling Somerset Liberty Cap-powered electricity coursing from Langley, Austell has arrived on the starting line of the human race. And when he looks into Langley's face, behind which a rogue cluster of cancerous cells eat away at his friend's friable brain, Austell realises he belongs somewhere, that he is loved and that his only friend in the world is going to die.

PART 5

THE AFTERGLOW

DEATH CROUCHES IN
THE SHADOWS

It has been two years since maverick psychiatrist Dr Joseph Langley and conservative doubter Dr Robert Austell started their experiment that led to the formation of *Bardo*. And now in the run up to their second Christmas at the farm their fledgling hospital remains in a state of happy chaos. Austell and Langley take a backseat and the other staff run the project.

Claire Castle, who is studying psychology part-time at college in Taunton, prepares new clients for the MDMA programme, supported by Andy who runs the post-combat groups. The Psilocybin and LSD tracks are respectively managed by John and Kathleen, who are now married. Kathleen Rattick is training as a complimentary therapist and John Patterson studies towards a pharmacology qualification. Their wedding was a glorious Rastafarian affair in which the whole farm was decorated from head to toe. Every tree and animal was painted red, gold and green, with bunting slung from the rooftops and apple trees. Amidst reggae music the stoned couple stood before a joyous congregation in the orchard and recited their vows:

Rastafari can't be married.
Rastafari don't worship in no church, so how can Rastafari
have a church to be married in?
Don't need no paper to say ya married; 'specially if it be da
babylon who created dat paper.

You got to know ya roots so is you know where you is comin'

from.
It is in I n I hearts.
Love is the truth, Jah see.
Bless up

Elsewhere in the UK, under the banner of the offshoot organisation, the *Scientific Hallucinogen Research Organisation for Opening Minds (SHROOM)*, Austell supervises the development of new clinical centres, disseminating the psychedelic tendrils of the *Bardo* model to groups of like-minded therapists. It is a cottage industry with minimal profits, corporate-free and cooperatively owned by those in charge. Collaborating laboratories supply the home-grown operation and the whole set-up is as far removed as it can be from Big Pharma.

Langley, now largely bedbound, spends much of his time in palliative recline. Avoiding conventional doctors who only want to prescribe drugs that mask symptoms, he prefers to embrace the complimentary therapies and takes a daily cup of ginger and mushroom tea. He insists on getting to know this dreadful parasite as it eats its way through his mushy cranium.

'It really is working, Joe,' says Austell, sitting on the bed with his friend. '*Bardo* is running itself.'

Langley pulls himself up and coughs. When he speaks his voice is thin but as authoritative as ever.

'It's a wonderful sight to behold, Bob, this coming to fruition of our embryonic idea. We have explored psychedelics as treatments for addictions, anxiety disorder, depression, OCD and PTSD, but you know there is still one study left to do. One crucial area of research we have not yet touched upon.'

274

Austell is curious, 'What have we missed?'

'Don't pretend you don't know! We haven't looked at the connection between psychedelics and *death*. Come on Bob, you know this. The links between hallucinogens and death are as old as the hills and don't you think this is something we should explore here at *Bardo*?'

Austell reaches for his friend's hand. It is limp and has lost its turgor. Over recent weeks the light in Langley's eyes has dimmed. As he slips from this world a lifetime of knowledge goes with him; knowledge achieved from selfless meanderings exploring primitive cultures and their reasons for living. As a scientist Langley has embraced nature and now it is embracing him in the most unimaginably cruel manner.

'Bob, listen to me,' he rasps. 'We must find a way to examine the existential process of death. We mustn't let my condition go unexplored.'

'You want to be the experimental subject of your own death?' Austell has to chuckle at this ludicrous suggestion. 'Joe, tell me you're not serious.'

'Of course I am. We *must* do this. We can use my fortuitous passing to capture and record the essential essence of the death process. I want you to help with an experiment to monitor the death experience under the influence of psychedelics.'

The room is dank. Austell gets up and throws open the window, letting in the sounds and smells of Somerset air on the eddying wind. 'OK, Joe. I will think about it. But right now my mind is on the Royal College conference. You will just have to cling on for a little while longer.'

Langley closes his eyes and sinks into a meditative state. 'I promise I'll try.' A smile spreads across his pallid face. Out in the corridor Death lurks, crouching in the shadows, watching the two psychiatrists, waiting to pick his moment to slink into the room.

STANDING NAKED
IN FRONT OF THE ELDERS

True to his promise Langley holds off death and makes it through Christmas and into the New Year. In the spring the core staff of *Bardo* take the train up to the Royal College of Psychiatrists Annual Conference. *SHROOM* is heralding a new direction for medicine and *Bardo* leads the way. It is a momentous invitation to deliver the keynote speech at The Royal College conference.

When he stands up to deliver his presentation in the conference hall Austell is bathed in applause from over a thousand psychiatrists from all over the world. Before him sit row upon row of esteemed colleagues from three generations of psychiatry awaiting his opening line; primed with expectation by the positive results that have flowed out from a humble farmyard in Somerset into the front pages of peer-reviewed scientific journals and popular newspapers throughout the world.

An eerie silence then descends over the great hall. Austell looks down at the front row, catching the eye of Langley, in a wheelchair wrapped in blankets, weary and thin but beaming no less than the rest of the gathered *Bardo* staff. For Austell this presentation is the pinnacle of the last two years since he started this tumultuous journey. He wants the crowd to experience the same thrill he felt when he sat there in San Francisco and first heard Langley. This talk is a very public thank you to his friend.

'Good afternoon,' he says. 'I will start at the beginning. *This* is the beginning. It is here in this hall today that we write history and herald in a new beginning for psychiatric treatment of mental disorder. Today we will take these sacred plants of ancient times and place them firmly into the arena of modern psychiatry. But before I start I want to say how grateful I am to all of you who have made this journey achievable. Thank you for inviting me to stand here in front of such an illustrious collection of academics, doctors, therapists and health professionals. But most of all thank you to the patients, the most unfortunate members of our so-called civilised society, whom we are privileged to work alongside. I am humbled so many of you have travelled so far to listen today.

'Our medicines are the compounds LSD-25, Mescaline, Psilocybin, DMT, MDMA, Ketamine, Phencyclidine, Ibogaine, Salvia divinorum and Cannabis. All of these drugs produce alterations in consciousness and induce perceptual distortions. They are also spiritual tools that have been used for millennia by non-Western cultures as part of religious ceremonies all over the world. So why is that we in the West know them only as illegal and dangerous drugs of abuse? As addictive compounds, not to be distinguished from cocaine and heroin, the cause of an individual's, if not the entire *society's*, destruction? This is wrong. We must challenge the so called 'War on Drugs' and embrace these fascinating substances as tools to further our understanding of the nature of consciousness. They are safe medical treatments to aid psychotherapy and they alleviate the symptoms and course of mental disorder. It is time to wake up to this realisation.'

The crowd murmurs their recognition with a sea of nods.

'Art, literature and music have been dedicated to the subject of hallucinogens. The psychedelic excursions of Huxley, Byron, de Quincey and James are legendary and through their writings

278

we catch a glimpse of the psychedelic landscape, but there is still no comprehensive, systematic and scientific understanding of the psychedelic experience. This needs to change! If Freud called dreaming '*The royal road to the unconscious'*, then surely psychedelic substances are the technicolor super-highway?'

Austell looks down at Langley and memories of their mushroom walk pass between them on invisible strings of morphic resonance. With his eyes closed and ears open Langley nods gently; absorbed by the lecture, knowing his friend is looking at him. Austell feels something of an imposter. It should be Langley up on the stage. These words are his. As far as Austell is concerned all of his words, thoughts or deeds of recent years belong to Langley. He is doing this for him.

'But are these drug experiences really spiritual or do they just *feel* spiritual? And what does this tell us about the workings of the brain? How can an organic substance make us at least *believe* we are talking to God?'

Langley smiles. His student is doing a splendid job, standing naked in front of the elders of his profession exposing his opinions for all to see. Austell pauses and takes a sip of water. So far he has been reading from a script behind the plinth but now he decides to continue without his prompts. He strides out from behind the podium, revealing an old pair of battered tennis shoes.

'Since the end of the 1960s, the subject of psychedelic medicine has fallen off the radar for doctors. It is as if all that work in the fifties never happened. But now, after a hiatus of over 40 years, there are new research projects underway. At *Bardo* and *SHROOM* we have successfully completed a raft of double-blind placebo controlled trials. Over sixty patients have completed the program in

279

Somerset – all with overwhelmingly positive results – and projects are now underway with double-blind placebo-controlled studies involving six hundred and seventy five patients from nine separate treatment centres nationwide.

'Furthermore, for the last two years we have encouraged psychedelic drug users – both medical and recreational – to contact us with their histories and we have collated the reams of data pouring in to us from other clinical studies all over the world. This data is now being followed up by our R&D team and there are plans underway to conduct further placebo controlled RCTs at *Bardo* next year, testing MDMA, LSD and Psilocybin on patients for the treatment of cluster headaches, period pains, alcohol dependency, smoking cessation, post-natal depression, chronic fatigue syndrome, autism and defect state schizophrenia.

'But we must not underestimate the struggle it has taken to get this far. The ethical considerations with this sort of work are immense. They ought not to be – these drugs are, after all, far less toxic than methadone and Ritalin, which are used liberally throughout psychiatry – but because of the unhelpful, non-evidence based political agenda there have been great barriers to surmount to bring you this data. Nevertheless, what we have achieved at *Bardo* in the last few years is merely the tip of the iceberg and we give thanks to those that paved the way before us.

'However,' he continues. 'These drugs are *not* a panacea. They do not offer a magic wand to cure all the ills of society. It was that attitude that caused the downfall of the last psychedelic revolution. We need the medical profession and the general public to find new ways of looking at old problems. So I appeal to you – my psychiatry colleagues – disillusioned by the costly, ineffective and drug-company-lead policies, whereby patients are maintained indefinitely on antidepressants and other ineffective drugs, to look towards new and creative solutions for our patients. Society needs new directions. It is this belief that has driven me. That is why we do this. Because we have hope. We have some hope for the future of psychiatry.'

Austell is nearing his final sentence. Without warning he feels a tear come to his eye. Sometimes he surprises even himself with these flows of emotion, especially in the turmoil of the last two years. For a split second, probably imperceptible to the homogenous carpet of faces below him, he feels dissociated from the scene. He is beyond the conference hall, floating, looking down on this stage, watching himself deliver a speech to the Royal College of Psychiatrists. On the front row, where Langley, Claire, John and the others sit, Austell sees people, not just his colleagues, but kindred spirits, folk who trust and respect him...*love* him. His friends. This is what it is all about, he realises. *This is the reason for my existence.* And then, as he steps to the front of the stage with his eyes glistening and a shiver rising through his body Austell glances at Langley, whose eyes snap open and fix on Austell.

'So, a lot of water has flowed under the bridge since the '*Turn On, Tune In and Drop Out*' days of the sixties. And if we look beyond our preconceptions of these compounds I believe – *we* believe – if clinicians can remain dispassionate and stay true to the principles of evidence-based medicine, we can reconsider the therapeutic possibilities of psychedelic drugs. And if we can do this then there is a chance these fascinating chemicals can play a positive role in the future of psychiatry and neuroscience. That much we owe to the population of patients with resistant psychological illnesses that may

281

benefit from this novel approach. We have shown this is possible at *Bardo*. We have taken the first tentative steps towards bringing these treatments into the fold of mainstream medicine forever. Thank you all, very much.'

He steps back, accepting the applause and beckons his friends to join him on the stage. As Claire and John climb up, the clapping increases and then the row behind them stands up and soon the whole hall is on its feet. Langley stays in the seat of his wheelchair, confined by his lack of mobility, until Claire drags him up too. The frail man is raised onto the platform and the volume of applause increases. He and Austell warmly embrace and are soon circled by a mass of people asking questions, shaking their hands and clambering to talk.

Austell is ushered away to the side of the stage to pose for photographs and bunches of flowers are being thrust his way. Then there suddenly comes a terrific scream. Everyone swings around to look and Austell pushes his way through the crowd to see Langley collapsed on the stage; twitching horrendously in the throes of a convulsive seizure.

A BAG OF MEASURABLE ORGANIC COMPONENTS

Robert Austell makes his way up to the second floor of Taunton District General Hospital. Despite being a doctor he has always had a morbid fear of hospitals. In the case of Taunton DGH such terrors are well founded. A more decrepit hellhole masquerading as a clinical setting is hard to imagine. It was this way when originally conceived in the 1930s, and since then the Jenga stacking of prefab temporary buildings on top of existing condemned structures has done nothing to enhance its healing potential.

The over-worked under-paid staff at the nurses' station sigh at the mention of Langley's name. The dying psychiatrist has clearly made his presence felt on the ward. 'Professor Langley is not himself,' warns the staff nurse without looking up from her screen. She points the way down the corridor to the side-room where the staff have been obliged to place him. Austell wonders what she means by this.

He picks his way past mothballed broken beds and overflowing bags of discarded clinical waste – also known in the profession as patients - waiting for collection by absent stoned porters. The troublesome Langley is happy to see Austell and leans over to brush newspapers from the chair. He is tangled in pipes carrying drugs and oxygen into him and yards of tubes and wires carrying waste products and electrical data out. Books and papers litter the room amidst a scattered foliage of cards.

'Bob! Come in, welcome to my boudoir!' he chirps. Propped up in a hospital bed he looks smaller than usual. He pushes back his long greying hair and holds it in a ponytail, waving his other arm. 'Here. Pass me that…that bloody tying thing. There, that's better. I can see you now!'

'The nurse said you are not yourself, Joe.'

'Nurse? She's not a bloody nurse! She's only a *general* nurse, not a proper *psychiatric* nurse. What does she know about patient care? Now Betsy, now there'*s* a nurse! Good God, Bob, did I tell you about the time when Betsy and I got locked in the ECT suite at Gobslorvaski State Hospital during a power cut? Jesus. We were in there for two days. Two days! State bloody holiday I think. Freezing it was. That's when I discovered the warming power of the propofol-midazolam mixture. Also got to see an awful lot of Betsy. She not with you?'

'No, Joe. She's back at the ranch. I think she's coming up later. She's finishing off going through the data on the Ketamine studies. Looks like…'

'Ketamine! Now there's a beauty! Did I tell you about the time I got lost in the Guatemalan jungle trekking through the Mirador Basin with no guide and no food? All I had was seventeen vials of Ketalar, and those bloody owls, well, I think they were owls? Never actually saw the buggers. Do you get owls in Guatemala?'

'No, you never mentioned that Ketamine story. But I'm sure there are owls in…'

'And now every half-wit on the street is on the stuff! Dribbling bladders and all!' Langley's breathing is laboured. He coughs, pulling himself up with the hoist from the sweat-soaked pillows. Austell helps him and after some grunting and swearing the wiry man settles back down and falls silent again. Clearly the frontal lobes are failing to do their job of dampening the id. Pure unadulterated

Langley is on display. Austell sits quietly and they meditate in silence for a while. Eventually it is Austell that speaks. Times like this call for a depth of honesty that the two friends are welcome to respect.

'It doesn't look good, Joe.'

'I know.'

'Don't be scared.'

'Don't be scared? What a bloody stupid thing to say.'

'Yes, sorry, I was just trying to…'

'Of course I'm bloody scared! Wouldn't you be?'

'Yes, yes of course…'

'I'm going to die, man. Die! My days are well and truly over. I am stepping off the precipice. This is it, Bob. This it IT!''

'What have the doctors said?' Austell asks, knowing full well what the doctor's have said.

Langley tosses the MRI scans across the bed. The pictures show a great sprawling mass of uncontrolled matter bulldozing its way through Langley's brain.

'See how it has completely occluded the left ventricle and frontal lobes? That is why I am *not myself*. Whatever I once was is now being eroded. Eaten away. It's a wonder I'm with you at all, Bob. But the important question is whether or not you got my emails about Roland Cox?'

'Yes. I got them. I have been up to Cardiff and met him.'

'Great! Is it all set up and ready to go? I reckon I've got another week, maybe two. We mustn't delay. We have to go ahead with the plan.'

The plan in question has been the subject of much debate amongst the staff at *Bardo*. When Austell first shared Langley's proposal with the others he had hoped nothing more would come of it and they would all put it down to the mad man's amnesic ramblings. But rather than dismiss it the other staff embraced the idea wholeheartedly. Everyone wants to grant Langley his final wish. And Langley's determination to go through with it has not diminished one iota.

'This is going to be the most important study on consciousness that has ever been performed, Bob. Roland Cox is *the man* when it comes to neuroimaging. I know he has access to the hardware; I spoke to him about it in San Francisco.'

'In San Francisco? You spoke about this project with Roland Cox two years ago?'

'Well, not exactly,' says Langley, distractingly flicking through the drug chart at the end of his bed, copying the junior house doctor's handwriting to add some methylphenidate and morphine. 'I mean, we spoke about it when he was over giving his talk at Opening Minds. It is something we have both always wanted to do, but I have to admit, I never imagined the subject would be me! Look, I've been working on the idea some more.'

He passes some papers over to Austell and the two of them flick through his scrawled text.

'Do you really think this will work? I don't see how you can combine MRI simultaneously with MEG *and* PET all in one scanner. These machines are huge. No one has ever tried anything like this before.'

'Of course they haven't. But if we don't try it, Bob, we will never know. I am sure it can be done. And I know Cox is up for it.'

'Yes, he is. And he reckons it can be done. He says he's done something similar with primates. But you will be the first human to

286

undergo the procedure.'

'Well that's fine then, isn't it? I'm certainly feeling fairly primitive at the moment. If a psychedelic death was good enough for Aldous Huxley then it's good enough for me.'

Austell's meeting with Roland Cox had taken place in the scanning department at Cardiff University amongst the gleaming multimillion-pound imaging machines. The professor had chattered excitedly about his colourful hallucinogenic experiences with Langley and his own neuroscientific research into bandwidths, magnetic fields and neuroimaging. It was clear to Austell that Cox was perfectly at home with the kind of human phenomena that can only be picked-up by electrode probes.

'He said it was going to be a bit touch and go,' says Austell. 'He wondered whether it was your plan to actually *die* in the scanner? He seemed quite excited about the prospect.'

'I hope you told him that I am totally set on transforming the cancerous decay of my brain into a psychedelic metamorphic masterpiece? Existentially I see no difference between the physical site of my cancer and the spiritual manifestation of the hallucinogenic experience. Both are set to carry me into the unknown.'

'Yes, I said all that,' sighs Austell. 'It seems your man Cox perfectly understands your reasoning. He too has a fascination with the pathoneurological process that accompanies death. "Just as long we get home with the data," is what he said, as he tapped on his laptop, running simulations of glucose starvation in the face of your vascular meltdown.'

'Wonderful!' laughed Langley. 'I knew he'd pull it out the bag!'

'He estimates the frontal lobes will go first and then ischemia will spread through the rest of the cerebrum. He was hoping to measure whether there will be any degree of acute neuronal plasticity. To be honest, Joe, it was pretty hard hearing him talk in that way about your demise. I think he sees you as little more than a bag of measurable organic components.'

'Spot on, Bob. Cox is da man!'

'Yes, so you say. Anyway, he assured me how fond he is of you and promised to give you a terrific send off. But, Joe, what about the hospital here? They are never going to let you out for this. And how are we going to get ethical approval for such a project?'

'Oh, come on Bob, don't be such a stiff doctor about this. Remember what Hofmann said: *When the second psychedelic revolution is upon us we must not allow the medics to run the show.*'

'OK, fine, but can't we scale things down a little. You know, consider something a little more manageable?'

'Manageable!' snaps Langley. 'Bloody hell, I could be just seconds away from the bottomless pit of eternity with only multiform diabolic angels for friends! I hate hospitals and I'm not staying here a minute longer.'

Austell sighs and picks up Langley's plans again and skims through them further. He balks at what he reads.

'Joe, look at this. What's all this about a floatation tank? How can we scan you under water?'

'That's a homage to Lilly. We must do it!'

'Come on, that's out of the question, Joe, surely?'

'OK, fine! Forget the tank,' snaps Langley, agitatedly tossing the papers aside. 'There's a dolphin CD knocking around at the farm. That'll have to do. But the rest is perfectly do-able. Cox says he can make it work. This experiment will demonstrate the neuroanatomical site of the Freudian subconscious. It will be a world's first!'

He explodes into a fit of coughing and reaches for his oxygen mask. Austell hands him a glass of water and the surrounding machines beep their warnings. Without too much haste a nurse saunters into the room.

'You OK?' she says, huffing as she sees Langley. She switches off the alarms and pulls him back to a sitting position. 'Come on now Professor. What have I told you about getting all excited? Honestly.' Turning to Austell sternly, 'Look, you mustn't let the Professor get over stimulated.'

Langley pulls away from her, snapping, 'Over stimulated? I couldn't get stimulated in this cell if you put a thousand volts up my ass! What is this crap you're pumping into me anyway? Look, if you want my advice you'd tear down all these pathetic neuro-*depressants* and get some real bloody medicine into my veins. Here, Bob, did you bring that LSD I asked for?'

'Joseph!' Austell glances nervously at the nurse. But she has heard enough of Langley's eccentric mutterings to not take him seriously. She smiles warmly and fluffs up his pillows, rolling her eyes at Austell.

'Come on Professor. Settle down. No one's going to poison you with anything dangerous like LSD. Look, I'll bring you a nice cup of tea.' She trots out of the room, pausing for a second to glance at a colourful picture Langley has hung on the wall depicting a poly-headed Hindu Goddess in ecstatic copulation with a multi-membered Kali. Shaking her head she hurries out.

'You told them you were a Professor?'

'What the hell's she talking about? LSD isn't *poisonous*. It's a bloody sacrament. Look, we have no time to lose. We need to act fast. I am almost at full term. The time of my birth is practically upon us. Bob, I need your help. Honestly, you have to get me out of here or I'm going to die trying!'

OPERATION EMANCIPATION

Death is a dirty word. Defend oneself from it at all costs. Do not speak of death, especially not to children. And then it might not happen. A similar approach is applied to life. Nowadays even birth is merely a matter of opinion. And what lies between these two vague concepts is perhaps less meaningful still. Keep the economy alive. Do not stop spending. Diversify your portfolio. Buy To Let. Go into the loft. Keep the high street buoyant. Shop yourself out of the recession. Keep the factories open and keep those landfills stuffed.

By the time Austell gets into hospital again to see Langley his old friend has been stripped of everything except a plastic skin. He has a yellow-green pallor with a consciousness to match. From beneath a chemo-induced hairless scalp a tiny flicker of recognition flashes over the drained face.

'Bob, thank God it's you! You gotta get me outta here, man,' he whispers, sounding well beyond his years, using every calorie of strength being dripped into his flaking arms. 'You gotta bust me outta this joint.'

Austell has come prepared. He meets with the lead consultant and presents a watertight case for taking Langley back to the farm. *Bardo* now sports a clinical staff better resourced than any district general hospital. With assurances that his friend will receive nothing but the best clinical monitoring and emergency treatments the ward put up little resistance to the plan. Besides, they need the bed. Within minutes Austell is wheeling his colleague out of the building and into the back of Betsy's Land Rover. But they are not going to the farm. Operation Emancipation is underway. With no left turn unstoned they rush Langley straight over the Severn Bridge to Cardiff. Usually Death waits for no one but in Langley's case he is prepared to be flexible.

Cox has secured the department for their sole use and is standing by. He frowns at the ominous hum emanating from the scanner. They need nineteen thousand gigawatts of electricity to fire up the machinery. The Welsh National Grid is just going to have to go without for a few moments. His anxiety is momentarily distracted by the monitor showing Betsy's Land Rover pulling up outside. The test subject is hurriedly bundled onto a waiting gurney and buzzed in. Many of the *Bardo* staff members from the farm have also come along for the event. Cox smiles at the swathes of goggle-eyed voyeurs entering the imaging suite and admiring the machinery.

'Aint she a beauty? What you are looking at here is over seventy million pounds of state of the art imaging equipment. We have fully-integrated SPECT, PET, MEG, fMRI and CT scanning all rolled into one. This machine is capable of delivering a whopping sixty-six hecto-volts of current directly into a single dendrite. It can detect the passage of a mere thirty molecules of neurotransmitter across the synaptic cleft. I can pinpoint, to within one tenths of a nanometre, the tiniest alteration in brain chemistry and electrical activity.

'In short,' he gulps, 'with this machine I can virtually *see* Joseph Langley's thoughts.'

The limp and practically lifeless unit of study is lifted up and placed on the slab. His legs and arms are bound with straps and a series of wires and tubes are connected. Needles are placed deftly into his veins, arteries and spinal cavity. Langley even insists on an anal probe in tribute to Area 51. The machine stirs around them.

292

Deep inside the electronic bulk of brushed metal and cabling there lies an almost dead psychiatrist, surrounded by spinning magnets, glowing copper coils, atomic accelerators and proton emitting diodes. A pathetic specimen of human flesh waiting to be subjected to ultra-high pressure X-rays, simultaneously shot through with magnetic charge fired out of a bank of superconducting quantum interference devices. Cox ushers everyone away from the patient and into the control room safely behind the magnetic-proof glass.

'How does it work?' asks Austell.

'Do you really want to know?'

Cox's Asperger charm is whetted. He doesn't usually get to talk about his work. Most other brains cannot understand what he does with his working day.

'Yes, I do,' Austell is bold enough to say. 'Do tell me.'

'Great. Well, you know the way a radionuclide redistributes itself slowly through the tissues of the brain when not subjected to the body's normal planar gamma ferromagnetic implant dipole segregation?'

'No.'

'Well, the fundamental problem of bio-magnetism is that the weakness of the signal relative to the sensitivity of the detectors and the competing environmental noise means…hang on a sec…okay, here we go! Start her up!'

The background hum starts climbing to a whine. Cox, anxious to continue the explanation of his work calls out above the din.

'So, what I have done here is made sure that any electrical current that is extracted or introverted *away* from Langley's brain, the stuff that is usually lost into the atmosphere, will instead be tunnelled back *into* his head in order to produce an orthogonally oriented magnetic field. Should work a treat. OK, simmer down everyone.'

This is the biggest event since the birth of the universe, which means the collected staff of *Bardo* are celebrating the occasion with a special cocktail punch that has been mixed in strict accordance with Langley's final wishes. It is starting to kick in.

'So when Joe first told me he wanted to capture the essential essence of the death experience I knew I had to find a way of boosting the signal. I decided to run it through a Fourier transformation loop. There is no way we can glimpse the numinous White Light unless we first localize the algorithms by expectation-maximization.'

'Obviously.'

'So I have primed the system by reversing the polarity of the couplings. I did this by charging the detectors picking up micro-currents coming from bundles of neurons orientated tangentially to the scalp surface. That's what we are doing right now. It won't take a moment. This is all part of the warm-up process. These detectors also act as transmitters at this level of charge, so they project measurable portions of the magnetic field outside of the head *right back into* the bundles typically located in Joe's cerebral sulci. Of course, the system can't run cold. It has to be initialized to allow for the exact volume of integrated high-end multi-detector-row radionucleotide throughput. Joe was insistent we did it this way. He said that would be the most effective method to harness the entities.'

'Entities?'

'Yes, something he is calling his 'Fungal Buddies'. Don't ask me. But he wanted it this way.'

'Right.'

'Well usually, with the wind behind it, this sucker kicks right in, but sometimes I have to run it very fast to encourage any remaining

294

static charge to come off the sending-electrodes and gather on the collection plates. That is the only way to allow for high-resolution 3D datasets. I would usually use a T_1 reducing gadolinium contrast agent before *and* after administration of the contrast agent in order to compare the difference. But in Joseph's case – his brain being what it is – I think the T_1-weighted scans are going to provide perfectly good grey/white matter contrast.'

'Yes, of course.'

'So come on, let's get it underway. Then we can start measuring. But before I do *any* of that we need to just…can you press that switch there please? That red one…'

'This one?' asks Austell tentatively, his finger hovering over an alarming-looking button.

'Yes, please.'

Austell presses the switch. Nothing happens.

'What is it?'

'That's the kettle. First things first, let's have a cup of tea.'

Inside the scanner Joseph Langley's petrified sack-of-shit that he used to call a body, so soon to be transformed into pure energy, shivers slightly. It is not a convulsion in the usual sense of the word but rather a gigantic emerging development of existential vigor building from the deepest part of his brain and bulging its way out through his Shatner's Bassoon. The alignment of the known planets and parallel universes tremble; each threatening to tumble off the beaten track and spiral away into new uncharted celestial waters. Langley is willing them to do so.

'OK, so here we go…throw open the switches on the sonic oscillator! Set the uranium-oxide pseudospheric spin protectors to eleven! Let's get those babies moving!'

Then Austell raises his hand and beckons for silence. The rabble in the control room is reduced to a whisper and Cox flicks on the intercom.

'Can you hear me, Joe?' Everyone is waiting anxiously for a sign of life from the patient as the machine begins its computerized sequence of neuroimaging.

Inside the metal tube Langley can just about make out a crackled voice through his headphones.

'Yes, yes, I can hear you,' he limply replies into the microphone suspended above his puckered, toothless mouth. His eyes have been taped shut – not because there are fears his sight might be damaged by the extreme magnetic fission (it will, of course, the eyeballs are among the first of the organs to burst under these high pressures) but rather because Cox does not want any distracting occipital lobe stimulation interfering with what is destined to be the world's greatest extra-visual visualization of mental phenomena ever not-seen.

From the control room there is astonishment as representatives from NICE and the Ethics Committee arrive to be part of the action. Crowds of Cardiff University staff have also gathered outside the building wondering why they have lost all power to their departments. From his darkened void Langley prepares himself for the first imaging sequence. Austell leans towards the control room microphone, 'I…I love you, Joe.'

For Langley in the scanner these words resonate with immense emotional vitality. The resulting neural network activity is immediately picked-up by the probes and diodes positioned throughout his brain. Langley can see Austell in his mind's eye; making out the shape of the man he first glimpsed in San Francisco, that clever, able man so riddled with senseless self-doubt and under-achievement. He has watched Austell grow, imparting into him all his years of wisdom and expectation. This is their moment. But rather than talk, Langley *thinks* a reply to Austell.

Bob, don't be fearful. Let go. Step into the flow of this experience. It is you who has taught me how to live. You are the lifeblood of Bardo, *and you are not so very different from me. We are two halves of an essential whole. You have brought closure to my existence and helped me to attain my life's dream. Thank you for saving my life. I love you too.*

Across the banks of screens in the control room there flickers a series of peaks and spikes. Illuminated regions of the spinning three-dimensional image of Langley's brain registers concentrated emotional activity. Cox's buzzing magnets, proton accelerators and high voltage lasers focused onto Langley's head pick up the depth of his cognitive output. It is Cox who is the first to speak.

'Joe, I think we got that. Every non-spoken word of it. By God, this thing actually *works*!' A great cheer goes up in the control room. Professor Cox's machine can actually detect specific thoughts. Langley knew it would. From deep within his near-comatose state in the scanner he is picking up the conversation offered by his friends in the control room. They are all joined by a mutual connectivity of vibrating particles and love is the medium in which they swim.

'Joe,' says Cox excitedly. 'Listen, I want you to think something else for me. I want you to…to think about your childhood…can you do that for me? Can you focus on any deeply emotional and visual picture of your childhood? Okay. When I give the signal…'

The neuroscientist leans across the desk and adjusts the wall of controls. Raising the cosmic background radiation into the red-shift spectrum of visible light he pushes gently on the mouse wheel and increases the machine's output of charge-coupled spectroscopic magneto-hydrodynamic particle accelerators.

'Okay, Joe, taking her up a notch or two. And we're starting the chemical inputs. Are you ready for the first infusion?'

From inside the spectral tube Joseph Langley nods and whispers a subtle affirmative.

'Betsy, start infusion mixture A.'

Betsy, as ever, is the assigned nurse responsible for all psychedelic neurochemical administrations. She presses a button linked to an electronic syringe plunger, which begins its discharge of solution into the arterial central line in Langley's neck. It is a concoction of DMT, LSD and Ketamine, all in the exact proportions to perfectly mimic the combined neuronal conditions of a Tibetan monk and a newborn baby. The molecules tumble over one another and gush their way into the portholes of Langley's withering brain.

'Good…okay, fine. Begin sequence 2.1,' calls out Cox. And what had started as a gentle whine now crescendos to an uncomfortable barrage of screeching. 'Joseph…Joe, can you hear me?'

'Yessssssss…' comes the drawn out response from inside the tube. The molecules of oblivion are clearly delivering their juicy goodness right on cue.

'Okay…I want those childhood memories, thoughts only, not words, in 5 seconds, 4,3,2,1…go!'

Fired, shot through a spiraled vortex of streaming checkerboard underground passages of blinding light, Langley explodes into a childhood vision of his mother's breast.

I am a newborn baby. I am my mother. My father is a towering giant, the protector. I am part of my mother, enveloped deep inside

298

her, but not all the way in because my powerful father blocks me. And now I am a beautiful three-year-old scruffy-haired boy, standing at my mother's feet tugging on her skirt in the kitchen. My father towers over me with his strength and containment. I adore him. But I am my mother. This is the natural order of things. My father will never know or love my mother in the way I love her, and she loves me.

'Great...great. Beautiful imagery Joe,' says Cox, his eyes scanning the array of figures pouring across the screens. 'It's all looking very Oedipal. Typical psychiatrist! Keep it up. I now want you to take your thoughts into adolescence please? Can you do that?'

But what's this? There is a dragon in the woods. Over the hill, beyond the meadows, further than the known extremities of the village lurks a beast. Many have travelled there but no one has ever returned – at least not as boys. All who go there come back as men, or not at all. And now I, Joe, must slay the dragon in order to overcome the strangling love for my mother and the excruciating conflict with my father. Then I will transcend from childhood into a functioning adult. The elders of the village have taught me through their campfire stories that this is the natural order of life. Jung and Freud have also told me so. They are with me now in this peri-adolescent lucid wet dream. My mother is not here. But instead there is another woman. It is Betsy.

Langley is really going to town with this one.

I am Betsy's man. She wants her father. He is me. Now I realise I do not need my mother like I need Betsy. I am strong and magnificent now, just like him. I have snared a mother of my own and the circle is complete.

In the control room the computers are going mental. Literally.

Digital signals are rising beyond their intended purpose and transcending into analogue, the gaps between the peaks and troughs of the binary code are becoming smoothed into a continuous wave. Modernity itself is spontaneously reverting back to archaic times. The laboratory's computers have spurned their links to the city's mainframe and are now drawing their own source of energy directly from Langley's brain, which vibrates with infinite frequency as it nears its endpoint of absolute singularity.

Beautiful and transcendent though this moment might be, no one at the desk can escape the smell of burning that now permeates the room. It is mingled with the smell of incense and cannabis coming from the mind-blowing party going on all around them. It is a Hindu festival on the banks of the Ganges at Varanasi. Hundreds, no *thousands*, of well-wishers from near and far have swarmed into the place to throw confetti, paint, streamers and smoke in all directions as they wade into the sacred waters surrounding the guru, whose flaming sarcophagus floats on the steamy river surrounded by a sea of candles.

Alongside Austell stands Mountain Spirit, the Orgone Man and reams of other grey-haired pony-tailed Californian psychedelic nut burgers, all of whom have gathered to watch the machine of death/birth/re-death/re-birth clatter away, vying for aural space with the drums, guitars, sitars and bells of the ceremony. The streets are pouring forth with thousands, no, *millions* of revellers. Love and beauty are the over-riding emotions. Everyone on the planet is here in Cardiff for this event.

Cox taps furiously on the controls. Austell clings to the desk and holds Betsy in his arms. She is weeping for Joseph and their children; pouring forth with endless streaming memories of their time spent together. These tales are picked up by the microphones dotted around the control room and transmitted directly back to Langley. In memory of Kesey and the Pranksters, the *Bardo* team have the place wired for sound; every draw and insufflation is echoed around the suite, intermingled with the brain-popping screech of a million volts of electricity being pumped into and out of Joseph Langley's rapidly heating skull.

'I had no idea it would be like this!' yells Austell. 'No idea it would be this intense!'

'I did,' screams Betsy back at him. 'Joseph's brain is not going to give up easily! There is so much love in there…so much waiting to get out!'

From the scanning room the transient vessel of Langley's pathetic remains quiver and shake and then bursts into a full blown convulsive seizure. All around him the scanners are whirling, twirling, tearing their way from this planet to the next, recording every nanosecond of the journey. Austell prays that the ten inches of lead set into the thick concrete wall holds out.

'Joseph!' he screams. 'Joseph! Where are you now?'

In the tiny centre of Langley's frying brain there exists, for an infinitely small moment of time, according to all the data, an infinitely dense, infinitely focused pinpoint of light that contains the sum total of all the energy in the universe. *The Pinealarity*. This boldest, newest – but also most ancient - of treatments, the Psychedelic Experience, is being recognised and embraced by doctors all over the world. It can now be applied globally to improve the lives of millions of sufferers of mental illness and rescue the psychiatric profession from its own self-inflicted fate. These thoughts of Austell's are transmitted into the flaming body of Joseph

Langley.

There was some light and some more light. Then even more light. Then, quite suddenly, all the noise and confusion stops dead for Dr Joseph Beefheart Langley, who amidst the screeching turbines of the fracturing scanning equipment is now falling ecstatically towards the earth and merging into it. A tree grows instantly in the spot at which his evaporated body hits the ground. And for a brief second before the tree immediately decays, on each leaf there is the face of all the people Joseph Langley has ever known and loved. These faces are now merging with the face of a bird on the wing, far above the earth. Everything is merging; the air and trees and birds and sky and all that is Joseph Langley. All his life and all his friends' lives, everything they will become and all of history since the beginning of time, everything that has ever happened and will ever happen and everybody whoever was and will be are all there with him together concentrated at this precise moment in the here and now.

It is a return; that is what it is. Joseph Langley is crossing the river….each step is laboured by the strong pull of the current on his legs as he wades perpendicular to the surge…the river keeps flowing…then he steps onto the bank and looks back, smiling to see the river's graceful course. He knew it would be like this. It just keeps on going; even without him it never stops. It just keeps on flowing.

Smoke is pouring not only from the machine but also from the body of the patient, who has ceased to even tremble. It is a funeral pyre. Those fifteen trillion volts of electricity are effectively cremating the brilliant psychiatrist. Everyone in the control room leans forward following Austell's gaze and Cox declares that this is now a genuine emergency situation. People rush in and out of the

302

building, flinging open doors, flailing extinguishers and letting off alarms. A tide of heavily tripping psychedelic on-lookers stumble outside, crying tears of joyous cosmology, making love in the street and staring with stoned expressions at the slowly turning blue lights of the gathering fire trucks.

The End